D0884323

MILITARY RULE IN LATIN AMERICA

MILITARY RULE
IN
LATIN AMERICA

320.98
R285

KAREN L. REMMER

Boston
UNWIN HYMAN
London   Sydney   Wellington

181618

© 1989 by Unwin Hyman, Inc.
This book is copyright under the Berne Convention. No reproduction
without permission. All rights reserved.

Unwin Hyman, Inc.
8 Winchester Place, Winchester, Mass. 01890, USA

Published by the Academic Division of
Unwin Hyman Ltd
15/17 Broadwick Street, London W1V 1FP, UK

Allen & Unwin (Australia) Ltd,
8 Napier Street, North Sydney, NSW 2060, Australia

Allen & Unwin (New Zealand) Ltd in association with the
Port Nicholson Press Ltd,
Compusales Building, 75 Ghuznee Street, Wellington 1, New Zealand

First published in 1989

Library of Congress Cataloging-in-Publication Data

Remmer, Karen L.
Military rule in Latin America/Karen L. Remmer.
p.   cm.
Includes index.
ISBN 0-04-445479-1
1. Latin America—Politics and government—1948-   2. Military
government—Latin America—History—20th century. 3. Chile
—Politics and government—1973-   4. Military government—
Chile—History—20th century.   I. Title.
F1414.2.R36   1989
322'.5'098—dc20

British Library Cataloguing in Publication Data

Remmer, Karen L.
Military rule in Latin America.
1. Latin America. Military governments
I. Title
322'.5'098
ISBN 0-04-445479-1

Typeset in 10 on 12 point Palatino by Fotographics (Bedford) Ltd
and printed in Great Britain by Billing and Sons Ltd,
London and Worcester

For My Parents

Contents

List of Figures

List of Tables

Preface

Military Rule in Latin America begins where most other literature on the subject ends, namely, with an analysis of the origins of authoritarianism. It is concerned less with the *causes* of military takeovers than with their *consequences*. Do military regimes make a difference? What is their economic and political impact, and how does it differ from that of other regimes? What factors shape the functioning, dynamics, and outcome of military rule? These questions have guided this study. The attempt to answer them has pushed the subsequent analysis beyond a purely societal-centered understanding of military rule to take into account the role of institutional forces and state actors in Latin American politics.

Precisely because scholarly attention has focused on coups d'etat at the expense of their sequel, the importance of institutional variations among military regimes has been seriously neglected. This study attempts to remedy this deficiency by underlining the link between institutional arrangements and political outcomes. How state power is structured subsequent to military takeovers affects the durability of military rule as well as its impact. Consequently, to explain key similarities and differences among military regimes, it is necessary to consider not only their social underpinnings but also the organization of the state.

The book is divided into two parts. Part I provides an overview of military rule in Latin America. Chapter 1 considers the social conditions associated with the emergence of military rule, and chapter 2 proceeds to show that major variations among military regimes cannot be explained solely in terms of those conditions.

Chapters 3 and 4 present empirical analyses of the economic and political impact of military rule. Given the problems of assessing that impact on the basis of selected and possibly unrepresentative cases, not to mention the obstacles to gathering comprehensive information about political and economic performance for the whole continent, the analyses focus on two sets of empirical data. The first resembles what Harry Eckstein has described as a "most-likely" or "must-fit" case: that is, a data set that in theoretical terms is especially tailored to invalidate a theoretical proposition—in this instance, the proposition that military regimes have a strong and distinctive economic impact. The specific focus of this analysis is economic stabilization, which is perennially regarded as *the* area of policy performance in which military regimes enjoy significant advantages over their civilian counterparts. The second set of data, which was designed to assess the political impact of military rule, was chosen for precisely the opposite reason: it resembles a "least-likely" case in the sense that it establishes an unusually strong basis for arguing that military rule is capable of effecting far-reaching political change. Specifically, the data explore the impact of military rule on political party systems, which are considered exceptionally resistant to change and which, therefore, offer a crucial test of the capacity of military regimes to alter the political status quo ante. The results of these analyses of the consequences of military rule fly directly in the face of conventional wisdom. They suggest that the economic impact of military regimes has been rather consistently exaggerated, while their political impact has been grossly underestimated.

Part II of *Military Rule in Latin America* examines a theoretically anomalous case of military rule—the Chilean. The scope and depth of the changes effected by the Pinochet regime, together with its durability and personalistic character, pose a number of significant questions. Why did such an unusually durable military regime emerge in a country with a strong constitutional tradition? What factors allowed the Pinochet regime to have such an unusually deep policy impact? Why did the rule of a highly professionalized military assume such a personalistic face? The analysis attempts to show that the answers to these questions are important not only for the study of the Chilean experience, but also for the comparative analysis of military rule more generally. Building on the discussion presented in Part I, chapters 5 and 6 examine how social class forces and institutional structures interacted to produce a durable and personal military regime with an unusually profound social impact.

The concluding chapter returns to the theme of regime transition. It explores the shift away from authoritarianism that began in the Latin American region during the late 1970s and speculates about the course of future political events. This chapter shows that the organizational structure of military rule is important not only for understanding what happens between the military's seizure of power and its retreat to the barracks; it also has significant implications for transitions from authoritarianism and the consolidation of democracy.

The process of researching and writing this book has stretched over nearly five years. In that time, I have incurred many intellectual debts. Special thanks are due to Guillermo O'Donnell, whose original theoretical insights provoked me to think long and hard about the issue of military rule. I also owe a large debt of gratitude to many Chilean friends and colleagues, particularly Genaro Arriagada, Manuel Antonio Garretón, Carlos Huneeus, and Augusto Varas, for helping me to understand the realities and complexities of military regimes. For reading, criticizing, and discussing key portions of the manuscript, I thank Diego Abente, Edward C. Epstein, Peter Gregory, Jonathan Hartlyn, Scott Mainwaring, Frederick Nunn, John Sheahan, Thomas E. Skidmore, Alfred Stepan, and Alexander W. Wilde. The author also gratefully acknowledges the assistance of Martin C. Needler and James A. Morris and the research support provided by the Heinz Endowment, Mellon Foundation, and Research Allocations Committee of the University of New Mexico. Above all, thanks are due to Gilbert W. Merkx for his encouragement, advice, and boundless willingness to thresh out the ideas presented in this work.

Earlier versions of portions of chapters 3, 4, and 5 appeared in the journal *Comparative Politics* (New Brunswick, NJ: Transaction Publishers) as "Redemocratization and the Impact of Authoritarian Rule in Latin America," XVII (April 1985): 253–295; "Neopatrimonialism: The Politics of Military Rule in Chile," XX (January 1989): 149–170; and "The Politics of Economic Stabilization," XIX (October 1986): 1–24. A preliminary version of chapter 6 appeared as "State Change in Chile, 1973–1988" in the journal *Studies in Comparative International Development* 24, 3 (Fall 1989, New Brunswick, NJ: Transaction Publishers).

MILITARY RULE IN LATIN AMERICA

PART I

*Comparative Perspectives
on Military Rule in Latin America*

CHAPTER 1

Military Rule in Latin America

The differences among military regimes are as profound as the differences between dictatorship and democracy. Factionalized military regimes coexist with cohesive ones, technocratically oriented regimes with corrupt and politicized ones, radical regimes with reactionary ones, and intensely personalistic regimes with others of a faceless nature. Hence, while General Omar Torrijos of Panama railed about oligarchical control and encouraged the lower class to participate in politics, his contemporary, General Juan Carlos Onganía of Argentina, governed in alliance with business interests, welcomed foreign investment, and repressed labor organizations. The military regime headed by General Juan Velasco Alvarado in Peru distributed land to nearly a quarter million families, while in neighboring Chile a military coup terminated an ongoing process of agrarian reform. Similarly, political power became concentrated in the hands of General Juan Perón in Argentina and General Alfredo Stroessner in Paraguay, but over the course of a decade executive control passed almost routinely from one military officer to another in El Salvador. The variations in the political stability of military regimes are no less striking. In 1979 the governments of Colonel Alberto Natusch of Bolivia and General Anastasio Somoza Debayle were both overthrown; but whereas Natusch had ruled only 17 days, Somoza's ouster marked the end of a political dynasty that had survived for more than 4 decades.

Given the wide disparities in ideology, class alliances, policies, structure, and durability that exist just within Latin

3

America, generalizing about military rule is problematic. One must either ignore the wide range of phenomena falling under the rubric of military rule or settle for platitudes and tautologies. The difficulties are illustrated by the long-standing effort to find a common denominator behind coups d'etat. Three decades of research have yielded little beyond a set of truisms. One truism is that the military acts to protect its institutional interests. The proposition is virtually unfalsifiable because competing conceptions of the military's political role are invariably defended in terms of institutional needs. Coup supporters and opponents alike thus claim to be protecting the corporate self-interest of military officers. Whatever the outcome of such a conflict, it can be defined as meeting institutional requirements. The search for policy commonalities among military regimes also has produced few positive results. The similarities uncovered are basically those built into the definition of military rule; for example, military regimes limit political liberties and competition. Such similarities require no explanation. The heterogeneity of military regimes poses the key theoretical challenge.

Inclusionary Versus Exclusionary Authoritarianism

The distinctions that have been drawn between inclusionary and exclusionary authoritarianism provide a basic point of entry into the complex topic of regime heterogeneity.[1] Inclusionary (or "populist") military regimes attempt to create a popular base of support for military rule by mobilizing new sets of political actors around reformist and nationalist projects. The popular sector, which encompasses the lower middle class and lower urban and rural class, is thereby drawn actively into politics—often for the first time. The regime of Juan Perón provides a classic example. Beginning in late 1943, Perón organized Argentine workers into a powerful political force by establishing new social benefits for industrial workers, introducing new labor legislation, encouraging the reorganization and expansion of the trade union movement, and intervening in the collective bargaining process. The Peronist loyalties and organizational strength of the Argentine working class remain a lasting tribute to the efficacy of his efforts. Perón's other principle base of support was local industry, which welcomed high tariffs and other policies designed to enhance national economic independence, whereas his leading opponents represented export-oriented agricultural interests and international capital.

Not all instances of reformist militarism come as close to the extreme inclusionary end of the political spectrum as the Argentine. Popular-sector elements, particularly urban workers, played an unusually important role within Perón's ruling coalition, accentuating his regime's nationalist and populist thrust. Many other countries within the Latin American region, however, have experienced one or more periods of military rule that at least approximate the Argentine case. The two most recent instances are those of Peru during the 1968–75 period and Panama under Omar Torrijos (1968–81). Parallels also exist outside the Latin American region in such cases as Nasserism in Egypt and the Armed Forces Movement in Portugal (1974–76).

Exclusionary military regimes represent the opposite end of the continuum. Instead of incorporating new social elements into the political arena, such regimes attempt to limit popular participation and physically repress trade unions and other vehicles for lower-class political activity. Their central thrust is demobilizational rather than mobilizational. Popular-sector groups thus become a principle source of opposition to military rule, rather than a base of support. Exclusionary authoritarianism is built instead on a foundation of middle- and upper-class support, and internationally oriented economic interests dominate the governing coalition. As a result, reactionary, rather than reformist, impulses guide public policy. Such an orientation does not preclude major policy change, but the economic nationalism and concern for social inequity that shape policy under inclusionary military rule are scuttled in favor of closer ties to the international economy and an overriding concern with economic efficiency. The military regime of General Augusto Pinochet, which seized power in Chile in 1973, provides a prime example of an exclusionary military regime, but there are many others. Rule by the military to the socioeconomic and political exclusion of the over-whelming majority of citizens also characterized Uruguay between 1973 and 1985, Argentina in both the 1966–73 and 1976–83 periods, Brazil between 1964 and 1985, Bolivia under General Hugo Banzer (1971–78), and post-1954 Guatemala. Similar regimes have also emerged outside of Latin America in countries such as Greece (1967–74).

As these examples indicate, exclusionary rule is not the product of a single level of modernization or capital accumulation. Both comparatively well-industrialized Latin American countries, such as Brazil and Argentina, and unindustrialized ones, such as Bolivia and Guatemala, have succumbed to exclusionary authoritarianism. The political experiences of the latter set of countries simply cannot be placed in a separate category, such as *traditional authoritarianism*, without ignoring the political similarities that exist across the spectrum of development. Likewise, whether or not a regime is personalist or institutional, or based on a professional or an unprofessional military, has little to do with the basic distinction between exclusionary and inclusionary authoritarianism. Professionalization may inhibit civilian penetration of military governments, limit the scope for corruption and individual gain, and enhance the political role of technocrats; but professionalized militaries have promoted both political inclusion and exclusion, as have comparatively unprofessionalized ones.

Explaining Regime Differences

The extent to which a military regime approximates the inclusionary rather than exclusionary end of the political spectrum hinges on the social class coalition supporting military rule. Exclusionary rule presupposes a process of class polarization that pits popular-sector groups against propertied interests and their international allies; inclusionary rule, on the other hand, requires a lack of solidarity among dominant class groups and the formation of political alliances that cut across class lines and include popular-sector elements. The coalition behind any given military regime typically falls somewhere between such extremes, but which of the two tendencies predominates, conditioning regime ideology and policy, is a product of three sets of factors: the socioeconomic structure of a nation, the dynamics of its political process, and specific international conjunctures.

The relationships between these variables and modes of political domination in Latin America can be further clarified if we follow the recommendations of Robert A. Dahl[2] and classify regimes in terms of two theoretical dimensions. One dimension is conventionally used to differentiate democracy from dictatorship and involves freedom of opposition and competition. The right of political leaders to compete for support as well as the classic liberal freedoms of speech, press, and assembly are indicators of competitiveness. The other dimension, which measures the breadth of participation in political affairs, refers to the inclusiveness of a given regime. The two dimensions are distinct such that high levels of competition may coexist with limited popular participation in politics. Similarly, regimes that place strict limits on political opposition may nevertheless encourage political involvement.

As indicated in figure 1.1, the classification of regimes along these two dimensions produces four extreme or polar types, which are labeled exclusionary and inclusionary democracy

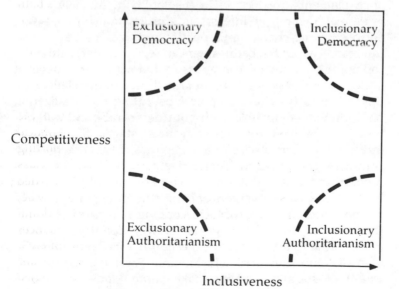

Figure 1.1
Two-Dimensional Classification of Regimes

and exclusionary and inclusionary authoritarianism. Most regimes, of course, do not fit neatly into any of the four corners of figure 1.1 but fall somewhere in between. Indeed, the virtue of the figure, as opposed to the more conventional terminology of regime classification, is precisely that it emphasizes this point, thereby averting endless terminological disputes as well as unproductive controversies about whether a given case is democratic or authoritarian, corporatist or populist, or even inclusionary rather than exclusionary. Moreover, all regimes can be located within the parameters of the figure, thereby facilitating comparison and avoiding the confusion associated with efforts to define regimes in terms of ideal types or syndromes of related traits. The long-standing debates surrounding the concepts of fascism, totalitarianism, and bureaucratic authoritarianism are all cases in point.[3]

Authoritarian regimes, which are typically military in the case of Latin America, can be located somewhere in the bottom half of figure 1.1; regimes that are described as competitive or democratic in the top half. Regimes incorporating popular-sector elements are located in the right half; those excluding such elements are located in the left half. In view of the perennial theoretical interest in the relationship between socioeconomic change and politics, what is perhaps most interesting about the Latin American region is that neither the top nor the bottom half can be associated with a single level of socioeconomic development, nor can the left or right half of the figure. The early stages of import-substituting industrialization have proven compatible with both democracy and authoritarianism, as have the more advanced stages. Similarly, as indicated earlier, exclusionary regimes have emerged in countries characterized by relatively high levels of social modernization as well as in those with exceptionally low levels. Nevertheless, few observers of Latin American politics would discount the importance of socioeconomic structure in shaping the rules of the political game. How a country has been integrated into the international economy, its degree of social diversity and industrial development, and the nature and extent of social inequality make some kinds of political arrangements more probable than others. Although complex, the relationships can be briefly specified.

8

Socioeconomic modernization neither increases not decreases the probability of competitive or democratic rule. The point is not that all modes of political domination are equally probable at all levels of socioeconomic modernization. Yet for every authoritarian option that exists at a given level of industrialization, literacy, or urbanization there also exists a competitive or "democratic" alternative. The level of modernization is important primarily for understanding the nature of those democratic and authoritarian alternatives.

As socioeconomic modernization produces a society that is increasingly urbanized, industrialized, and literate, the probability that a competitive regime will assume an exclusionary or oligarchical form steadily declines in favor of inclusionary democracy. Until very recently, oligarchical democracy constituted the modal rather than the exceptional form of competitive rule in Latin America due to the region's high level of socioeconomic inequality. That inequality creates enormous incentives and opportunities for political exclusion. People at the bottom of the socioeconomic pyramid have everything to gain from a change in the status quo, whereas those at the top have everything to lose. Moreover, inequality concentrates resources in the hands of the few, facilitating the exclusion of the many. As political observers as far back as Aristotle have noted, political inclusion is therefore problematic under conditions of severe inequality. Exclusion, however, does not require authoritarianism with its attendant legitimacy costs. It can be achieved equally well under competitive political arrangements, providing that pressures from below can be contained. Lower levels of literacy, industrialization, and urbanization facilitate such containment.

In Latin America elite dominance of competitive institutions proved comparatively easy until the 1960s, particularly in the Andean countries, where the preservation of traditional and highly inegalitarian agrarian structures allowed landowners to manipulate sizable blocs of rural votes. Buttressed as well by literacy requirements, the overrepresentation of rural areas in legislative bodies, controls on peasant organization, and other comparable mechanisms, conservative forces could depend on competitive political arrangements to protect their interests. The relative stability of competitive institutions in Andean

9

nations, such as Colombia and Chile, can be understood in this light, as can the somewhat lukewarm support of Latin American labor organizations for political democracy.

In countries in which a traditional peasantry did not exist (as in Argentina) or was displaced from the land by the integration of the rural sector into the international economy (as in El Salvador), oligarchical democracy never took hold. Elsewhere its viability declined dramatically during the 1960s due to rapid urbanization, increased literacy, and the sociopolitical transformation of the countryside. The associated upsurge in authoritarianism swept aside even rather well established Latin American democracies, such as Chile. By the mid-1970s, most of the continent was ruled by the military, lending credibility to arguments that socioeconomic modernization under conditions of dependent development produces dictatorship, not democracy.[4] An equally dramatic shift away from military rule occurred in the late 1970s and early 1980s, however, producing in such countries as Brazil, Ecuador, and Peru civilian regimes that were much more inclusionary than their competitive predecessors. In Peru, for example, the return to competitive rule in 1980 entailed a 171.6 percent increase in the voting population and a major political realignment highly unfavorable to conservative forces.[5] These more recent trends indicate that democracy is neither a purely cyclical phenomenon in Latin America nor a form of governance destined to vanish in the face of socioeconomic modernization. The breakdown of competitive rule that began in the 1960s marked the crisis of a particular form of democracy, the prevalence of which will continue to decline in response to socioeconomic modernization, paving the way for other types of political arrangements. These relationships are summarized in figure 1.2.

The relationship between socioeconomic modernization and exclusionary authoritarianism in Latin America is curvilinear, such that exclusionary military regimes are most likely to emerge at relatively low and advanced levels of industrialization, urbanization, and educational attainment. Inclusionary military regimes, on the other hand, are most likely to emerge at middle levels of socioeconomic modernization. These relationships are depicted in figure 1.3. Again the probabilities

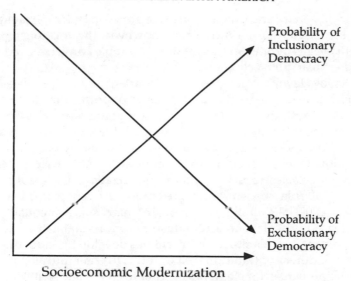

Figure 1.2
Socioeconomic Modernization and Competitive Regimes

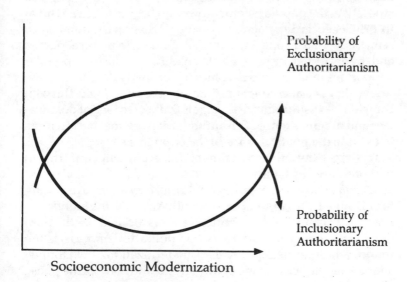

Figure 1.3
Socioeconomic Modernization and Authoritarian Regimes

of inclusionary and exclusionary rule appear as mirror images. In the case of authoritarian rule, however, the relationships with socioeconomic modernization resemble converse curves rather than intersecting lines.

At low levels of socioeconomic modernization, privileged social elements have few incentives or opportunities to form alliances with the popular sector. Without industrial development, the interests of elites are comparatively homogeneous, trade unions are unlikely to be powerful or easily organized, and low levels of literacy and communications development create obstacles to mass political mobilization. Exclusionary forms of rule consequently predominate over inclusionary ones, especially under conditions of high social inequality. Increased urbanization and industrialization establish a basis for a change in this situation. Incentives develop for industrialists and other nontraditional elite groups to enter into alliances with popular-sector elements in order to challenge established oligarchies, foreign interests, and the policies associated with their dominance. The chances of inclusionary rule of both the democratic and authoritarian variety increase accordingly. Such alliances develop strains, however, as the political strength of the popular sector grows and begins to pose a threat to privileged groups across society. Inclusionary democracy remains a political option, but as allegiances to political parties and trade union organizations solidify, mobilizing popular support for military rule becomes increasingly difficult. To the extent that social conflicts cannot be accommodated through competitive institutions, the stage is thus set for social polarization and the emergence of an authoritarian regime that attempts to exclude the political voice of the popular sector.

To some extent the structure of this argument conforms to that presented by Guillermo O'Donnell in his influential work, *Modernization and Bureaucratic-Authoritarianism*. According to O'Donnell, "In contemporary South America, the higher and lower levels of modernization are associated with non-democratic political systems, while political democracies are found at the intermediate levels of modernization."[6] O'Donnell singled out the "easy stage of import substitution" as the phase of industrial development most conducive to inclusionary rule, of either the competitive or authoritarian variety, and the

12

exhaustion of this stage as the critical juncture shifting the odds toward exclusion. In his formulation, the first phase of import substitution, which is characterized by the expansion of consumer goods production and the growth of the domestic market, creates the basis for political coalitions incorporating lower middle- and working-class groups. As the possibility of further growth on the basis of consumer goods production declines, the viability of these coalitions diminishes. Inflation, foreign exchange shortages, and other developmental bottle-necks generate pressures for major policy shifts. At the same time the strained economic situation leads the popular sector to become increasingly active in defense of its interests, accelerating its political isolation. Propertied sectors come to perceive its demands as an obstacle to further growth and as a serious threat to existing social arrangements, including the class structure and international alignment of the country. O'Donnell argued that the resulting political polarization highlights the strong class component of the situation, "facilitating the collaboration of most of the propertied sectors in accepting a political 'solution' that supposedly would eliminate such threats by the political exclusion of the popular sector."[7] That political solution is exclusionary military rule, or what O'Donnell called "bureaucratic-authoritarianism."

Partially because he pulled together several intellectual traditions that have tended to remain disparate, O'Donnell recast the debate over the relationship between social change and politics in Latin America and made an original contribution to the ongoing critique of modernization theory. His line of argument also drew attention to the relative ease with which multi-class coalitions have been constructed around the relatively dynamic phases of import-substituting industrialization in Latin America but floundered in the face of foreign exchange constraints and export-oriented policies. O'Donnell thus provided a basis for understanding the persistence of military rule in Latin America, even in countries that have achieved high levels of modernization. The difficulty is the socioeconomic determinism of his argument, which exaggerated the fit between stages of economic growth and forms of political domination. O'Donnell failed to recognize that the initial phase of industrialization in Latin America occurred under a variety of political conditions other than populism.[8] O'Donnell also treated bureaucratic authoritarianism strictly as a product of advanced socioeconomic development, ignoring parallels between repressive modes of political domination in Central and South America. Indeed, O'Donnell explicitly dismissed the importance of such parallels by classifying authoritarian regimes at medium or low levels of development as "populist-authoritarian" or "traditional-authoritarian,"[9] reserving the term "bureaucratic" for those found at more advanced levels. In his own words,

> the term "bureaucratic" suggests the crucial features that are specific to authoritarian systems of high modernization: the growth of organizational strength of many social sectors, the governmental attempts at control by "encapsulation," the career patterns and power-bases of most incumbents of technocratic roles, and the pivotal role played by large (public and private) bureaucracies.[10]

The continuing weight of the Weberian tradition, with its insistence on the misleading dichotomy between traditional and modern societies, is evident here; but even more problematic for comparative analysis, regimes come to be classified in terms of the properties of the societies in which they emerge, rather than in terms of regime properties per se. The linkages between social change and politics as well as the importance of political similarities and differences among countries are thus established definitionally rather than on the basis of empirical investigation. The same tendency is evident in O'Donnell's treatment of competitive rule, which he defines as a product of a particular phase of the industrialization process rather than as a form of governance that represents an alternative to authoritarianism at all phases. At lower levels of social modernization and industrial development, the chief alternative to exclusionary authoritarianism is exclusionary competition or oligarchical democracy. At middle levels, where inclusionary authoritarianism is most probable, the chief alternative is inclusionary democracy. At high levels, the alternative modes of political domination are inclusionary democracy and exclusionary authoritarianism.

The probability that a democratic or authoritarian mode of political domination will prevail at a given level of modernization and industrialization is conditioned by four major sets of factors: the structure of social inequality, mode of international economic integration, international political conjunctures, and the dynamics of the political process established over time in response to these other factors. The probability of exclusionary authoritarianism is enhanced by extreme socioeconomic inequality, which fuels social polarization at all levels of industrialization. How countries are integrated into the international economy is relevant as well.[11] As indicated earlier, the traditional landowning pattern of the Andean nations provided comparatively fertile ground for exclusionary democracy, whereas exclusionary authoritarianism has predominated in nations integrated into the international economy on the basis of capital intensive agricultural production. Whether an economy depended on a declining export product, such as copper, or a relatively buoyant one, such as oil, during most of the postwar era, is also significant. As the Christian Democrats discovered in Chile during the administration of Eduardo Frei (1964–70), maintaining a multiclass democratic coalition is much more problematic in a country facing severe foreign exchange restraints than in a country enjoying an export boom, such as Venezuela in the 1960s, where oil revenues provided democratic reformers with the resources necessary to overcome tensions within their political alliance.

To these aspects of the socioeconomic setting, one must also add two sets of variables that are more strictly political in nature. The key variables are the specific international conjuncture in which political actors make their calculations and the political dynamic established by prior political events and choices. The first variable is particularly important for understanding the origins of inclusionary authoritarianism. The more the United States is involved in the hemisphere, rallying local allies against the dangers of leftist movements, the smaller the chances of inclusionary military rule. It is hardly coincidental that the most outstanding examples of inclusionary authoritarianism in the Americas emerged in conjunction with the Great Depression of the 1930s, World War II, and the Vietnam War. These international events created openings for the Cárdenas regime

15

in Mexico (1934–40), Peronism in Argentina (1945–55), the regime of Omar Torrijos in Panama (1968–81), and General Juan Velasco Alvarado's reformist government in Peru (1968–75). The relative fragility of inclusionary militarism also can be understood partially in these terms because the political openings created by power vacuums in the inter-American system are inherently temporary.

Relationships also exist between specific international conjunctures and other political options. Democratization in Latin America has characteristically occurred in waves, with peaks occurring in the late 1950s and mid-1980s. The prospects for democratic consolidation also appear to be influenced by such cycles. Competitive regimes that have not emerged as part of a broader international trend, such as Argentina (1973–76) and Honduras (1971–72), have not lasted, whereas the most durable Latin American democracies (Colombia, Costa Rica, and Venezuela) were consolidated in conjunction with waves of democratization. Exclusionary military rule has also waxed and waned in cycles, with 1976 marking the most recent peak. Again, countercyclical patterns of regime change have created a fragile basis for regime consolidation. The two military takeovers that occurred during the 1957–62 period of democratization produced exclusionary regimes that lasted less than two years in power.

Traumatic international events and the exercise of U.S. hegemony in the hemisphere have influenced these patterns. The Mexican, Cuban, and Nicaraguan revolutions all fueled U.S. interventionism and generated intense outside pressures for competitive elections, even in environments as unpromising as Nicaragua in the 1920s and Guatemala in the 1980s. Such pressures clearly have contributed to major democratizing cycles. At other times, however, the banner of anticommunism has been raised to promote exclusionary militarism (e.g., Guatemala in 1954, Brazil in 1964, Chile in 1973) and has undermined competitive rule. The lack of any consistent U.S. foreign policy trajectory, except that pertaining to inclusionary authoritarianism, consequently has produced a constantly shifting political environment that undermines the stability of all forms of political domination. The uncertainties of democratic consolidation, even at the relatively high levels of social diversity and industrial development, are greater in Latin America than in Southern Europe precisely for this reason. The international context, including regional institutions, trade arrangements, defense agreements, and international political contacts, closes the door much more firmly to military rule in Western Europe than in Latin America.[12]

The relationship between socioeconomic modernization and the form of political domination is conditioned, finally, by what may be described as the political dynamic that has been established by political actors and institutions over time. The importance of this variable is emphasized by the experience of Central America. Composed primarily of countries dependent on export-oriented agriculture with high levels of socio-economic inequality, limited industrial development, and literacy and urbanization levels that do not begin to approach those of the rest of the region, Central America has been enmeshed in a cycle of reformist pressure and repressive response that has discredited moderates, radicalized popular-sector forces, and created a political dynamic highly unfavor-able to inclusionary rule. Outside intervention, far from breaking the dynamic, has merely intensified the tendency toward political inflexibility, reliance on violence, and polarization of political forces. In Salvador and Guatemala, the resulting pressures for repressive exclusion have easily matched those emerging in the Southern Cone during the 1970s, despite the obvious differences in levels of socio-economic modernization. In short, events at one time set up expectations that influence later events, broadening or limiting the available range of political options. The cycle does not necessarily favor polarization and exclusionary rule. Successful compromise, such as that achieved in Venezuela in the wake of the Colonel Marcos Pérez Jiménez dictatorship, begets com-promise, enhancing opportunities for democracy and discouraging military intervention. Likewise, competitive regimes create opportunities for the development of strong political parties that enhance future prospects for democratic rule, whereas continuing military involvement in political affairs undermines democratic institutions and contributes to a political dynamic favorable to continuing military inter-vention.

The Dilemmas of Military Rule

As this general overview indicates, military regimes assume so many different forms and rule in such a wide variety of different ways because their power corresponds to radically divergent sets of sociopolitical conditions. Factors that contribute to the polarization of social forces favor the emergence of exclusionary military regimes; inclusionary ones emerge under diametrically opposite circumstances. The causes of the breakdown of inclusionary and exclusionary rule differ accordingly.

The central dilemma of military regimes is that they alter the conditions favoring their emergence and thereby risk undermining their own viability. The risk is particularly serious in the case of inclusionary military regimes. As Marx emphasized in *The Eighteenth Brumaire of Louis Bonaparte*,[13] conflicts among privileged groups that create political stalemates allow for the emergence of regimes rising above dominant class interests. Such stalemates, however, are typically short-lived. As inclusionary authoritarianism threatens privileged groups and strengthens popular-sector forces, social polarization begins. A military that opens the door to inclusionary rule either cedes power to other forces, as in Guatemala in the 1940s, or succumbs to mounting opposition and internal division, shifting the dynamic back in the direction of exclusion. The international context within which Latin American regimes operate intensifies these tendencies. As indicated early, the exercise of U.S. hegemony in the hemisphere has created few openings for inclusionary authoritarianism, and all those have been temporary.

Inclusionary militarism consequently tends to be both a rather unusual and precarious form of rule. Only three inclusionary military regimes in the postwar era have survived more than a decade, and in all three cases the inclusionary character of the regime was severely diluted well before its official demise. The Peruvian military regime of the 1968–80 period shifted its political course dramatically after Velasco Alvarado's removal from office in 1975. In the other two instances of relatively durable inclusionary military rule, those of Argentina and Panama, policy reversals within a few years of regime emergence signaled important changes in political direction.

Exclusionary military regimes also confront a central predicament. Over time the social polarization associated with their emergence tends to wane, reversing the prior political dynamic. As a result the regime's base of social support narrows, divisions widen within the governing coalition, and opportunities grow for linking up opposition agenda to cracks within the state apparatus. The vulnerability of exclusionary military rule to such developments, however, varies widely. Although some have collapsed after short periods in power, in the postwar era exclusionary military regimes in nine countries (Uruguay, El Salvador, Guatemala, Brazil, Haiti, Chile, Nicaragua, Paraguay, and the Dominican Republic) have lasted long enough to celebrate a decennium or more in power. Of these the record for regime durability clearly belongs to Nicaragua, which was ruled by a single regime for more than four decades. As of 1989, no competitive regime in Latin America could match this record, much less any inclusionary military regime.

Exclusionary military rule obviously has not provided the only basis for political stability in the region. By almost any standard, authoritarian regimes in Mexico and Cuba have proved well institutionalized as have competitive regimes in Venezuela, Colombia, and Costa Rica. Yet in contrast to other parts of the Third World, where military regimes cluster toward the unstable end of the continuum of political stability, it cannot be said that military rule in Latin America is "inherently unstable."[14] Due to the durability evinced by exclusionary authoritarianism in the region, military regimes range along the full continuum of stability to instability.

The relative durability of exclusionary military rule in Latin America has been enhanced by the region's socioeconomic structure. Under conditions of severe inequality, the problems of maintaining exclusionary rule pale in comparison with those confronting an inclusionary regime. By promoting social polarization, inequality sustains exclusionary authoritarianism but undermines inclusionary authoritarianism. The regional environment also has been less consistently hostile to exclusionary militarism than to inclusionary militarism. The former has not only been tolerated but even encouraged at times. But even more important, the structure of capitalism and the associated constraints on state autonomy create funda-

19

mental asymmetries between exclusionary and inclusionary military rule. As Charles E. Lindblom has argued so persuasively, the capacity of state actors in market-oriented societies to pursue goals that conflict with those of dominant economic interests is distinctly limited.[15] Inclusionary authoritarian regimes, attempting to mobilize support behind reformist and nationalist programs, are much more likely to run up against these limitations than are their exclusionary counterparts.

In Latin America, exclusionary military rule consequently has predominated over inclusionary military rule. Indeed, the single most prevalent form of political domination in Latin America since World War II has been the exclusionary military regime. Of the 20 countries conventionally included in the region, only 3 (Colombia, Mexico, and Costa Rica) have avoided exclusionary military rule. Several have experienced little else. The key questions about military rule in the Latin American context consequently are questions about exclusionary authoritarianism.

Notes

1 For an elaboration of these distinctions, see Alfred Stepan, *The State and Society: Peru in Comparative Perspective* (Princeton: Princeton University Press, 1978), 73–113.
2 Robert A. Dahl, *Polyarchy: Participation and Opposition* (New Haven: Yale University Press, 1971), 5–8.
3 See, for example, Jerry F. Hough and Merle Fainsod, *How the Soviet Union Is Governed* (Cambridge, MA: Harvard University Press, 1979) 518–29; Ernest A. Menze, ed., *Totalitarianism Reconsidered* (Port Washington, NY: Kennikat Press, 1981); A. James Gregor, *Interpretations of Fascism* (Morristown, NJ: General Learning Press, 1974); Walter Laqueur, ed., *Fascism: A Reader's Guide* (Berkeley: University of California Press, 1976); Karen L. Remmer and Gilbert W. Merkx, "Bureaucratic Authoritarianism Revisited," *Latin American Research Review* XVII, 2 (1982): 3–40; David Collier, ed., *The New Authoritarianism in Latin America* (Princeton: Princeton University Press, 1979).
4 For the classic statement of this view, see Guillermo O'Donnell, *Modernization and Bureaucratic-Authoritarianism: Studies in South American Politics* (Berkeley: Institute for International Studies, University of California, 1973).
5 Evelyne Stephens, "The Peruvian Military Government, Labor Mobilization, and the Political Strength of the Left," *Latin American Research Review* 18, 2 (1983): 57–93.

6 O'Donnell, *Modernization and Bureaucratic-Authoritarianism*, 51.

7 Ibid., 72.

8 For an elaboration of this criticism, see Ian Roxborough, "Unity and Diversity in Latin American History," *Journal of Latin American Studies* 16 (May 1984): 1–26; Robert Kaufman, "Industrial Change and Authoritarian Rule in Latin America: A Concrete Review of the Bureaucratic-Authoritarian Model," in *The New Authoritarianism*, ed. David Collier, 61–98.

9 O'Donnell, *Modernization and Bureaucratic-Authoritarianism*, 114.

10 Ibid., 95.

11 The seminal work on this topic is Fernando Henrique Cardoso and Enzo Faletto, *Dependency and Development in Latin America* (Berkeley: University of California Press, 1978), which was originally published in Spanish in 1969. For a recent analysis of the installation and consolidation of democracy that draws on Cardoso and Faletto, see Evelyne Huber Stephens, "Capitalist Development and Democracy in South America," paper prepared for the meeting of the Midwest Political Science Association, Chicago, April 1988.

12 For a cogent analysis of the differences between the two regions, see Laurence Whitehead, "International Aspects of Democratization," in *Transitions from Authoritarian Rule: Comparative Perspectives*, ed. Guillermo O'Donnell, Philippe C. Schmitter, and Laurence Whitehead (Baltimore: Johns Hopkins University Press, 1986), 3–46.

13 Karl Marx, *The Eighteenth Brumaire of Louis Bonaparte* (New York: International Publishers, 1963).

14 Eric A. Nordlinger, *Soldiers in Politics: Military Coups and Governments* (Englewood Cliffs, NJ: Prentice-Hall, 1977), 139.

15 Charles E. Lindblom, *Politics and Markets: The World's Political-Economic Systems* (New York: Basic Books, 1977). For a recent reassessment of this argument, as well as the stronger versions of it that form the core of Marxist theories of the state, see Adam Przeworski and Michael Wallerstein, "Structural Dependence of the State on Capital," *American Political Science Review* 82 (March 1988): 11–29.

CHAPTER 2

The Analysis
of Military Regimes

Why does repressive military rule rapidly disintegrate in one Latin American country but last a generation in another? What variables account for major differences in policy and performance within the broad categories of exclusionary and inclusionary authoritarianism? Under what conditions does military rule produce fundamental sociopolitical change? Such questions make it apparent that the distinction between exclusionary and inclusionary authoritarianism merely provides a basic point of departure for the analysis of military rule in Latin America. As we attempt to move beyond this distinction and explain variations in the structure, policies, durability, and impact of military regimes, the limitations of the literature on military rule in Latin America become apparent.

The central difficulty is that military rule has been studied more in terms of processes of transition to and from democracy than as a political system in its own right. The revised edition of *Armies and Politics in Latin America*,[1] which offers an overview of recent research, provides a concrete indication of this tendency. Only 3 of its 18 chapters are devoted to the analysis of military rule. The majority either focus on the structural, ideological, and situational preconditions for military seizures of power or provide analyses of transitions from military to civilian governance. The volume is representative of research trends over the past two decades.

During the 1970s, when Latin America experienced its biggest wave of militarism since the Great Depression, the literature on military rule centered around the causes of democratic breakdown. Authoritarianism had been taken for granted in Central America and other less modernized settings, but its resurgence in the more industrialized nations of South America, such as Argentina and Brazil, provoked a major reassessment of the relationship between socioeconomic modernization and forms of political domination. The center-piece of this theoretical endeavor was the bureaucratic-authoritarian model linking military rule to the structural constraints of dependent capitalism.[2]

Following a series of democratic transitions during the late 1970s and early 1980s, a new intellectual cycle began. The focus of scholarly attention shifted away from the etiology of authoritarianism to the causes of democratic transition. Concommitantly, *virtù* and *fortuna* displaced structural forces from the center of theoretical analysis. Whereas the debate over the rise of authoritarianism had revolved around such issues as class polarization, foreign economic penetration, and the exhaustion of the "easy" phase of import substitution, efforts to account for its demise stressed the importance of accident, leadership choice, and "underdetermined social change."[3] Apart from theoretical symmetry, what was lost in this intellectual *volte-face* was any analysis of the role of institutional forces in Latin American politics and a related incapacity to explain important variations among military regimes. Scholars moved from the study of democratic breakdowns to the study of democratic transitions without pausing to analyze the authoritarian phase that came in between.

The monographic literature on the military in Latin America largely conforms to the same pattern. For every book written about the consequences of military rule in Chile, for example, probably ten or more examine its causes. To make matters worse, the monographic literature that does deal directly with the subject of military rule is largely descriptive and idiographic in character, reflecting on the peculiarities of a given national experience rather than placing that experience in a broader theoretical perspective. Hence, we have studies of the Torrijos regime in Panama and the Velasco Alvarado regime in Peru, but no systematic comparison of the two contemporaneous instances of inclusionary authoritarianism. Likewise, studies of military rule in Brazil abound, but few have been conceived within a comparative theoretical framework. The result is a body of literature that fails to add up or to provide a solid basis for theorizing about military rule.

Bureaucratic Authoritarianism

The tendency for research to emphasize regime transitions and neglect the comparative analysis of military rule is evident even in the most theoretically sophisticated body of work available on Latin American militarism—that dealing with bureaucratic authoritarianism.[4] Beginning with the seminal writings of Guillermo O'Donnell, the central focus of this literature has been the origins of military rule in the more economically advanced nations of South America. As a result, the debate over the bureaucratic-authoritarian model has consistently revolved around a set of questions having to do with typological similarities among the cases that O'Donnell labeled "bureaucratic-authoritarian." What differentiates the authoritarianism found in the more advanced South American nations from other forms of military or authoritarian rule in Latin America? Is bureaucratic authoritarianism a new phenomenon? Are there enough generic similarities among cases to warrant placing them in a separate category? If so, what are the key identifying features? Is there an inherent link between advanced industrialization and exclusionary authoritarianism in Latin America? Is Mexico a case of bureaucratic authoritarianism or a crucial exception to the model? These questions have guided the debate. Differences among the set of regimes classified as bureaucratic authoritarian, which call for a different level of analysis, at best have been considered issues of secondary theoretical relevance.

The focus on the origins of military rule, as distinct from its functioning, dynamics, or impact, was particularly pronounced in O'Donnell's initial work on the topic of bureaucratic authoritarianism. Analyzing the breakdown of democracy in Brazil and Argentina during the 1960s, O'Donnell highlighted the similarities between the two countries to support his argument that there is an "elective affinity" between high modernization and repressive military rule in Latin America.

Differences between the Argentine and Brazilian military regimes were addressed only in passing and explained in terms of the constellation of forces triggering military intervention. According to O'Donnell, the more successful performance of Brazilian authoritarianism and its higher degree of consolidation reflected differences in the ideology, organizational strength, and autonomy of the popular sector. The Brazilian popular sector was more easily defeated or "deactivated" because it was weaker and at the same time perceived by established sectors as more threatening than the popular sector in Argentina.[5]

O'Donnell's subsequent work focused more directly on the workings, dynamics, and impact of bureaucratic authoritarianism. Nevertheless, the overall theoretical preoccupation with regime origins remained, leading O'Donnell to continue to link variations among cases with the social underpinnings of military rule. According to his analysis, bureaucratic authoritarianism originates because popular-sector political activation convinces dominant classes and sectors that the existing socioeconomic order is threatened. The perception of threat thus accounts for the generic similarity among bureaucratic-authoritarian regimes. Variations over time and between cases are related to the same variable. O'Donnell argues that the higher the threat level, the greater the degree of class polarization, dominant-class cohesion, political repression, popular-sector deactivation, economic orthodoxy, and military unity.[6] The following quotation illustrates the nature of his argument.

> What do these differences in threat level imply? The general answer is that the greater the threat level, the greater the polarization and visibility of the class content of the conflicts that precede the implantation of the BA. This, in turn, tends to produce a stronger cohesion among the dominant classes, to prompt a more complete subordination of most middle sectors to them, and to provoke a more obvious and drastic defeat of the popular sector and its allies. . . . A higher threat level lends more weight, within the armed forces, to the "hard-line" groups . . . and closely connected, a higher threat level leads to . . . more systematic repression for the attainment of the political deactivation of the popular sector.[7]

To put it crudely, "more threat, more bureaucratic authoritarianism." Thus, according to O'Donnell, the configuration of social class forces existent at the time of regime emergence not only constitutes the principle explanation for the origin of exclusionary authoritarianism in the advanced Latin American nations, but also accounts for major differences across cases in the durability, policies, and performance of exclusionary military rule.

A similar line of analysis characterizes the work of Alfred Stepan. Like O'Donnell, Stepan's work has concentrated heavily on the origins of military regimes.[8] Also like O'Donnell, Stepan has carried over this theoretical preoccupation to the analysis of military rule. In his study of military rule in Peru, Stepan traced the failures of the Velasco Alvarado regime back to its origins, arguing that the factors promoting regime installation inhibited regime institutionalization.[9] In a more recent essay analyzing exclusionary authoritarianism, Stepan has taken a somewhat different tack, but the emphasis on regime origins remains. Contrasting patterns of state-society relations in Argentina, Brazil, Chile, and Uruguay are attributed to variations in the depth of the crisis surrounding the installation of military rule in the 1960s and 1970s. For example, the greater orthodoxy of the Chilean military regime as compared to that of the Uruguayan is related to the attitudes associated with military takeovers in the two countries. According to Stepan, "the Chilean bourgeoisie believed far more strongly than its Uruguayan counterpart that its economic and social survival was threatened."[10] Similarly, to explain the unusual strength of the Chilean state relative to civil society, Stepan argues:

> The intensity of class conflict during the period that preceded the regime made it relatively easy for the regime to gain acceptance of its "project" in the upper and middle classes. Equally important, fear of the possible recomposition of the Marxist opposition helped maintain the internal cohesion of the state apparatus itself.[11]

Hence, Stepan, like O'Donnell, finds within the preconditions for the military's seizure of power the principal explanation of subsequent events.

Although the causes of military coups are unquestionably relevant to any understanding of their consequences, comparative evidence casts considerable doubt on the adequacy of such explanations. Even if attention is limited to the set of regimes that fall squarely within the bureaucratic-authoritarian category, the depth of the crisis provoking military takeovers cannot be persuasively linked to variations in regime cohesion or durability. During the 1970s, highly repressive forms of exclusionary authoritarianism emerged in Argentina, Chile, and Uruguay. According to O'Donnell's formulation, all three regimes originated with "high threat"; nevertheless, their durability varied significantly. Within a few years of the seizure of power, Argentine authoritarianism had begun to disintegrate, whereas Chile's military government weathered a long series of crises and challenges to rule on into the late 1980s.

The Argentine case is telling in itself. The military coup of 1966, which brought General Onganía to power, occurred in an environment of virtual civic indifference, whereas a profound economic crisis and rapidly escalating guerrilla activity provoked the military coup of 1976. Dominant social groups in Argentina consequently perceived events surrounding the 1976 coup as posing a much more pronounced threat to the basic parameters of capitalist society than did those in 1966. Yet, contrary to O'Donnell's explanatory model, the military regime of the 1970s proved no more cohesive or durable than the Onganía regime of the 1960s. In both cases the unity of the military regime broke down, fostering additional coups and paving the way for the restoration of control to elected governments within seven years of the initial military seizure of power. This similarity between the military regimes of the 1960s and 1970s cannot be dismissed on the grounds that the disintegration of military rule in the later period was a product of military defeat rather than of internal political dynamics. The decision to embark on a military adventure in the Malvinas Islands was a consequence, not a cause, of the Argentine regime's internal divisions and domestic policy failures.[12]

Because O'Donnell's work has centered on the Argentine case, the lack of correlation between threat perceptions and regime cohesion or durability is particularly damaging. The theory of bureaucratic authoritarianism rescued Argentina from the status of a deviant case by arguing that the fragility of democracy in the most modernized country in Latin America was predictable, rather than anomalous or paradoxical. In terms of that theory, Argentina thus approximates a "crucial case."[13] If O'Donnell's hypotheses do not fit Argentina, they can hardly be expected to shed much light on the question of regime variations elsewhere.

The point is not that the degree of threat or class polarization associated with the emergence of exclusionary military rule is irrelevant or unimportant for understanding postcoup developments; however, the impact of that variable is incapable of adequately explaining variations across cases. One reason is that the viability of military rule increases with threat but declines with the political activation of the popular sector. Popular-sector organization and mobilization may contribute to the perception of threat and thereby enhance incentives for dominant class groups to rally around exclusionary authoritarianism. As suggested by the theoretical model presented in figure 2.1, however, the obstacles to establishing and maintaining an exclusionary regime also increase *pari passu* with the activation of the popular sector. Its political strength limits regime autonomy and raises the costs of repression. O'Donnell

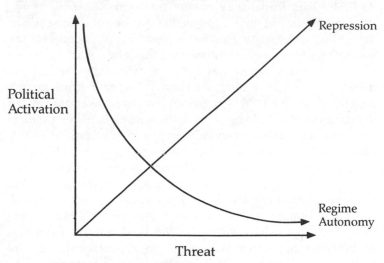

Figure 2.1
Threat, Repression, and Popular-Sector Activation

recognized this point in his original analysis of exclusionary military rule. Speculating about the reasons for the greater degree of authoritarian consolidation achieved in Brazil as compared to Argentina, O'Donnell argued that labor market differences created a stronger popular sector in Argentina. Political deactivation was consequently more difficult to achieve without extreme repression and its attendant high social costs. O'Donnell noted that in the Argentine case these costs "would soon have reached a critical threshold where the degree of social dislocation they produced would have made it very unlikely that the Brazilian type of 'success' could have been achieved."[14]

From this perspective, it is hardly surprising that the Brazilian case stands out as the most successful and durable example of bureaucratic authoritarianism in Latin America to date. Precisely because the working class was not autonomous or well organized prior to the 1964 coup, political demobilization was achieved without the legitimacy costs associated with high levels of political repression and without a total break in institutional continuity. After 1964, the military retained both an electoral arena and a legislature. Hence, as such scholars as Stepan and O'Donnell claim, high levels of class polarization and perceived threat may create conditions favorable to the implementation of orthodox economic policies, strengthen "hard-line" elements in the armed forces, augment the autonomy of state actors, or enhance the cohesion of dominant classes; but to the extent that threat reflects political activation, it implies stronger resistance from below and fundamental problems of political exclusion, institutionalization, and legitimation. Precisely because of the tension between political activation and exclusionary military rule, O'Donnell's hypotheses about regime cohesion, autonomy, and durability are not compatible with available evidence. Of the cases O'Donnell has explicitly identified as bureaucratic authoritarian, to date the greatest regime durability has been found in Brazil, where the threat was comparatively low, and in Chile, where the threat was extremely high. The least durable examples of bureaucratic authoritarianism, on the other hand, are the two Argentine cases, one of which was an instance of low threat (1966–73) and the other of high threat (1976–83). The

30

relationships that may be drawn between regime origins and other variations in regime functioning and impact are equally tenuous.[15]

The inadequacies of existing literature, however, are not merely a function of the explanatory weaknesses of the threat variable. A more fundamental problem is that theoretical formulations stressing the importance of originating crises suggest that the course of authoritarian rule is fixed *ab origine*— a deterministic vision curiously at odds with the emerging literature on democratization. Indeed, because some of the same pens have written on both topics, the theoretical contrasts between the literature analyzing the emergence of authoritarianism and that concerned with its breakdown are fascinating. Whereas the former has emphasized the importance of structural forces, the latter has taken us on a vertiginous descent down the ladder of abstraction and left us abruptly immersed in the complicated and unpredictable manuevers of individual actors. It is rather as if undesirable outcomes (the emergence of repressive military regimes) are the result of ineluctable historical forces or structural forces, whereas desirable outcomes (the breakdown of authoritarianism, liberalization, and democratization) respond to human choice and action. However comforting, such theoretical asymmetries underline the limitations of our understanding of military rule. Rather than promote *virtù* and *fortuna* to major roles, it might be more appropriate to begin thinking about authoritarianism in terms that are less societal centered and less preoccupied with the conditions associated with the installation and breakdown of democracy. The forces that shape authoritarian rule are not fixed at the time of regime emergence. The factors that explain the origins of military rule are not necessarily the same as those that account for varying patterns of postcoup development. And the level of analysis appropriate for understanding the contrasts between inclusionary and exclusionary military rule is not necessarily the most useful for understanding variations within these broad regime categories.

The Centrality of State Structures

Two decades ago Samuel P. Huntington asserted, "Military explanations do not explain military interventions."[16] Most scholars would agree. The main causes of military takeovers are to be found in the sociopolitical structure of a given society and the transnational context in which it functions. It does not necessarily follow, however, that the dynamics, functioning, and impact of military regimes can be understood solely in terms of larger social forces. A more adequate theoretical model for analyzing military rule in Latin America must consider a second element—state institutions. Because research has neglected institutional analysis in favor of societal forces, this second element has received relatively limited attention; but, to cite the title of a recent book,[17] "bringing the state back in" is essential to the study of authoritarianism.

The emergence of an authoritarian regime tips the balance of power sharply in favor of state actors, whose capacity to proceed relatively independently of societal pressures expands in response to the closure of avenues for political participation and the expression of class interests. Instead of simply processing societal inputs, aggregating individual preferences, or serving as an arena for class struggles, state actors under authoritarianism may ignore or go beyond the demands and interests of social forces to effect profound change in their societies. To the extent that they succeed in doing so, political opportunities and choices will be governed less and less by precoup conditions. The analysis of military rule consequently should be predicated on the assumption that the answers to basic questions about variations among authoritarian regimes are to be found in the dynamic interaction between social class forces and state institutions.

Foremost among those institutions are the armed forces, which—at least in the abstract—represent the quintessence of the state. Their basic role is defined in terms of issues that represent core interests of the state: national sovereignty, security, the defense of territorial integrity, and international status. Likewise, the power to coerce and enforce authoritative decisions, which is fundamental to both Marxist and Weberian conceptions of the state, is embodied more concretely in the military institution than in any other structure or set of political actors. Indeed, the relatively naked exercise of this power is the hallmark of military rule.

Focusing on state actors and state institutions takes us away from purely societal-centered analyses of military rule. As the recent literature on the state has reminded us, state actors may pursue goals, interests, and activities that are not readily reducible to those of the middle class, oligarchy, or any other set of social interests. By analytically separating state and class structures and defining the state in relatively concrete terms as a set of administrative, legal, coercive, and extractive organizations that dominate a given territory and population, it becomes possible to conceive of state actors as playing a potentially (albeit atypically) independent social role. Likewise, as the dominant state institution under military rule, the armed forces may be seen as having concerns that potentially differ from the class interest of the bourgeoisie as a whole. Those concerns revolve around such issues as professional status, internal unity and discipline, career patterns, institutional resources, corporate identity, and decision-making autonomy. Consequently, even though the military may act as an agent or voice for a particular set of class or sectoral interests, it is also a state actor with its own institutional interests, resources, and goals.

Although it is often overlooked, military institutions also have their own history. The historical dimension is critical because the central characteristics of a military are not forged on the eve of a military takeover but shaped in response to longer-term influences and past events. As Stephen D. Krasner has put it, "It is necessary to understand both how institutions reproduce themselves through time and what historical conditions gave rise to them in the first place. Current institutional structures may be a product of some peculiar historical conjuncture rather than contemporaneous factors."[18] To the extent that the histories of national militaries evince major dissimilarities, those differences are likely to create important contrasts among military regimes.

Given the distinctive interests, resources, goals, and history of the military institution, the organization of the state sector becomes a question of major importance. The political impact of military rule will obviously vary with the capacity of the military institution to express its views and exercise political power. In some military regimes the distinctive perspectives of that institution are heard loudly and clearly in government corridors. In others the military voice is muted, distorted, confused, or simply not heard. Which of these patterns prevails is a function of the institutional structure of military rule. How involved is the military as an institution in governance? Is the military a captive of the government or vice versa? Is political power concentrated in the hands of a single military leader or dispersed throughout the military institution as a whole? These kinds of questions need to be asked to understand significant variations among military regimes.

Institutional Structures and Regime Durability

Foremost among these significant regime variations are similarities and differences in the stability of authoritarian rule. Whereas the life span of some military regimes is measured in weeks, others persist for decades. Huntington's dictum that "the most important political distinction among countries concerns not their form of government but their degree of government"[19] overstates the case; but such variations in stability are nevertheless important. If regime change matters, so logically does regime stability.

The recent literature on transitions from authoritarian rule provides few insights into the question of regime stability. The emphasis placed on the role of individual leadership and historical accident represents an admission of theoretical inadequacy, not an explanation of the widely varying survival rates of military regimes. As indicated earlier, theoretical frameworks stressing the "threat" generated by the alignment and correlation of class forces at the time of regime emergence are equally unsatisfactory. Threat is important for understanding the social class basis, ideological proclivities, and policy orientations of military regimes, but its impact is highly ambiguous with respect to the important question of regime durability. As recent Southern Cone experience suggests, the survival of military regimes depends not merely on the alignment of domestic and international social forces, but also on coercive capability. To quote Guillermo O'Donnell and Philippe C. Schmitter, "No transition can be forced purely by opponents against a regime which maintains the cohesion, capacity, and disposition to apply repression."[20] Central to this issue is the institutional structure of military rule.

The relationships between institutional arrangements and regime durability are clarified if we conceptualize military regime structure in terms of two distinct theoretical dimensions. The first dimension, which corresponds to the horizontal axis in figure 2.2, is the nexus that develops between the military as an institution and the military as a government. At one end of the spectrum are military regimes in which the two roles are fused. Military participation in the process of governance, as indicated by such data as cabinet participation, is high; the military is actively involved in policy formation and implementation; and the most powerful uniformed, active-duty officer in the armed forces is either the chief of state or closely linked, both personally and professionally, to the head of the government. Given the extremely close and even overlapping

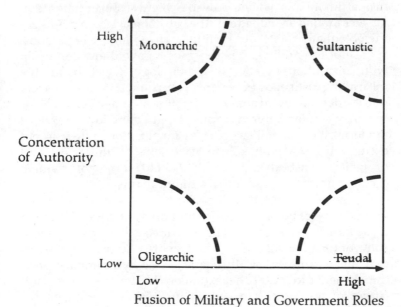

Fusion of Military and Government Roles

Figure 2.2
Theoretical Dimensions of Institutional Structures

relationships, it is impossible to determine where the govern-. ment begins and the military ends. Either the government is militarized or the military politicized. At the other end of the spectrum, lines are drawn between the military and the government. Military participation in the cabinet and other government positions is low; the chief of state is not an active-duty military officer or at least not the most powerful of such officers; and the military institution is insulated against the inevitable crises of governance.

The second dimension, corresponding to the vertical axis in figure 2.2, is the degree to which power under a military regime is concentrated in the hands of a single individual rather than exercised on a collegial basis. At the lower end of this spectrum are regimes that can be described as bureaucratic, which, contrary to the literature on bureaucratic authoritarianism, may or may not be regimes that emerge in countries that are highly modernized or have highly professional military institutions. In such regimes power rotates routinely among military officers. At the other extreme are regimes that can be described as neopatrimonial in which power is highly concentrated and radiates around an individual. The patrimonial label emphasizes the potentially stable and institutionalized nature of personal rulership; the prefix *neo* is designed to avoid any confusion with conventional Weberian terminology, which builds the misleading distinction between modern and traditional society into the definition and analysis of state structures. Personalistic rule may assume different forms at higher and lower levels of modernization or military professionalization, but it is not exclusively linked with "oligarchic society,"[21] "the lowest level of military institutionalization,"[22] "old forms of *caudillo* domination,"[23] or "traditional authoritarianism."[24]

The results of this two-dimensional conceptualization are four extreme or polar types of institutional structure. Although these four types might also be described by means of a more conventional fourfold table, the use of continua emphasizes that military rule is typically characterized by a combination of the elements found at the extremes. In the lower left-hand corner of the figure are sets of institutional arrangements labeled "oligarchic," in which political power is exercised on a collegial basis but without a high degree of day-to-day

36

involvement of the military institution in the process of governance. Among recent Latin American military regimes, Brazil in the post-1974 period resembles this extreme as does Uruguay (1973–85). In the upper left-hand corner are regimes described as "monarchic," which are characterized by a combination of personal rulership and separation of military and government power. The Onganía regime, which governed Argentina in the late 1960s, probably provides the best example of such a regime. As a retired military officer, General Juan Carlos Onganía exercised minimal control over the military institution but maximal control over government appointments and the policy process, which he jealously guarded against military participation or interference. After the 1966 coup the military junta was dissolved, leaving Onganía with complete legislative and executive authority.

Argentina in the 1976–83 period, on the other hand, provides an example that falls in the lower right-hand side of the figure. One cabinet minister who served under both Onganía and General Leopoldo F. Galtieri (1981–82) described the differences between Argentine military rule in the 1960s and the later period in the following terms: "Onganía was a king; Galtieri was a Prime Minister."[25] But the difference is not just the relative power of the head of state over the government or the relative degree of collegial control. A high level of participation by the armed forces in the process of governance characterized the military regime that seized power in 1976. Whereas under Onganía most cabinet officials, governors, heads of state banks and enterprises, and other important decision makers were civilians or retired military officials, after the 1976 coup the state apparatus, not to mention Argentine society, was militarized. Together with the collegial structure of military rule, this fusion of military and government roles produced a set of institutional arrangements that were highly feudal in nature.

In the fourth corner of the figure, labeled "sultanistic," can be placed such cases as Nicaragua under the Somoza dynasty, Chile under General Augusto Pinochet, and, with some qualifications due to the demilitarization of the regime over time, Paraguay under General Alfredo Stroessner. Peru under General Juan Velasco Alvarado (1968–75) and Bolivia under Colonel Hugo Banzer Suárez (1971–78) evinced some of the characteristics of this form of institutional structure as well; however, the military as an institution retained too much power in the two latter cases to include them in the sultanistic category. The government was more of a captive of the military than the other way around.

Whether or not military rule in Latin America has approximated feudal, monarchic, sultanistic, or oligarchic forms has had little to do with levels of social modernization, industrialization, or military professionalization. As the cases cited indicate, sultanistic forms of military rule have emerged in Latin American societies that are quite modern (Chile) and comparatively traditional (Paraguay) and feudal forms in both highly industrialized (Argentina) and unindustrialized (Ecuador) ones. Likewise, highly professionalized militaries have governed through all four types of institutional arrangements. The relationships that may be drawn between the alignment and correlation of social class forces and the organization of military rule are equally tenuous. Feudal institutional arrangements have been associated with highly exclusionary military rule (Argentina, 1976–83) as well as inclusionary authoritarianism (Peru, 1968–75). What shapes the structure of military regimes is less their social underpinnings than the specific institutional history of the armed forces in question.

The extraordinary concentration of personal power achieved by Pinochet is a case in point. Neither the professional character of the Chilean armed forces nor the social class composition of the governing coalition explains Pinochet's rise to preeminence; it was, rather, the distinctive traditions of the Chilean armed forces that created opportunities for the construction of a personal dictatorship. As chapter 5 explores in more depth, these traditions created a rigidly hierarchical organization that was socially isolated, virulently anti-Marxist, and oriented around norms of professionalism, non-deliberation, and constitutionalism. After the coup Pinochet drew on these traditions to restore the cohesion of the armed forces and to weather repeated outside challenges to his authority. *Inter alia*, a Prussian-style respect for verticality combined with the social isolation of the military cast Pinochet in the powerful role of sole interlocutor between the armed forces and the rest of society.

38

Similarly, Pinochet drew on the nondeliberative tradition to label any efforts to check his power as "political" and, hence, "unprofessional." The constitutionalist tradition was equally useful, especially after the introduction of the 1980 constitution, which extended Pinochet's presidency into the late 1980s.

The importance of institutional history is also evident in the regime structures established by the Argentine military. Following the confrontation between rival military factions known as the *azules* and *colorados* in the early 1960s, which represented the nadir of Argentine military professionalism and organizational unity, every effort was made to avoid direct involvement of the armed forces in the process of governance. The prestige and capability of the military was seen to revolve around the maintenance of strictly defined professional boundaries. The Onganía regime, in which the government and the military were relatively autonomous from one another, was the result. As an influential subsecretary in the Onganía government later wrote, "It was made clear that the armed forces neither governed nor cogoverned. But they existed and apart from personal prestige, were his [Onganía's] only base of support."[26] The lessons of that experience were incorporated into the structure of power that emerged after 1976. Prior to the coup against the Peronist government, the rival service chiefs agreed on a ruling formula that guarded against personal rulership by providing for the rotation of the presidency and the dispersal of power among the services.[27]

Table 2.1 presents data that underline the relationship between regime structure and durability. Due to the weight of international forces in the evolution of Central American authoritarianism, the table is limited to South America, but it includes all of the military regimes that have governed in that region since 1965. Classifying a large number of highly disparate regimes in terms of the vocabulary of extreme types poses obvious problems, not only because most military regimes represent diluted or combined versions of these types, but also because the institutional structure of military rule usually evolves over time. The Peruvian regime of the 1975–80 period, for example, initially combined sultanistic and feudal features but shifted in a more purely feudal direction following the ouster of Velasco Alvarado in 1975. Likewise, the Banzer

Table 2.1
Military Regime Structure and Durability[a]

Monarchical Military Regimes	*Sultanistic Military Regimes*
Argentina, 1966–73	Chile, 1973–89
Bolivia, 1964–71 (Barrientos)	Paraguay, 1954–89
Average durability: 6.9 years	Average durability: 25.1 years
Oligarchic Military Regimes	*Feudal Military Regimes*
Brazil, 1964–85	Argentina, 1976–83
Uruguay, 1973–85	Bolivia, 1971–79
	Bolivia, 1980–82
	Ecuador, 1963–66
	Ecuador, 1972–79
	Peru, 1968–80
Average durability: 16.3 years	Average durability: 6.5 years

[a] Differences among categories significant at the .05 level.

regime in Bolivia, which began with a somewhat monarchical set of institutional structures, changed character substantially over time, shifting in a feudal direction. Nevertheless, even crude classifications of the type presented in the table are revealing with respect to the relationship between institutional structure and the stability of military rule.

The table suggests that two types of institutional patterns have provided a basis for stable military rule: the oligarchic, which lasted nearly 12 years in Uruguay and more than 20 in Brazil, and the sultanistic, represented by the Pinochet and Stroessner regimes, whose durability compares favorably with that of all other forms of military rule. Although the long-standing weight of international pressures in Central America raises questions about the significance of data from that region, it should be noted that regimes in that area also appear to comport with the pattern suggested by the table. The records for regime durability in that region are held by the rather oligarchic regime of El Salvador (24.8 years) and the sultanistic regimes of Haiti (28.3 years) and Nicaragua (43.1 years).

Lesser stability has been associated with feudal and monarchic forms of military rule. Indeed, the table significantly exaggerates the stability of the latter two forms by following the convention of treating all but one of the periods of military rule as if a single regime had governed continuously. The exception is Bolivia, where the Barrientos regime has been separated from the

Banzerato that followed. Even in the case of Bolivia, however, the stability of feudal and monarchical forms of military rule is seriously overstated. The 1964–71 period was punctuated by coups that brought four different presidents to power after the death of General René Barrientos in 1969; likewise, between the overthrow of Banzer in 1978 and the brief restoration of civilian rule in 1979, two successful military coups occurred.

Considerable instability also characterized other periods of military rule listed in the feudal and monarchical categories. By 1970, the Onganía regime in Argentina had unraveled, leading to the ouster of the president in June 1970 as well as of his successor, General Roberto Levingston, the following year. In the case of the regimes listed in the feudal category, the level of instability is even more understated. Every one of the periods of feudal military rule listed in the table was interrupted by one or more military coups and unscheduled changes of leadership. Some of these changes left the basic rules of the game defining the regime unchanged, but in other instances, notably Peru in the post-1968 period, the ouster of an established leader led to important shifts in the character of the regime in question. No coups interrupted the periods of military rule listed in either the sultanistic or oligarchic categories. It is also worth noting that variations in durability within the feudal category reflect the extent to which individual regimes approximated the institutional structure of one of the more stable types. Significantly, the longest lasting regimes in the feudal category were the Bolivian and Peruvian, which initially combined sultanistic and feudal features.

The question is why do institutional arrangements make a difference to the stability of military rule? Are institutional arrangements epiphenomenal in the sense that some underlying set of conditions determines both regime structure and regime stability? One obvious candidate is military factionalism. The problem in the first instance with such an explanation is operational. Military factionalism is characteristically assessed on the basis of regime stability, leading to a tautological pattern of explanation. More significantly, however, the argument that regime structures produce factionalism is much more plausible than is its opposite. The seizure of power by highly unified militaries has resulted in feudal and monarchical power structures; likewise, factionalized militaries have established regimes with sultanistic and oligarchic power structures. The unity of the Argentine military in 1976, for example, was no less impressive than that of the Chilean military in the immediate aftermath of the 1973 coup, but the former resulted in a feudal institutional structure and the latter in a sultanistic one. The Chilean case is not anomalous. The unity of the Paraguayan military was also anything but a given during the early stages of the Stroessner regime. It was Stroessner and Pinochet's consolidation of personal control that created military unity rather than the other way around. Stated another way, sultanistic regimes do not reflect military unity; they forge it by repressing dissent within the armed forces. Similarly, feudal patterns of military rule are more a cause than a consequence of military factionalism. Collegial rule combined with a high level of military involvement in the process of governance shatters military unity and thereby undermines the principal institutional basis for regime stability.

As the recent literature on transitions from authoritarian rule demonstrates, explaining regime stability or breakdown in terms of underlying structural forces is equally problematic. The correct conclusion, however, is not that regime durability depends on leadership or chance, but rather that the impact of the structural forces is mediated by political institutions. Given a high level of institutional involvement by the armed forces in the process of governance, the political divisions evident in the wider society tend to become replicated within the military institution itself. Unless power becomes highly concentrated, every government crisis is thus translated into a regime crisis. Monarchical regimes are vulnerable for a different reason. The separation of military and government roles protects the regime from the military disunity that develops under feudal institutional arrangements; but highly centralized governments that do not fuse control over the military with control over the government become more and more out of touch with their institutional base and degenerate over time into feudal regimes. Looking at the question from the perspective of opposition forces, provoking a regime crisis is much more difficult if military unity has been protected by oligarchic rule or imposed by sultanistic rule.

International Forces, Social Structure, and Institutional Forms

Developing a more adequate understanding of military rule consequently presupposes that analytical frameworks incorporate three different sets of factors, corresponding to three rather different levels of social analysis. As indicated in the previous chapter, the basic course of military rule is conditioned at the broadest level by the international context, which in the Latin American region has created an environment much more hospitable to exclusionary than to inclusionary military rule. National social structures, as well as the political dynamic that has been established in response to them over time, constitute a second set of variables. The extent to which a military regime is inclusionary rather than exclusionary is determined primarily by these larger social conditions. Knowing something about the factors that shape the basic orientation of military regimes, however, does not take us very far in analyzing other issues. A large gulf separates regime origins from regime outcomes, creating room for major variations in the dynamics, functioning, and impact of regimes that are armed with similar ideologies, international allies, and bases of social class support. To understand these variations, it is necessary to move beyond the analysis of structural conditions shaping the basic contours of military rule and grapple with the question of state institutions.

By definition the armed forces are the dominant force in the state apparatus under military rule. The nature of the armed forces and how they exercise their role are consequently of central importance to the analysis of diachronic and cross-sectional variations in the political outcomes of military regimes. Particularly significant is the institutional relationship that develops between the armed forces and the government. That relationship, which is not a simple function of socio-economic conditions, provides a basis for understanding the varying capacity of military regimes to weather changes in the configuration of international and social class forces associated with their emergence. As argued in the following chapter, regime durability in turn shapes other political outcomes. The longer a military regime stays in power, the greater its political impact.

Notes

1 Abraham F. Lowenthal and J. Samuel Fitch, *Armies and Politics in Latin America*, rev. ed. (New York: Holmes & Meier, 1986).

2 For a more complete overview of these developments and their larger theoretical significance, see David Collier, "Introduction," and "Overview of the Bureaucratic-Authoritarian Model," in *The New Authoritarianism*, ed. David Collier, 3–32; idem, "Industrial Modernization and Political Change: A Latin American Perspective," *World Politics* 30 (July 1978): 593–614.

3 See, in particular, James M. Malloy, "The Politics of Transition in Latin America," in *Authoritarians and Democrats: Regime Transition in Latin America*, ed. James M. Malloy and Mitchell A. Seligson (Pittsburgh: University of Pittsburgh Press, 1987), 235–58; Guillermo O'Donnell and Philippe C. Schmitter, *Transitions from Authoritarian Rule: Tentative Conclusions about Uncertain Democracies* (Baltimore: Johns Hopkins University Press, 1986).

4 The major contributions to this literature revolve around the work of Guillermo O'Donnell. They include O'Donnell, *Modernization and Bureaucratic-Authoritarianism*; idem, "Reflections on the Patterns of Change in the Bureaucratic-Authoritarian State," *Latin American Research Review* 13, no. 1 (1978): 3–38; idem, *Bureaucratic Authoritarianism: Argentina, 1966–1973, in Comparative Perspective*, trans. James McGuire (Berkeley: University of California Press, 1988); Collier, ed., *The New Authoritarianism*; Karen L. Remmer and Gilbert W. Merkx, "Bureaucratic-Authoritarianism Revisited," *Latin American Research Review* 17, no. 2 (1982): 3–40.

5 O'Donnell, *Modernization and Bureaucratic-Authoritarianism*, 101–103.

6 Guillermo O'Donnell, "Reflections," *Latin American Research Review* 13, no. 1 (1978): 3–38; idem, "Tensions in the Bureaucratic-Authoritarian State and the Question of Democracy," in *The New Authoritarianism*, ed. David Collier, 285–318.

7 O'Donnell, "Reflections," 7.

8 Alfred Stepan, *The Military in Politics: Changing Patterns in Brazil* (Princeton: Princeton University Press, 1971); idem, "State Power and the Strength of Civil Society in the Southern Cone of Latin America," in *Bringing the State Back In*, ed. Peter B. Evans, Dietrich Rueschemeyer, and Theda Skocpol (Cambridge: Cambridge University Press, 1985).

9 Stepan, "State Power," 290–316.

10 Ibid., 325.

11 Ibid., 320.

12 See Andrés Fontana, "De la crisis de Malvinas a la subordinación condicionada: conflictos intramilitares y transición política en Argentina," Working Paper No. 74, Kellogg Institute (Notre Dame, IN: Kellogg Institute, 1986); Aldo C. Vacs, "Authoritarian

Breakdown and Redemocratization in Argentina," in *Authoritarians and Democrats*, ed. Malloy and Seligson, 15–42; David Pion-Berlin, "The Fall of Military Rule in Argentina: 1976–1983," *Journal of Interamerican Studies and World Affairs* XXVII, 2 (Summer 1985): 55–76.

13 Harry Eckstein, "Case Study and Theory in Political Science," in *Handbook of Political Science*, Vol. VII: *Strategies of Inquiry*, ed. Fred I. Greenstein and Nelson W. Polsby (Reading, MA: Addison-Wesley Publishing, 1975), 118.

14 O'Donnell, *Modernization and Bureaucratic-Authoritarianism*, 101n.

15 Remmer and Merkx, "Bureaucratic-Authoritarianism Revisited," 3–40.

16 Samuel P. Huntington, *Political Order in Changing Societies* (New Haven: Yale University Press, 1968), 194.

17 Evans, Rueschemeyer, and Skocpol, eds., *Bringing the State Back In*.

18 Stephen D. Krasner, "Approaches to the State: Alternative Conceptions and Historical Dynamics," *Comparative Politics* 16 (January 1984): 225.

19 Huntington, *Political Order in Changing Societies*, 1.

20 O'Donnell and Schmitter, *Transitions from Authoritarian Rule*, 21.

21 Huntington, *Political Order in Changing Societies*, 201.

22 Abraham F. Lowenthal, "Armies and Politics in Latin America," in *Armies and Politics in Latin America*, rev. ed., ed. Abraham F. Lowenthal and J. Samuel Fitch (New York: Holmes & Meier, 1986), 19.

23 Fernando Henrique Cardoso, "On the Characterization of Authoritarian Regimes in Latin American," in *The New Authoritarianism*, ed. David Collier, 35.

24 O'Donnell, *Modernization and Bureaucratic-Authoritarianism*, 112.

25 Author's interview with Nicanor Costa Méndez, Buenos Aires, May 1986.

26 Roberto Roth, *Los años de Onganía: relato de un testigo* (Buenos Aires: Ediciones La Campana, 1981), 45. See also Guillermo O'Donnell, "Modernization and Military Coups: Theory, Comparisons, and the Argentine Case," in *Armies and Politics in Latin America*, ed. Abraham Lowenthal and J. Samuel Fitch (New York: Holmes & Meier, 1986), 96–133; idem, *Bureaucratic Authoritarianism: Argentina 1966–1973*.

27 Rubén M. Perina, *Onganía, Levingston, Lanusse: Los militares en la política argentina* (Buenos Aires: Editorial de Belgrano, 1983, 173n.

CHAPTER 3

The Political Impact of
Military Rule

In September 1955, Juan Perón took refuge on a Paraguayan gunboat in the port of Buenos Aires. Eighteen years later a crowd of one million Argentines gathered outside Ezeiza airport to welcome the former dictator back from exile. If anything, the efforts of two exclusionary military regimes to destroy the Peronist movement had enlarged the political stature of its leader. Shortly before his seventy-eighth birthday, Perón won more than 60 percent of the vote in competitive presidential elections.

Perón's durability as a political figure is not unparalleled. A striking feature of Latin American politics is the number of leaders who have enjoyed exceptionally prolonged political careers. José María Velasco Ibarra of Ecuador, after having been ousted from the presidency by military coups on three separate occasions, ran successfully for office a fifth time in 1968 at the age of seventy-five. Víctor Paz Estenssoro, the leader of the 1952 Bolivian revolution, won a third presidential term at the age of seventy-seven. In the case of Peru, the prominent figure is Víctor Haya de la Torre, who led the Peruvian Aprista party from its founding in 1924 until his death in 1979. Such instances of leadership survival involve more than a simple fact of longevity. In such countries as Argentina, Peru, Bolivia, and Ecuador, military rule has contributed directly to unusually prolonged political careers by disrupting the process whereby new political leaders achieve recognition, gain popular followings, and move up the recruitment ladder. Hence, although military regimes routinely announce their deter-

47

mination to alter the political life of their countries, their capacity to effect such change is not unlimited.

Just how extensive is the capacity of military regimes to transform the political situation associated with their emergence? Under what conditions is military rule likely to produce major shifts in the preexisting alignment and correlation of political forces? Does authoritarianism disrupt the process through which political beliefs, partisan loyalties, and cleavage structures are established and maintained? What factors limit the capacity of military officers to alter the status quo ante? Such questions shift attention away from the causes of military regimes to their consequences and open the door to an analysis of the factors producing, as well as inhibiting, political change over time.

Theoretical Perspectives

Existing literature offers few insights into the political impact of authoritarianism. As indicated in the previous chapter, theoretical analyses of military rule have rather consistently downplayed the capacity of state actors to induce political change, emphasizing instead the impact of societal forces and originating conditions on the political evolution of authoritarianism. The exceptional durability of Latin American political leaders is compatible with this theoretical perspective, as is much of the literature on political party systems.

Political scientists have long been impressed with the tendency of party systems to persist fundamentally unchanged over time, despite significant shifts in socioeconomic structure. In their comparative analysis of Western European party systems, for example, Stein Rokkan and Seymour Martin Lipset pointed to the "freezing" of major party alternatives in the wake of the extension of the suffrage, emphasizing that *"the party systems of the 1960s reflect, with few but significant exceptions, the cleavage structures of the 1920s."*[1] The reasons for this stability remain somewhat unclear, but the intergenerational transmission of party identification, the self-perpetuating character of party structures, the closure of organizational space, and the related narrowing of what Rokkan and Lipset have called the "support market" all appear to have contributed to the persistence of electoral loyalties, partisan alternatives, and issue polarities over time.

Given the importance of political parties in shaping and reflecting political attitudes, linking mass publics with political elites, and recruiting political leaders, the durability of party systems can be seen as limiting the capacity of military regimes to alter the preauthoritarian political situation. The Western European experience suggests that continuities between pre- and postauthoritarian democratic regimes may be impressive even when party systems that have not been well established through an extended series of national elections fall victim to a protracted period of authoritarian rule.[2]

Yet, as emphasized in the previous chapter, the impact of state actors also needs to be taken into account. The inability of military regimes to effect lasting political change simply cannot be taken for granted. A completely new cadre of political leaders may emerge in response to the imprisonment, exile, and execution of former democratic officials and well-known political activists. As authoritarian rule introduces new sources of cleavage and conflict into a society, it may also lead to the redefinition of political beliefs and loyalties along a pro- versus antiauthoritarian political continuum. Restrictions on the dissemination of political information and constraints on party, interest group, and electoral activity may similarly contribute to important discontinuities between pre- and postauthoritarian regimes. Prohibitions against political party and trade union meetings, for example, are likely to widen the gap between leaders and rank-and-file activists, to undermine the ability of political groups to secure funds and recruit new members, and to contribute to ideological and organizational fragmentation. Authoritarian rule also frequently entails a reorientation of public policy. To the extent that this reorientation involves significant social and economic change, the political status quo ante may be fundamentally altered. In addition, the redefinition of electoral regulations and other political rules, which typically accompanies the process of regime transition, is likely to create major contrasts between postauthoritarian party systems and their democratic predecessors. From this perspective, the political continuities

49

between pre- and postauthoritarian democratic regimes, which have been observed in the Western European context, might be seen as the product of a special set of historical conditions or dismissed altogether as the imaginary products of an exaggerated historicist version of political reality. In the absence of any clearly defined objective standards, one observer may see impressive political continuities where another is struck by massive change and discontinuity.

The contradictory predictions that began to emerge in the late 1970s about the contours of postauthoritarian politics in Chile illustrate these divergent perspectives on the impact of authoritarian rule. Some scholars argued that the Pinochet regime would be unlikely to introduce lasting change, because of the Chilean party system's deep historical roots and/or because military rule had tended to freeze the status quo ante by eliminating the forums through which new leaders, parties, and ideological tendencies develop a base of popular support.[3] Other scholars, however, emphasized that the far-reaching sociopolitical changes effected by the Pinochet regime were eroding the bases of the preexisting party system, creating possibilities for fundamental change in the alignment and correlation of political forces.[4]

The impact of such variables as repression on the process of regime transformation likewise can be viewed from contradictory theoretical perspectives. If authoritarian rule tends to freeze political life by disrupting the processes through which new sets of political alternatives become recognized, then high levels of repression are likely to preserve characteristics of the preauthoritarian political situation more fully than do low levels of repression. On the other hand, high levels of repression might be linked with major discontinuities between pre- and postauthoritarian regimes on the grounds that repression decimates political leadership ranks, creates new sources of cleavage, alters political beliefs and attitudes, undermines the social bases of existing organizations, and otherwise contributes to sociopolitical change. The impact of the duration of authoritarianism is equally debatable. If authoritarian rule limits change in the status quo ante, then variations in regime survival rates should have little effect on the degree of continuity between pre- and postauthoritarian party systems. The same is true if, as Arturo and J. Samuel Valenzuela have argued, "The political landscape is more or less impermeable to change once it has been firmly established. Periods of authoritarian rule, however long, do little to undermine it."[5] But if authoritarian rule promotes political change, longer regime survival rates should produce greater discontinuities.

In short, the political consequences of military rule are open to question. The capacity of military regimes to promote political change can plausibly be seen as extensive or limited. Likewise, existing literature provides no unambiguous guidelines for assessing how characteristics of the preauthoritarian political order or variables, such as regime durability or political repression, condition the impact of authoritarian rule.

Redemocratization in Latin America

The importance of analyzing military rule in terms of the dynamic interaction of social forces and the state is emphasized by the experience of countries that have undergone processes of redemocratization. Such experiences offer crucial insights into the impact of military rule because pre- and post-authoritarian elections provide us with concrete bench marks against which to assess shifts in political beliefs, partisan loyalties, and cleavage structures. Aggregate electoral statistics, which supply meaningful information about partisan loyalties, political alignments, and other characteristics of democratic regimes, are available for most countries over long time periods. No comparable source of data exists for measuring the political impact of authoritarianism in nondemocratic settings.

There are also strong theoretical advantages in focusing on experiences of redemocratization. The political histories of countries in which periods of democratic rule have been interrupted by authoritarianism provide a basis for evaluating continuities and discontinuities in party systems. Precisely because party systems are widely considered to be resistant to change, they offer a crucial test of the capacity of military regimes to alter the status quo ante. Party systems are the *least likely* area in which to find evidence of the impact of military regimes. Hence, data suggesting that authoritarianism can produce major discontinuities in party systems establish a very strong basis for dismissing the notion that originating conditions exercise a decisive influence over the evolution of military rule. The finding that military rule can alter party systems creates a strong presumption that authoritarianism can transform most aspects of political life.

The subsequent analysis explores all cases of redemocratization in Latin America between 1940 and 1988 in which democratic regimes were displaced by authoritarian ones lasting at least three years.[6] To fall within the redemocratization category, national political leadership positions must have been filled by means of competitive elections, both before and after the imposition of military rule. Excluded from consideration are such cases as Guatemala, in which electoral competition has been restricted by massive fraud. Also excluded are cases of what Alain Rouquié has called "supervised democracy,"[7] in which efforts to legitimize authoritarian rule have involved the creation of an official party or a controlled party system. In doubtful cases, an attempt has been made to err on the side of inclusiveness.[8]

Given the prevailing tendency to view Latin American politics in terms of alternating waves of military and civilian rule, surprisingly few cases fit the criteria outlines above. Nearly half of countries in the region either did not experience a period of competitive rule between 1940 and 1988 (Mexico, Paraguay, Panama, Nicaragua, El Salvador, Guatemala, and Haiti) or remained under authoritarian rule after the breakdown of political democracy (Cuba and Chile). Of the remaining countries, 9 fit the criteria outlined earlier: Argentina, Brazil, Bolivia, Colombia, Ecuador, Honduras, Peru, Uruguay, and Venezuela. Three of them (Argentina, Honduras, and Peru) have experienced redemocratization more than once, resulting in a total of 13 different cases. To assess the impact of authoritarian rule in each of these cases, data were collected on the competitive national elections that most immediately preceded the authoritarian seizure of power (time 1 or T1 election) as well as those elections associated with redemocratization (time 2 or T2 election). These data, together with other relevant facts about the 13 cases, are summarized in tables 3.1 and 3.2.

Table 3.1
Cases of Redemocratization in Latin America, 1940–88

	Years of Authoritarian Rule	T1 Election Year	T2 Election Year	% Pop Voting at T1	% Electoral Increase	Years of Dem. Regime Survival[a]
Argentina	1946–58	1946	1958	18.3	218.9	4
Peru (I)	1948–56	1945	1956	6.3	189.5	6
Venezuela	1948–58	1946	1958	31.9	92.2	29+
Colombia	1953–57	1949	1958	16.6	110.9	30+
Honduras (I)	1963–71	1957	1971	20.0	79.0	1
Bolivia	1964–82	1960	1980	28.5	50.8	6+
Argentina (II)	1966–73	1965	1973	41.3	27.9	3
Peru (II)	1968–00	1963	1980	17.8	171.6	8+
Ecuador	1972–78	1968	1978	14.7	78.9	9+
Honduras (II)	1972–81	1971	1981	23.4	80.7	6+
Argentina (III)	1976–83	1973	1983	49.9	20.2	5+
Uruguay	1973–85	1971	1984	56.6	16.7	3+
Brazil	1964–85	1962	1986	19.6	369.0	3+

Sources: Kenneth Ruddle and Philip Gillette, eds., *Latin American Political Statistic* (Los Angeles: Latin American Center, University of California, 1972); John D. Martz *Ecuador: Conflicting Political Culture and the Quest for Progress* (Boston: Allyn and Bacon, 1972), 128; Howard Handelman, "Ecuador. A New Political Direction? *American Universities Field Staff Reports*, South America Series, No. 47 (1979); Rafae Roncagliolo, *Quien Ganó: Elecciones 1931–80* (Lima: Centro de Estudios y Promoción del Desarrollo, 1980), 38, 80, 83; *Hispanic American Report, X:* 10 (October 1957): 523 James A. Morris, "Honduran Elections and Patterns of Party Support," Centra American Working Group Paper, New Mexico State University (Las Cruces, 1982) Operations Policy Research, Inc., Institute for the Comparative Study of Politica Systems, *Bolivia: Election Factbook* (Washington, DC, Institute for the Comparative Study of Political Systems, 1966); *Foreign Broadcast Information Service* 14 (July 1980) C1; Donald L. Herman, *Christian Democracy in Venezuela* (Chapel Hill, NC University of North Carolina Press, 1980), 27–31; Gregorio Badeni, *Comportamient electoral en la Argentina* (Buenos Aires: Plus Ultra, 1976); Darío Cantón, *Materiale para el estudio de la sociología política en la Argentina*, Vol. I (Buenos Aires: Institut Torcuato Di Tella, 1968); *La Nación* (International Edition), 7 November 1983, 1 *Keesing's Contemporary Archives* (London, 1960–88); Christian Anglade, "Th Brazilian Elections of November 1986," *Electoral Studies, VI*, 6 (1987): 165; Charles G Gillespie, "Activists and Floating Voters: The Unheeded Lessons of Uruguay's 198. Primaries," in *Elections and Democratization in Latin America, 1980–85*, ed. Paul W Drake and Eduardo Silva (San Diego: University of California, San Diego, 1986), 22' Juan Rial, "The Uruguayan Elections of 1984: A Triumph of the Center," in *Election and Democratization in Latin America, 1980–85*, ed. Drake and Silva, 248.
[a] As of 1988.

Table 3.1 provides basic information about the cases, including the years in which the T1 and T2 elections were held, the size of the electorate and its increase between the two elections, the years of authoritarian rule separating the elections, and the length of time that the reconstituted democracies survived. Note that in nearly all of the cases the pre- and postauthoritarian elections were separated by a decade or more, allowing considerable time for socioeconomic change as well as electoral growth. On average, the electorate grew 115.9 percent in the 13 cases, a figure that reflects not only population growth, but also changes in electoral eligibility enfranchising women (Colombia; Argentina, 1946–58; Peru, 1948–56; and Venezuela), illiterates (Brazil and Peru, 1968–80), and 18 to 21 year olds (Argentina, 1966–73; Brazil; and Peru, 1968–80). These figures on the growth of the electorate alone provide a basis for anticipating major discontinuities in the party systems of the 13 cases over time.

Table 3.1 also underlines the importance of specific historical conjunctures for understanding the process of redemocratization and its outcome. In 11 of the 13 cases, redemocratization was linked with the cyclical shifts away from military rule of the late 1950s and late 1970s—periods in which the international environment created a relatively favorable set of political conditions. In the 2 remaining cases (Argentina, 1966–73, and Honduras, 1963–71), the process of redemocratization was countercyclical and proved exceptionally ephemeral. Thus, not only has redemocratization rarely occurred in isolation from broader Latin American political trends, but historical timing also appears to affect possibilities for the consolidation of competitive political institutions. The same is true of prospects for the consolidation of military rule. Democratic breakdowns that have occurred in conjunction with democratizing cycles have produced durable military regimes. Hence, the Peruvian and Argentine coups of 1962, which interrupted the process of redemocratization before political authorities could pass power on to constitutionally elected successors, brought only short-lived caretaker governments to power. By 1963, competitive institutions had been restored in both countries. When the process of redemocratization has been countercyclical, on the other hand, the breakdown of competitive rule has resulted in the consolidation of authoritarianism.

Table 3.2, which presents data on the electoral shifts that took place between T1 and T2 elections, provides a basis for assessing the political impact of authoritarian rule in each of the 13 cases. The first column of the table measures changes in the fortunes of political parties receiving more than 5 percent of the vote in T1 or T2 congressional elections. The figures in this column were calculated as the sum of the differences between major party vote shares at T1 and T2 elections, as illustrated by the hypothetical example presented in table 3.3.

The second column in Table 3.2 reports changes in the percentage of the total vote received by minor parties. Although in general the minor party share of the vote was small and

Table 3.2
Shifts in Electoral Outcomes between Pre- and
Postauthoritarian Elections

		Change in Major Party Vote Shares	Change in Minor Party Vote Shares	Index of Party System Discontinuity
Colombia	1953–57	8.1	0.4	8.5
Uruguay	1973–85	8.3	1.9	10.2
Honduras	1972–81	16.9	4.0	20.9
Honduras	1963–71	45.3	0.0	45.3
Argentina	1966–73	34.3	14.0	48.3
Venezuela	1948–58	53.7	5.7	59.4
Argentina	1976–83[a]	47.9	15.8	63.7
Peru	1963–80	48.0	17.6	65.6
Ecuador	1972–78[a]	96.4	1.0	97.4
Peru	1948–56[b]	108.6	0.0	108.6
Argentina	1946–58[c]	113.6	5.3	118.9
Bolivia	1964–82[a]	135.5	12.4	147.9
Brazil	1964–85[d]	165.4	3.4	168.8

Sources: As for table 3.1.

[a] Presidential election results.

[b] Data adjusted in accordance with Hugo Neira's estimates of Aprista voting strength in "Peru," *Guide to the Political Parties of Latin America*, trans. Michel Perl (Middlesex, England: Penguin Books, 1969), 420. Calculations based on legislative seats.

[c] Data adjusted in accordance with Peter G. Snow's estimates of Peronist voting strength in "Parties and Elections in Argentina: The Elections of 1962 and 1963," *Midwest Journal of Political Science* IX (February 1965): 5.

[d] Based on legislative seats.

Table 3.3
Hypothetical Shifts in Party Vote Shares

Party	% Vote T1	% Vote T2	% Change
Conservative	40	45	5
Liberal	35	30	5
Communist	25	25	0
		Aggregate Change in Major Party Vote Shares =	10

registered little change over time, in some cases, notably Peru in 1980 and Argentina in 1983, the process of redemocratization was associated with a major shift in the political fortunes of minor parties.

The statistics presented in the final column of Table 3.2, which were calculated by adding the first two columns, represent a summary measure of changes in electoral outcomes and party fortunes over time. To simplify subsequent discussion, this measure, which is designed to facilitate comparisons among the 13 cases, is called the Index of Party System Discontinuity, or PSD Index.

Perhaps the most striking feature of Table 3.2 is the enormous variation that exists among the 13 cases. At one extreme, represented by Colombia, the data show that authoritarian rule produced little or no change in a preexisting competitive party system. Indeed, what might be called the *freezing hypothesis* appears to fit the Colombian case remarkably well. Greater electoral shifts took place between the Colombian congressional elections of 1939 and 1949 than between the competitive elections of 1949 and 1958, which preceded and followed the 1953–57 period of military rule. The democratic 1958–68 period also witnessed more change in electoral outcomes than did the preceding decade, as measured by shifts in the distribution of both the interparty and intraparty vote.[9]

A similar tendency toward party system freezing is evident in the Uruguayan case. Greater change took place between the elections of 1962 and 1966 and between those of 1966 and 1971 than between the pre- and postauthoritarian elections, which were separated by 13 years. On the other hand, significant shifts in intraparty forces did occur between 1971 and 1984, cutting in half the vote of the right wings of both major parties.[10]

The relationship between authoritarianism and party system stability is even more ambiguous in the Honduran case. Since 1940, there have been no extended periods of competitive party rule with which to compare the political shifts that occurred between the 1957 and 1971 or 1971 and 1981 elections. The only available reference point is the October 11, 1954, general election. Nevertheless, the change in the distribution of the vote between that election and the election of 1957 does suggest that authoritarian rule in Honduras failed to produce much political change. The PSD index for shifts occurring between the 1954 and 1957 elections equals 26.9, as compared to 45.3 and 20.9, respectively, for the longer 1963–71 and 1972–81 periods, which were characterized by authoritarian rule (see table 3.2).

At the other extreme stand the cases of Bolivia, Argentina (1946–58), Peru (1948–56), and Brazil, where periods of military rule were associated with major political changes. Indeed, in all of these cases discontinuties between T1 and T2 elections were so great as to pose serious dilemmas with respect to the problem of measuring and comparing political change. These difficulties are compounded by the paucity of data for electoral results.

In the case of Peru, where published data on the vote in congressional elections remain exiguous and often contradictory, it is necessary to rely on presidential election results to assess political change over time. For the 1945 and 1956 elections, these data are unfortunately rather inadequate. The Aprista party, which has provided the Peruvian party system with its principal element of continuity over time, did not compete openly in presidential elections until 1962. It participated instead in ad hoc electoral coalitions that dissolved rapidly in the wake of elections: the Frente Democrático Nacional, which brought President J. L. Bustamente y Rivero to power in 1945, and the Movimiento Democrático Pradista, which successfully backed Manuel Prado in 1956. If these coalitions were treated as parties for the purposes of calculating the indicators in table 3.2, Peru's PSD index would approach 200—a figure suggesting that all of the major parties competing in the 1945 elections had disappeared by 1956. Given the active role played by the Apristas in both elections, such an index would obviously be highly misleading. The figures in table 3.2 have therefore been based on Hugo Neira's estimates of Aprista strength in 1945 and 1956. These estimates err on the side of exaggerating continuities.[11] Nevertheless, Peru's PSD index for the 1948–56 period still remains very high, largely because political cleavages had yet to crystallize around a well-defined set of partisan alternatives. To some extent, disjunctions between the 1945 and 1956 elections also reflect the rise of a significant new force in Peruvian politics, the Acción Popular led by Fernando Belaúnde.

Discontinuities in the case of Brazil resulted more directly from military rule. To establish its political legitimacy, the Brazilian military regime maintained an electoral arena and engaged in intensive efforts at party system engineering. The high PSD index in table 3.2 reflects these efforts. Between 1964 and 1986, political conflict in Brazil crystallized along pro- versus anti-regime lines, displacing and subsuming older issues and organizational loyalties. The overwhelming majority of voters in the 1986 elections cast their ballots for one of the two parties that had emerged after the 1964 coup. This crystallization of conflict creates problems in calculating Brazil's PSD index inasmuch as a high percentage of votes in the baseline election of 1962 went to local and ad hoc party coalitions. To avoid exaggerating the real extent of party discontinuity, the PSD index for Brazil has therefore been calculated on the basis of the distribution of legislative seats.

Discontinuities in the other two cases ranking at the bottom of table 3.2 reflect rather different sets of political circumstances. In the case of Bolivia, the fragmentation of the Movimiento Nacionalista Revolucionario (MNR), the country's dominant political force from 1952 to 1964, produced the high PSD index reported in table 3.2, although a lack of continuity in opposition forces also played a role. As in the Peruvian case discussed earlier, the preauthoritarian party system consisted largely of one party and a host of disorganized elements.

The division of a major political party, the Unión Cívica Radical, also gave rise to significant discontinuities in the 1946–58 Argentine case. In 1946, the Radical party campaigned as the chief alternative to Peronism; in 1958, two Radical parties, the Unión Cívica Radical Intransigente (UCRI) and the Unión Cívica Radical del Pueblo (UCRP), competed to secure a plurality of the popular vote. Restrictions on Peronist participation in the 1958 elections also contributed to discontinuities between 1946 and 1958 and left Peronist supporters with a choice of voting for the UCRI or casting blank ballots. The 1946–58 case thus poses problems similar to those of Peru (1948–56) inasmuch as the strength of one of the country's major political parties cannot be assessed accurately from electoral results. As a consequence, estimates of electoral strength have been used to avoid exaggerating discontinuities between the pre- and postauthoritarian elections.

The remaining five cases in table 3.2 fall between the extremes of Colombia, Uruguay, and Honduras and Peru (1948–56), Argentina (1946–58), Bolivia, and Brazil. Of these five, Argentina (1966–73) most closely resembles the three cases characterized by high party system continuity, inasmuch as change resulted chiefly from the strengthening of the electoral position of the dominant party and the erosion of the minor party vote rather than from major reversals in party fortunes or the appearance of new electoral forces. In the other four cases, major shifts occurred in the relative strength of different political tendencies. In the 1983 elections, the Unión Cívica Radical (UCR) displaced Peronist forces to become the nation's largest party, chiefly by wooing votes away from smaller parties. In Peru (1968–80), the return of competitive elections brought the same man, Belaúnde, back to the presidency. Yet his victory disguised a basic change in the status quo ante. Between 1963 and 1980, the right-wing share of the Peruvian vote fell from 25.5 to 10.2 percent, while the left, although fragmented among a large number of small parties, emerged as a significant electoral tendency for the first time. A similar, albeit much less pronounced, change occurred in Ecuador in the wake of the 1972–78 period of military rule. The 1978 elections were marked by the disappearance of the previously dominant and highly personalist Federación Nacional Velasquista, a sharp decline in the political fortunes of the traditional Conservative and Liberal parties, and the rise of the left-of-center Concentración de Fuerzas Populares (CFP) and Izquierda Democrática (ID). Finally, in Venezuela the elections that followed the collapse of the Pérez Jiménez dictatorship were characterized by a notable erosion in the electoral position of Acción Democrática, whose share of the vote fell from 78.4 in 1946 to 47.5 in 1958, and a marked increase in the popularity of the Unión Republicana

Democrática, which temporarily displaced COPEI as the nation's second largest political party.

Variations in the Political Impact of Authoritarian Rule

The data in table 3.2 clearly demonstrate that authoritarian rule leads to much more political discontinuity in some cases than in others. What accounts for its variable impact? Is the amount of change registered between pre- and postauthoritarian elections related to characteristics of the military regime in question, such as its longevity, or to other variables, such as the level of political participation? If the latter, are the political experiences of the cases of moderate and high party system discontinuity necessarily incompatible with the argument that authoritarian rule limits rather than promotes political change? Would more or less change have occurred under liberal democratic regimes?

Such questions are exceptionally difficult to answer because national party systems tend to be rather unique historical products with dynamic properties that may vary considerably over time. To complicate matters further, comparative reference points are few and far between. Only two of the medium and high discontinuity cases experienced, either before or after authoritarian rule, an uninterrupted series of national elections extending over a time period comparable to that separating T1 and T2 elections. In the case of both Ecuador and Venezuela, there have been periods of competitive rule characterized by just as much party system discontinuity as those periods interrupted by military intervention. In addition, moderately high indices of party system discontinuity in these two countries have reflected similar sets of changes under both competitive and authoritarian regimes. Significant erosion of the electoral strength of Acción Democrática in Venezuela, for example, contributed to party system discontinuities both before and after 1958. Similarly, the volatility of support for personalistic political parties has contributed to limited electoral continuity in Ecuadorean politics for decades. At the same time, generalizing from these two cases poses major hazards. Neither affords the opportunity for comparisons of continuity with *both* pre- and postauthoritarian periods. Moreover, there is no reason to regard the experience of these two countries in any way as prototypical.

Turning to cross-sectional evidence does little to resolve questions about the relationship between military rule and party system discontinuities. Not only have few countries in Latin America enjoyed extended periods of competitive rule, but their experience is also decidedly mixed. Although the Colombian and Uruguayan party systems have consistently displayed greater stability than have most of the cases listed in tables 3.1 and 3.2, the reverse is true for the Costa Rican and Chilean ones.

Comparisons among the 13 cases of redemocratization offer more significant insights into the relationship between authoritarianism and political change. One of the clearest signs that authoritarian rule promotes rather than inhibits political change is the strength of the relationship between the duration of authoritarian rule and the degree of party system discontinuity. The 4 cases characterized by the least party system discontinuity experienced on average only 8.3 years of authoritarian rule, whereas the average for those at the upper end of the spectrum was 15.3 years. The importance of this relationship is underlined in table 3.4, which shows a strong correlation between years of authoritarian rule and party system discontinuity. This correlation cannot be dismissed on the grounds that political change reflects the passage of time rather than the impact of authoritarian rule per se. Otherwise, the PSD index should be correlated more strongly with the time interval between the T1 and T2 elections than with the duration of authoritarian rule. As table 3.4 indicates, this is not true. The PSD index is actually correlated more strongly with years of authoritarian rule than with the time interval between T1 and T2 elections, although the difference is not statistically significant. In short, the freezing metaphor fails to capture the real impact of authoritarian rule. The longer an authoritarian regime remains in power, the more it changes the political status quo ante.

Other authoritarian regime characteristics, although difficult to assess quantitatively, appear less important in understanding variations in party system discontinuity. Authoritarian

Table 3.4

Correlations between PSD Index and Selected Indicators[a]

Years of Authoritarian Rule	.6996*
Time Interval Separating Pre- and Postauthoritarian Elections	.6683*
Electoral Growth between Pre- and Postauthoritarian Elections	.6270
Combined Age of Major Parties (T1 Elections)	−.7579*
Percentage of Population Voting (T1 Elections)	−.3773

[a] Simple Pearson product-moment correlations.
* Significant at the .01 level.

regimes that have adopted a reformist ideology can be found at both ends of the spectrum of political change, as can conservative regimes. Whether or not military regimes attempt to legitimize their rule through noncompetitive elections appears marginally more important, although the search for electoral legitimacy is also related to regime duration. Hence, although all four of the regimes with high party system discontinuity held elections, so did five of the six regimes that lasted ten years or more. Moreover, as indicated in table 3.5, elections have also been linked with limited party system discontinuity, as in the case of Uruguay. The critical issues here appear to be not simply the existence of a noncompetitive electoral process, but rather the nature of that process and the extent to which it has been used to mobilize and amplify the regime's base of social support. Fraudulent elections not involving efforts to create a base of support for authoritarian rule, such as those held in Honduras in 1965, have contributed more to continuity than to change. At the other extreme, major discontinuities have ensued when the search for legitimacy has involved a series of quasi-competitive elections, the organization of pseudo-democratic institutions, the creation of a new cadre of political leaders, and the mobilization of support behind a regime-supported party, as indicated especially by the Brazilian and 1946–58 Argentine cases. In Argentina, military rule in the 1940s gave rise to one of the nation's two major electoral forces as well as to the overriding political cleavage between Peronists and anti-Peronists. The durability of the pro- and antiregime cleavage that emerged in Brazil in the 1986 elections remains to

Table 3.5
Indicators of Authoritarian and Preauthoritarian Regime
Characteristics

	Preexisting Party System Continuity[a]	Elections under Authoritarian Regime	Level of Political Repression	Two-Party System
Colombia	Yes	No	1	Yes
Uruguay	Yes	Yes	3	Yes
Honduras (1972–81)	Yes	No	1	Yes
Honduras (1963–71)	Yes	Yes	1	Yes
Argentina (1966–73)	Yes	No	2	No
Venezuela	No	Yes	2	No
Argentina (1976–83)	Yes	No	3	No
Peru (1968–80)	Yes	No	1	No
Ecuador	No	No	1	No
Peru (1948–56)	No	Yes	2	No
Argentina (1946–58)	No	Yes	2	No
Bolivia	No	Yes	3	No
Brazil	No	Yes	3	No

[a] Continuities were assessed on the basis of the answer to the following question: Were the two strongest parties in the two sets of competitive elections most immediately preceding military seizures of power the same?

be seen, but military rule clearly produced new electoral forces. Isolated plebiscites, such as those held by Pérez Jiménez in Venezuela, Odría in Peru, and the military in Uruguay, have had a lesser impact. Nevertheless, even these efforts to rally support behind an authoritarian regime have altered national party systems. Twenty-four years after General Odría left office in Peru, the Unión Nacional Odriísta was still competing in national elections.

A significant relationship also appears to exist between political repression and party system discontinuities, although serious problems are involved in measuring repression. Not the least of these are the multi-dimensional nature of repression and the lack of uniformity, both with respect to time and to potential targets, that characterize its application. Such problems cannot readily be solved by "averaging." The political impact of an authoritarian regime that employs a consistently moderate level of repression is likely to differ from the impact of one that severely represses all political groups and then relaxes repression. Moreover, repression is not a unidimensional concept; severe repression of some forms of political activity may coexist with ample freedom for others. Repression can also be applied differentially to political groups, as in the 1948–56 Peruvian case. Because of these difficulties, the levels of repression reported in table 3.5, which are based on expert assessments, lack precision and allow only for tentative conclusions.[12] Nevertheless, it appears that the level of repression is associated with variations in party system continuity. The average level of repression in the four cases at the lower end of the discontinuity spectrum was only 1.5 as compared to average levels of 1.8 and 2.5 at the middle and upper end of the spectrum, respectively.

Repression can also be linked to some very specific changes in the relative strength of political forces in the cases under consideration. For example, despite its previous experience with political repression, the Peruvian Aprista party emerged from the Odría dictatorship in a weakened condition. Differential repression also changed the correlation of political forces in such cases as Venezuela, where the Pérez Jiménez dictatorship almost completely destroyed the Acción Democrática's urban organizational network, and Argentina, where the political repression of the 1955–58 period eroded Peronist electoral strength.

Yet, although regime characteristics account for variations among cases, table 3.4 also underlines the impact of other variables. Properties of national party systems, in particular, explain why authoritarian rule has led to greater political change in some cases than in others. As the strong correlation between the combined age of the two strongest parties at T1 and the PSD index suggests, continuities between pre- and post-authoritarian democratic regimes have typically been greatest in countries with older party systems. Virtually by definition, such party systems are better institutionalized than others. They also tend to be more immune to the influence of leadership personality, even though they do not differ from more recently established systems in terms of the extent to which cleavages revolve around ideology rather than patronage. The most notable exception to these generalizations is Ecuador, because the combined age of its top parties provide an exceptionally misleading indicator of the preexisting stability of partisan alternatives and electoral loyalties. Despite its age, the Ecuadoran party system has not been institutionalized around long-standing partisan cleavages but has fluctuated in response to leadership alternatives.

Table 3.5 further emphasizes the importance of preexisting party system continuity. As indicated by the first column in the table, the cases with the least party system discontinuity are those in which elections prior to authoritarian rule had been characterized by major continuities. The cases with the highest PSD indices, on the other hand, had evinced major electoral discontinuities in the pre-authoritarian period. As a result, when a dummy variable for preexisting party-system continuity is entered into a regression equation along with years of authoritarian rule, it is possible to account for more than 75 percent of the variation in the PSD index. The relationships are too complicated, however, to analyze fully on the basis of a small number of cases. As indicated by the final column in table 3.5, two-party systems, which limit incentives and opportunities for the emergence of new political forces, tend to be more resistant to change than are multiparty systems. Type of party system is thus significantly correlated with the PSD index ($r = .7096$) as well as with preexisting party system continuity ($r = .7319$) and party system age ($-.6495$).

Is the strong correlation between the duration of military rule and party system discontinuity also a product of preexisting party-system stability? That is, does a strong and well-institutionalized party system limit the duration of military rule and thereby contribute to low party system discontinuity? The answers to such questions are negative. Comparatively durable military regimes have been established in countries with deeply rooted party systems, such as Uruguay. Military rule has also proved short-lived where political parties have not been well established, as in Peru (1948–56). The correlation between party system age and the duration of military rule is consequently not statistically significant.

Other political system characteristics appear unimportant for understanding variations in the dependent variables. In view of the European experience, which points to the crystallization of major party alternatives in the wake of suffrage expansion, one might expect to find that high rates of political participation

65

at T1 would produce more resistance to party system changes. Table 3.4, however, shows that no significant relationship exists between the percentage of the population voting at T1 and the PSD index. Widely divergent PSD indices characterize such cases as Colombia and Argentina (1946–58) with similar rates of electoral participation. Likewise, cases with nearly identical PSD indices rank very differently in terms of electoral participation. For example, the PSD indices for Honduras (1963–71) and Argentina (1966–73) are 45.3 and 48.3, respectively; yet the percentage of the population voting during the 1960s in Argentina was twice as high as in Honduras.

Part of the reason for the failure of the PSD index to correlate with electoral participation rates may be the relationship between electoral participation and political repression. Where political participation has been higher, authoritarian regimes have tended to employ more repression. Hence, in the four cases in which the percentage of the population participating in T1 elections exceeded 25 percent, the average level of political repression was 2.5. In contrast, repression levels averaged only 1.7 in the other cases, which were characterized by lower levels of participation.

Yet although the PSD index fails to correlate significantly with rates of electoral participation at T1, some relationship appears to exist between the growth in the electorate and party system discontinuities. As indicated by table 3.4, the greater the percentage increase in the size of the electorate between T1 and T2 elections, the more pre- and postauthoritarian regimes have differed. Obviously, the longer a regime holds power, the more the electorate is likely to increase in size. Hence, in the case of Brazil, where military rule lasted 21 years, seven out of ten voters were participating in competitive elections for the first time in 1986. In some families, two generations were inexperienced in competitive party politics. But more than population growth associated with the passage of time is involved here. Changes in electoral regulations enfranchising large sectors of the population without established partisan attachments occurred in all of the cases characterized by substantial electoral growth. These rapid widenings of the political support market made it relatively easy for new political forces, including those associated with the authoritarian regime, to compete with older parties for votes.

66

Changes in electoral regulations enfranchising new groups have been associated particularly with inclusionary or populist regimes that have attempted to mobilize a broad base of social support. Four of the five cases that experienced the greatest increases in electoral participation were governed by regimes of this type. The regimes with the most explicitly exclusionary and demobilizing orientation, on the other hand, left the smallest increases in electoral participation in their wakes (Bolivia; Uruguay; Argentina, 1966–73 and 1976–83). The observed relationship between electoral expansion and party system discontinuity thus reinforces the point made earlier about the significance of authoritarian regime characteristics. The more military regimes have sought to alter the status quo through the mobilization of popular support, the greater the party system discontinuity.

Some residual variation among the 13 cases under consideration can also be attributed to other types of changes in preexisting institutional arrangements. As Adam Przeworski has reminded us,[13] the process of redemocratization involves not merely the breakdown of authoritarian rule, but also the creation of a set of specific institutions that shape the relative capability of various parties and groups to realize their interests. This process does not necessarily entail the simple restoration of the status quo ante. Indeed, the Latin American experience demonstrates that such an outcome is highly improbable. In *every* Latin American case, the rules previously governing the democratic game have been changed in response to conflicts and compromises among groups struggling both for and against the restoration of democracy.

In some instances, changes in institutional arrangements have reflected conditions imposed by the outgoing military regime. In the 1946–58 Argentine case, for example, the Aramburu regime sought guarantees to prevent Peronists from returning to power. When the Frondizi government voided these guarantees and thereby eliminated a major source of discontinuity between the pre- and postauthoritarian electoral game, it was ousted by the military. In other instances, military regimes have played a more indirect role in changing institutional arrangements. The enfranchisement of illiterates in Peru, for example, was a product of political bargaining among rival groups in the 1978–79 constituent assembly. The 1968–80 military regime nevertheless influenced the outcome of this bargaining because it strengthened the forces favoring such a constitutional change.

Changes in institutional arrangements alone constitute evidence that military rule alters the status quo ante. In at least half of the cases under consideration, institutional changes also appear to have had consequences that are important for understanding the political outcome of the redemocratization process. These cases include Peru, where the expansion of the minor party and leftist votes between 1963 and 1980 might be explained partially in terms of constitutional alterations; Argentina (1946–58), where restrictions on Peronist participation contributed to a drop in the Peronist vote as well as to the partition of the Radical party; Argentina (1966–73), where changes in electoral rules discouraged minor parties; Ecuador, where a military ban on presidential nominees of non-Ecuadoran parentage eliminated frontrunner Assad Bucaram from the 1980 electoral race; and Colombia, where the National Front agreement restricting competition contributed to party system continuity rather than discontinuity. At the same time, it is difficult to assess precisely how much of an impact changes in electoral rules had in each of these cases. For example, existing information is too limited to assess how much of the shift in voting patterns in the 1968–80 Peruvian case can be attributed to the enfranchisement of illiterates. Other factors clearly contributed to the upsurge in the leftist and minor party vote.[14] Moreover, any gains made by the left through suffrage expansion were at least partially offset by changes in legal provisions beneficial to other political forces.

The utility of institutional changes in understanding variations among the cases is further limited by the rather country-specific character of such changes. Put another way, the array of phenomena that falls under the rubric of institutional change is so broad and disparate that comparative analysis is virtually impossible. Properly speaking, institutional change does not represent a single variable at all, but rather a whole category of variables with potentially differing and contradictory effects. Hence, although changes in the institutional rules governing democracy may be useful in understanding specific outcomes in individual countries, such changes do not significantly enhance our understanding of why the process of redemocratization has been associated with greater party system discontinuity in some cases rather than in others. Variations among cases are more effectively and economically explained in terms of the other two sets of factors analyzed earlier: authoritarian regime and party system characteristics. Further, changes in institutional arrangements have largely reflected the influence of these two sets of factors.

Finally, residual variation among the 13 cases can be attributed, of course, simply to acts of *fortuna*. Given the key role played by personalities in Latin American politics, death or disablement of major party leaders warrants special attention under this heading. The importance of this variable is particularly evident in the case of Ecuador, whose ranking on the PSD index is not adequately explained in terms of the factors analyzed earlier. As Howard Handelman has observed, modern Ecuadoran politics has been largely marked by the alternation of Velasquista populism and military rule.[15] The death of the country's five-time president, Velasco Ibarra, in March 1979 thus not only symbolized an end to a political era but also contributed directly to the chief contrast between the outcomes of the 1968 and 1978 elections: namely, the disappearance of the Velasquista party. The importance of human mortality can be noted in other cases as well. For example, the death of Haya de la Torre before the 1980 Peruvian elections undermined the Aprista party, whereas Acción Popular benefited from the survival of its leader, Belaúnde. Yet, in general, the relative importance of political leadership has been related inversely to party system age. Thus, although leadership longevity provides a basis for understanding political outcomes in specific cases, it sheds little additional light on the reasons for variations in party system continuities.

Military Rule and Political Party Systems

The Latin American experience with redemocratization indicates that military rule tends to promote political change rather than freeze preexisting political patterns. Whereas the freezing metaphor suggests that the degree of continuity between pre- and postauthoritarian regimes will not vary with the duration of military rule, the evidence presented here points in the opposite direction. The longer military regimes remain in power, the more party systems change. There are instances in which redemocratization has paved the way for previously dominant leaders and parties to return to power; but more frequently, redemocratization has entailed major shifts in party strength, electoral realignments, and/or the rise of new partisan alternatives. Because party systems have long been considered highly resistant to modification, the obvious implication is that military rule is capable of producing profound changes in all facets of political life.

How much change results from authoritarian rule is not merely a function of the length of time military officers remain in power. Party system continuity has also varied with the interaction between characteristics of the authoritarian regime and the preauthoritarian political situation. Military regimes ranking near the extremes of the continuum ranging from inclusionary to exclusionary rule are those evincing the greatest capacity to induce political change. Hence, the degree of party system discontinuity linked with redemocratization in Latin America over the past four decades is positively associated with electoral growth, political repression, and the organization of support in noncompetitive elections. In all of the four cases of pronounced party system discontinuity, military officers engaged in efforts either to mobilize or demobilize the populace. Political discontinuity also has been marked where the pre-existing party system was not well established. To a lesser extent, the political impact of authoritarian rule has been affected by continuities in political leadership and by institutional changes introduced as a result of military governance.

To restate these findings differently, the ideal situation for a military regime to effect major political change would be one in which political loyalties had not previously solidified around a clear set of partisan alternatives and in which authoritarian rule lasted for a long period, the electorate grew considerably, and the authoritarian regime in question was highly repressive and at the same time successful in mobilizing some degree of popular support. The opposite situation would be one in which the preauthoritarian party system was well established, the growth of the electorate limited, and the authoritarian regime in question short-lived, nonrepressive, and unwilling or unable to mobilize popular support.

The Brazilian case, which stands at the top of the party discontinuity rankings, evinces all of the features of the situation most likely to result in change. First, by 1986, Brazil had experienced more years of authoritarian rule than any Latin American country that has ever undergone a transition back to democracy. The sheer duration of military rule meant that Brazil had changed profoundly between the 1964 coup and the competitive elections of November 1986. The Brazil of the mid-1980s was a much more industrialized, urbanized, and literate society than was preauthoritarian Brazil. Moreover, rapid population growth had created a new generation of voters with no established attachments to the pre-1964 party system. Second, although repression was not as severe in Brazil as in such countries as Argentina and Chile, the restrictions on political liberties that were imposed in the wake of the 1964 coup dispersed party activists, undermined organizational net works, and disrupted the processes through which partisan loyalties develop. Third, military rule in Brazil entailed major efforts to develop a base of popular support and establish electoral legitimacy. The regime sponsored a long series of quasi-competitive elections and the formation of a regime-supported party. Fourth, the pre-1964 Brazilian party system was not well established or very stable. The three most important parties in the 1946–64 period only dated their origins back to 1945, and electoral outcomes in the years leading up to the 1964 coup were characterized by a high degree of instability.

The Colombian case most closely resembles the ideal combination of conditions for minimal political change. Military rule was brief, repression minimal, and the efforts of Rojas Pinilla to mobilize a base of popular support comparatively unsuccessful. What is more, the preexisting two-party system was deeply established, with both major parties dating their origins before the turn of the century. Except for two of the key variables conditioning the capacity of military regimes to effect durable political change, Uruguay also closely resembles the ideal situation for political continuity. Uruguay's

LIBRARY ST. MARY'S COLLEGE

precoup party system was even older and better institionalized than that of Colombia. The names of Uruguay's major parties derive from the colors raised by rival forces during the civil wars of the 1830s, and electoral results prior to 1973 were characterized by a comparatively high degree of continuity. Moreover, slow population growth combined with a high precoup rate of citizen participation left little room for electoral expansion or the mobilization of support behind new political structures. The military's efforts to rally support behind authoritarian rule ended in total disaster. In 1980 Uruguay's authoritarian government was forced to admit losing a plebiscite designed to legitimate its rule. Only in terms of the duration and highly repressive nature of military rule does Uruguay depart from the optimal conditions for continuity between pre- and post-authoritarian politics.

On the basis of this analysis, it should be possible to predict the outcomes of future transitions from authoritarianism to competitive rule in countries that have had prior democratic experience.[16] Future events will also expand the number of cases that fall within the redemocratization rubric, thereby expanding opportunities for analyzing the impact of military rule. Yet the study of that impact need not remain focused solely on cases of redemocratization in the Latin American context nor on the political structures and behaviors associated with competitive rule. The implications of the previous analysis are much broader. The Latin American experience with redemocratization points the way toward an improved understanding of military rule in other settings by indicating that the political impact of authoritarianism is not only conditioned by the preexisting political order, but also shaped by three key regime properties: durability, mobilizing capability, and repressiveness. These three characteristics reflect the extent to which a regime approximates the inclusionary rather than the exclusionary end of the political spectrum. As suggested in the previous chapter, however, regime durability is not merely a function of the international context or the configuration of domestic class forces. The capacity of military regimes to weather shifts in the conditions surrounding their origins and impose changes on their societies is also shaped by the institutional structure of military rule.

In conclusion, the evidence presented in this chapter about redemocratization in Latin America emphasizes that the analysis of military rule should not automatically begin with the assumption that, *plus ça change, plus c'est la même chose*. Military regimes in Latin America have modified electoral loyalties, restructured political cleavages, and contributed to the rise of new political forces. Because Latin American party systems are much older and better established than those in most Asian, African, or Middle Eastern countries, military rule presumably has an even greater impact in other parts of the world. Likewise, because the Latin American experience indicates that military rule can significantly alter party systems, which have historically demonstrated impressive resistance to change, there is every reason to suppose that military regimes leave an even deeper imprint on other types of political structures and activities.

Notes

1 Seymour M. Lipset and Stein Rokkan, "Cleavage Structures, Party Systems, and Voter Alignments: An Introduction," in *Party Systems and Voter Alignments: Cross-National Perspectives*, ed. Seymour M. Lipset and Stein Rokkan (New York: Free Press, 1967), 50 (italics in original). See also Joseph G. LaPalombara, *Politics within Nations* (Englewood Cliffs, NJ: Prentice-Hall, 1974), 547–48; Richard Rose and Derek W. Urwin, "Persistence and Change in Western Party Systems since 1945," *Political Studies* 18 (1970): 287–319.

2 Lipset and Rokkan, "Cleavage Structures," 52–53; Mattei Dogan, "Political Cleavages and Social Stratification in France and Italy," in *Party Systems and Voter Alignments*, ed. Lipset and Rokkan, 183–84; Juan J. Linz, "The Party System of Spain: Past and Future," in ibid., 264.

3 See, in particular, Arturo Valenzuela and J. Samuel Valenzuela, "Party Oppositions under the Chilean Authoritarian Regime," in *Military Rule in Chile: Dictatorship and Oppositions*, ed. J. Samuel Valenzuela and Arturo Valenzuela (Baltimore: Johns Hopkins University Press, 1986), 184–229.

4 See, for example, Kevin J. Middlebrook, "Notes on Transitions from Authoritarian Rule in Latin America and Latin Europe," Working Paper No. 82, Latin American Program, Woodrow Wilson Center for Scholars (Washington, DC, n.d.), 15–16.

5 Valenzuela and Valenzuela, "Party Oppositions," 205.

6   The three-year cutoff maximizes the number of cases considered
    without extending analysis to regimes that have acted solely in a
    "caretaker" capacity. The 1940 initiation point was chosen for
    three reasons: (1) it eliminates very few possible cases; (2) electoral
    data for the pre-1940 period are relatively scarce and often of
    dubious reliability; and (3) the pre-1940 political experience, which
    was characterized by extremely limited political participation,
    generally is not comparable to that of later years and appears to be of
    limited relevance in understanding and predicting political develop-
    ments today. Significantly, the largest and most important political
    parties in many countries emerged only after 1940. Examples include
    the Argentine Peronist party, the Bolivian Movimiento Nacional
    Revolucionario (MNR), the Costa Rican Partido de Liberación
    Nacional (PLN), Acción Democrática (AD) of Venezuela, and the
    Christian Democratic parties of Chile, Honduras, and Venezuela.

7   Alain Rouquié, "Demilitarization and the Institutionalization of
    Military-Dominated Polities in Latin America," Working Paper
    No. 110, Latin American Program, Woodrow Wilson Center for
    Scholars (Washington, DC, 1982).

8   Argentina (1946–58) is probably the most marginal case because
    the pre-1946 regime was not democratic. It has been included
    nevertheless because (1) the country had enjoyed an extended
    period of liberal democracy in the past, and (2) the 1946 elections
    were quite competitive and therefore allow for the same kinds of
    longitudinal comparisons as the other cases. The case of Brazil has
    likewise been included, even though the 1986 elections signified
    a less than complete restoration of democratic rule. In other
    instances doubts about categorization arise from restrictions on
    competition. Most notable in this regard are the cases of Honduras
    and Colombia, in which pacts between major parties strictly
    limited competition in either preauthoritarian (Honduras, 1972–
    81) or postauthoritarian (Colombia; Honduras, 1963–71) elections.
    See James A. Morris, *The Honduran Plan Político de Unidad
    Nacional 1971–1972: Its Origins and Demise* (El Paso: Center for
    Inter-American Studies, University of Texas at El Paso, 1975); and
    R. Albert Berry, Ronald G. Hellman, and Mauricio Solaún, eds.,
    Politics of Compromise: Coalition Government in Colombia (New
    Brunswick, NJ: Transaction Books, 1980). Yet, as Guy Hermet has
    pointed out, virtually all elections involve some restrictions on
    competition. See "State-Controlled Elections: A Framework," in
    Elections without Choice, ed. Guy Hermet, Richard Rose, and
    Alain Rouquié (London: Macmillan, 1978), 1–18. The key distinc-
    tion between competitive and noncompetitive elections is not the
    existence of restrictions on voters' freedom of choice. The
    important issues are whether voters have a choice and whether
    their choices determine who controls the government.

9   Departamento Administrativo Nacional de Estadística, *Colombia
    política: estadísticas 1935–1970* (Bogota: 1972), 154.

10 See Charles G. Gillespie, "Activists and Floating Voters: The Unheeded Lessons of Uruguay's 1982 Primaries," in *Elections and Democratization in Latin America, 1980–85*, ed. Paul W. Drake and Eduardo Silva (San Diego: University of California, San Diego, 1986).

11 In departments in which Aprista candidates ran in 1956, they received a much lower percentage of the vote than in 1945. See Frederick B. Pike, *The Modern History of Peru* (New York: Praeger, 1967), 295.

12 The figures for levels of repression reflect the combined opinions of three Latin Americanists with expertise in political history. Although admittedly crude, efforts to arrive at more precise measurements of repression in Latin American have not necessarily produced more accurate results. For example, Ernest Duff and John McCamant's annual repression scores for Latin America indicate that the Peronist regime in Argentina ranks among the most repressive regimes to have ruled in the region between 1950 and 1969. *Violence and Repression in Latin America: A Quantitative and Historical Analysis* (New York: Free Press, 1976), 39. Few Latin Americanists today would concur with this assessment.

13 Adam Przeworski, "Some Problems in the Study of the Transition to Democracy," in *Transitions from Authoritarian Rule: Comparative Perspectives*, ed. Guillermo O'Donnell, Philippe C. Schmitter, and Laurence Whitehead (Baltimore: Johns Hopkins University Press, 1986), 47–63.

14 Evelyne Stephens, "The Peruvian Military Government, Labor Mobilization, and the Political Strength of the Left," *Latin American Research Review* 18 (1983): 57–93.

15 Howard Handelman, "Ecuador: A New Political Direction?" *American Universities Field Staff Reports*, South American Series, No. 47 (1979), 1.

16 In this connection note that in 1984, prior to transitions from military rule in Brazil and Uruguay, I predicted on the basis of a preliminary version of this analysis that "a future transition from authoritarian rule in Uruguay is likely to give rise to a democratic regime very similar to that of its displaced predecessor. . . . Uruguay closely resembles the ideal situation for minimal change." With respect to Brazil, I wrote: "The Brazilian case most clearly resembles the ideal type of situation for the emergence of major discontinuities between pre- and postauthoritarian regimes. It can therefore be predicted that contrasts between the pre-1964 Brazilian democratic regime and any future one are likely to be unusually marked by comparative standards." "Redemocratization and the Impact of Authoritarian Rule in Latin America," *Comparative Politics* XVII (April 1985): 270, 272. As of late 1988, my predictions that redemocratization in Chile would place the country somewhere between the middle and upper end of the spectrum of political change had yet to be tested.

CHAPTER 4

The Economic Impact of Military Rule

"The agricultural, commercial, and industrial economies of the country are in a state either of stagnation or recession and inflation is rampant, but there are no signs whatever that the government is interested in them, except as a mere spectator."[1] With this official statement of September 11, 1973, the Chilean armed forces expressed a concern that occurs again and again in the pronouncements of coup leaders. In a similar vein, General Jorge Rafael Videla explained the need for the 1976 Argentine coup: "A vacillating and unrealistic economic leadership carried the country toward recession and the beginnings of unemployment, with its inevitable sequel of anguish and desperation, a condition which we have inherited and which we will seek to alleviate."[2]

However self-serving, such justifications for the overthrow of established governments do not necessarily distort economic reality. General Videla's remarks, for example, were made in the context of an acute economic crisis. In the months leading up to the military takeover, Argentina was experiencing negative economic growth, capital flight, and a more than 300 percent rate of inflation. The situation in Chile at the time of the 1973 coup was no better. Although it remains far from clear whether economic difficulties cause political crises or merely reflect and reinforce them,[3] the existence of a link between military coups and deteriorating economic conditions is beyond question. Open to debate is the ability of military officers to manage economic crises any better than civilians.

77

Military Regimes and Economic Performance

Comparative evidence provides no basis for arguing that long-term macroeconomic performance, as distinct from short-term crisis management, improves with military rule. The policy thrust of military regimes is too dissimilar and the impact of other variables on economic performance too powerful to leave much room for significant linkages between military rule and economic development. Hence, for every military success story of the Brazilian variety, it is possible to cite at least one example of abysmal failure. And whatever the expertise, commitment, and coercive capability of military governments, macroeconomic performance is conditioned by forces, such as commodity prices, that are beyond the control of any Latin American regime. The result is that no single type of regime can be linked with either developmental success or failure.

Table 4.1 illustrates the problem of explaining variations in the economic performance of Latin American nations in terms of broad regime similarities and differences. The table includes all cases of military rule since the mid-1950s that allow for comparisons with prior or successor competitive regimes. Out of a total of 21 comparisons of rates of economic growth, military regimes outperformed their nonauthoritarian predecessors or successors only 11 times. Ten of the comparisons were more favorable to competitive political arrangements. In other words, the odds that a military regime will promote growth more effectively than a competitive regime appear to be no more than fifty-fifty. The results are the same if the growth rates of military and competitive regimes are compared as a group, rather than on a country-by-country basis. There is no statistically significant difference between the growth records achieved by the military and competitive regimes included in table 4.1.[4]

These findings are fully consonant with previous research into the relationship between regime type and economic performance. Whether cross-sectional or diachronic, study after study has concluded that military rule makes little difference to long-term patterns of economic development.[5] Even research focusing on specific subtypes of authoritarianism has dismissed the importance of regime type for explaining economic performance. A case in point is a recent study of

Table 4.1
Economic Growth under Authoritarian and Competitive Rule
(Average Annual Rate of Increase in GDP)[a]

		Preauthoritarian	Authoritarian	Postauthoritarian
Argentina	1955–58	—	–0.8	5.0
Argentina	1966–73	3.6	3.4	2.4
Bolivia	1964–79	3.6[b]	5.6	–2.0
Brazil	1964–85	6.6	7.0	n.a.
Chile	1973–86	3.8	2.2	—
Colombia	1953–57	n.a.	2.9[c]	4.8
Dom. Repub.	1963–66	n.a.	6.2	7.7
Ecuador	1963–68	4.4[d]	6.8[e]	5.0
Ecuador	1972–79	5.0	13.4	24.3
Honduras	1972–82	4.4[f]	9.4	7.4
Peru	1968–80	4.7	3.8	–0.1
Uruguay	1973–85	0.6	1.5	3.6

Source: International Monetary Fund, *International Financial Statistics,*
1954–1987.
[a] Growth data were calculated as weighted averages, with the weights
determined by the months of regime initiation and termination. Only regimes
lasting two years or more were included in the table.
[b] For 1961–64 only.
[c] For 1956 and 1957 only.
[d] For 1959–63.
[e] Including interim and provisional presidencies of Clemente Yerovi Indáburu
and Otto Arosemena Gómez.
[f] For 1959–63.

bureaucratic-authoritarian regimes, which concluded "that
the evidence both within and across countries does not
support the proposition that the B-A [bureaucratic-authori-
tarian] regimes were better economic managers than the
competitive regimes."[6] The key area of exception was that of
short-run stabilization, in which B-A regimes did compile a
record of success.[7]

Short-run stabilization programs, as distinct from longer-
term growth strategies, also have been singled out by other
analysts as an exception to the conclusion that military rule
makes little difference to economic performance. Indeed, the
proposition that authoritarianism is a prerequisite for successful
economic stabilization has been accepted by Latin Americanists
as a piece of conventional wisdom.[8] Its obvious corollary is that
competitive regimes are virtually incapable of managing
programs designed to correct serious economic imbalances.

Is this conventional wisdom correct? Is military rule a prerequisite for successful economic stabilization in Latin America? Does the historical record sustain the view that military regimes are singularly well equipped to cope with serious macroeconomic disequilibria? Do conventional stabilization policies involving currency devaluations, wage and credit restrictions, and strict fiscal controls carry higher political risks for competitive regimes than for authoritarian ones? Under what conditions, if any, has democratic rule produced successful stabilization and authoritarianism resulted in failure?

Answers to these questions are central to theoretical debates over the relationships among regime, public policy, and economics in Latin America. Previous research suggests that economic stabilization is the *most likely* area in which to uncover performance contrasts between authoritarian and competitive regimes. If such contrasts do not emerge, it becomes very difficult to assert that military regimes have a distinctive economic impact. The politics of economic stabilization thus offer a crucial test of hypotheses regarding regime consequences.

The issue, however, is not merely theoretical. Given the linkage between economic crisis and military coups, the relative success of military regimes in restoring economic stability is also a question of real political importance. If military officers do have the edge in coping with macroeconomic disequilibria, then coup leaders have a concrete basis for their claims regarding the necessity of military rule. Likewise, prospects for competitive regimes confronting economic crises appear rather dismal.

Military Rule and Economic Stabilization

The proposition that authoritarianism is a necessary, albeit insufficient, condition for successful stabilization is buttressed by several highly plausible lines of argument. Most begin with the assumption that stabilization policies are inherently painful and unpopular. Particularly in Latin America, where extensive past experience with stabilization has left a legacy of cynicism

80

and distrust, simply announcing that an agreement has been reached with the International Monetary Fund (IMF)—the international agency charged with helping member nations carry out stabilization programs—may provoke political protest. Anticipated cuts in popular-sector living standards are not the only reason. Stabilization programs also alienate comparatively privileged political support groups. Local entrepreneurs, for example, are likely to react strongly to restrictions on credit, tariff cuts, or other measures designed to produce a more efficient allocation of resources. For governments dependent on consent rather than coercion, stabilization consequently poses a major dilemma. As Joan M. Nelson has emphasized, "The only alternative to planned and guided adjustment is chaotic adjustment, entailing higher costs in terms of controls, scarcities, inflation, unemployment, and atrophied output and growth."[9] Yet voters are unlikely to evaluate the costs and benefits of stabilization programs against some counterfactual alternative. Democratic leaders thus face strong pressures to postpone corrective action as long as possible or to abandon programs once their costs become palpable, particularly since any resulting economic hardship can plausibly be blamed on exogenous forces rather than on government actions.[10] It can be argued that under authoritarian rule the political calculus pushes policy makers in a rather different direction. The benefits of postponing corrective action are likely to appear less significant to regimes whose survival does not depend on popular approval, whereas the long-term dangers of inaction are likely to loom much larger.

A related line of argument stresses the greater capacity of popular-sector groups to disrupt or thwart the implementation of stabilization policies under democratic rule. Democracies not only offer more channels of protest and policy-making influence to subordinate groups than do authoritarian regimes, but they also create more favorable conditions for the development of strong and independent popular-sector organizations capable of resisting efforts to curtail private consumption. Policies designed to curb inflationary wage increases, for example, are obviously more likely to founder where workers enjoy the freedom to organize and strike than where trade unions are controlled or suppressed. As Robert R. Kaufman has argued with specific reference to the three large Latin American nations, "the ability to sustain stabilization initiatives . . . has varied inversely with the capacity of [popular-sector] forces and their leaders to escape the orbit of state supervision and control."[11]

The argument linking effective management of economic stabilization with authoritarianism may be related as well to characteristics of the policy-making process. The recent history of such countries as Chile suggests that technocrats are likely to enjoy considerable autonomy under authoritarian rule, whereas in liberal democracies control over government expenditures and other key aspects of stabilization programs may be left to persons lacking the convictions and technical competence necessary for program success. The concentration of political authority characteristic of authoritarianism would also appear to permit greater coherence in program implementation. Democratic rule fragments decision-making authority among branches of government and relatively independent loci of political power, allowing stabilization opponents to interfere with program design and implementation. The weaknesses of authoritarian regimes may also push in the direction of more effective program implementation. Lacking a firm basis of legitimacy, authoritarian regimes may weigh economic performance more heavily than would competitive ones.

Last, but not least important, the belief that a firm hand is necessary for successful economic adjustment places democracies at a distinct disadvantage. Such a belief reduces incentives for individual trade unions or business firms to respond to the appeals of democratic leaders for sacrifice, and the logic of collective action makes the incentives for program cooperation minimal even in the best of circumstances.[12] The level of confidence in program success also influences capital flows and the willingness of external banks and financial agencies to extend the additional credits necessary to overcome temporary economic dislocations. In short, the greater the skepticism about the possibility of program success, the greater the probability of failure.

Against these supposed advantages of authoritarianism in the management of austerity programs can be set the greater legitimacy and popular support typically enjoyed by democratic regimes, which increase the appeal of programs calling for short-term sacrifice on behalf of the whole nation. To the extent that policy information and feedback are vital to the success of stabilization programs, democracies may have other advantages as well, particularly as compared with authoritarian regimes that are not cohesive, technocratically oriented, or capable of overriding popular dissent and particularistic claims with coercion. At the very least, the advantages supposedly enjoyed by authoritarianism in managing stabilization programs would appear to be undercut by the greater support, legitimacy, and access to information available to democratic policy makers

The chief question mark about the theoretical linkage between authoritarianism and stabilization, however, has less to do with the reputed strengths of institutional democracy than with the explanatory power of the regime variable. Virtually by definition the process of policy formation varies with regime type; but other influences on policy outputs and outcomes are so numerous and the phenomena embraced by broad regime categories (such as democracy) so diverse, there is reason to question whether regime per se actually has any significant impact on the political sustainability of stabilization programs. The willingness and ability of governments to implement stabilization policies instead may depend on other factors. The level of industrial development and structure of trade unionism, for example, clearly condition the capacity of popular-sector groups to sabotage stabilization measures. Similarly, the degree of technocratic control over policy may reflect variations in educational infrastructure or bureaucratic traditions rather than regime type. Thus, certain nations might experience successful adjustment under both democratic and authoritarian regimes whereas the histories of others might be littered with records of failure. Failure at one time may also enhance the probability of subsequent failure. Carlos Díaz-Alejandro hypothesized that "the longer the history of failed stabilization plans, the smaller the chances of success (and/or the greater the costs of success of any new plan)."[13] Again, the obvious implication is that the success of stabilization efforts varies with national setting, not with regime.

The sociopolitical context in which stabilization is attempted may also be important for other reasons. Drastic regime change, in particular, appears to create exceptional space for the adoption of controversial programs.[14] Indeed, it is striking that the most widely cited examples of successful authoritarian stabilization in Latin America are those in which comparatively traumatic democratic breakdowns paved the way for the initiation of austerity policies. Such examples are often used to bolster arguments about the superiority of authoritarianism in addressing intractable economic problems. Yet they also provide a basis for optimism about the viability of democratic stabilization following the breakdown of authoritarianism.

Nonpolitical factors also enter the picture and call into question the significance of regime differences for explaining variations in the sustainability of stabilization programs. Stabilization has been easier in some time periods than in others, due to such factors as the availability of external funding, the dynamism of world trade, and the rate of imported inflation. Large countries have enjoyed easier access to funds and better terms in negotiating stabilization agreements.[15] Numerous other influences on the success of stabilization efforts should be mentioned as well, including the severity of economic problems at the start of the program, policy errors, price fluctuations for major export commodities, natural catastrophes, import and export elasticities, and the speed with which resources can be shifted to the tradables sector.

In short, although the theoretical arguments linking authoritarianism and economic stabilization are highly plausible, there are also grounds for questioning the explanatory power of the regime variable. If the capacity to adjust is chiefly determined by factors that vary independently of the type of regime in control, then the conventional wisdom about the politics of economic stabilization is seriously misleading.

Prior Research

Doubts about the theoretical significance of regime type for the analysis of economic stabilization are reinforced by previous research, which supplies surprisingly little support for the proposition that authoritarianism is a necessary condition for stabilization. Most of the evidence is confined to studies of the three largest Latin American nations. The most influential study of this type has been Thomas Skidmore's analysis of stabilization in the ABM countries (Argentina, Brazil, and Mexico). According to Skidmore's widely cited conclusions, the experience of these countries during the 1950s and 1960s demonstrates that

(1) governments in competitive political systems find it *extremely* difficult to reduce inflation, once it has exceeded 20 percent, and they have paid very high political costs for their efforts; (2) no such government has proved able to pursue a successful (as defined earlier) anti-inflation effort; (3) all the cases of successful stabilization have been carried out by authoritarian (or one-party) governments; and (4) even authoritarian governments must have a high degree of internal consensus to carry through a successful stabilization.[16]

Robert Kaufman's more recent study of stabilization in the ABM countries arrived at a similar conclusion. According to Kaufman, "Authoritarian regimes in the ABM countries are, in fact, so far the only ones in which stabilization programs have actually restored some degree of price and exchange equilibrium and a resumption of economic expansion."[17]

The difficulty is that the experiences of the large Latin American nations provide a fragile basis for broader generalizations about the relationship between regime and economic stabilization. In the first place, the ABM countries are rather atypical of the continent as a whole in terms of economic structure and bargaining power vis-à-vis international creditors and lending agencies. More important, authoritarianism has been the predominant form of political domination in the largest Latin American nations during the past few decades. Between 1965 and 1985, they had experienced less than five years of democratic rule among them. Countries in which democratic impulses are so weak are clearly inappropriate cases for assessing the relative strengths of democracy and authoritarianism in the management of stabilization programs. Because research has relied so heavily on the experience of the

85

ABM countries, it is quite possible that the tension between democracy and stabilization in Latin America has been exaggerated.

Research on other world regions points in the same direction. Because it explicitly considers the linkage between regime and policy, Stephan Haggard's study of IMF Extended Fund Facility (EFF) programs during the 1975–84 period is of particular interest. On the basis of an analysis of 30 cases (8 of them Latin American), Haggard dismissed any connection between stabilization programs and the collapse of democratic regimes.[18] He also challenged the assumption that authoritarianism facilitates adjustment. According to Haggard, the political capacity to adjust depends less on regime than on the economic ideologies of bureaucratic elites, the strength of administrative structures, and the availability of non-IMF resources.[19] Haggard's conclusions are echoed in Joan M. Nelson's recent work. Based on an analysis of 5 non-Latin American nations, Nelson also emphasized the wide variety of nonregime factors that condition the political sustainability of stabilization programs, including the prevalence of patron-client politics, the real and anticipated program impact, and the adequacy of mechanisms to control government spending.[20]

Previous research consequently leaves the relationship between authoritarianism and economic austerity very much open to question. The literature on stabilization in Latin America has consistently emphasized the significance of contrasts between authoritarian and democratic regimes. Comparative studies of public policy in Latin America, on the other hand, have consistently dismissed the explanatory importance of regime differences, as have comparative analyses of economic stabilization focusing on other world regions. The sole point of consensus among scholars is that politics affect economic stabilization. Even the IMF, which has traditionally ignored political risks in designing economic programs, concedes this point. An IMF staff review of agreements signed in the 1978–80 period, for example, concluded that "political constraints" and/or "weak administrative systems" accounted for 60 percent of the breaches of credit ceilings, whereas exogenous shocks, both domestic and external, led to only 26 percent of the breaches.[21] Critics of the

IMF might also cite inaccurate economic diagnoses and inappropriate policy targets to explain program failures; but for IMF supporters and detractors alike, the political sustainability of stabilization programs is a central issue.

IMF Programs in Latin America

To resolve some of the unanswered questions about the importance of authoritarianism to economic stabilization, this chapter provides both a cross-sectional and diachronic analysis of the implementation of IMF programs. The analysis focuses specifically on Latin American countries that attempted to implement at least one IMF standby arrangement under both democratic and authoritarian regime auspices during the 1954–84 period. Thus, countries that have not enjoyed any period of competitive rule between 1954, when the principles governing standby arrangements were first formalized, and 1984, when the debt crisis produced major changes in the process of stabilization,[22] are excluded from analysis (Mexico, Paraguay, Cuba, Panama, Nicaragua, El Salvador, Guatemala, and Haiti). Also excluded are 3 countries that have signed IMF agreements under only one kind of regime. The resulting sample, which encompasses more than half of the total number of conditional lending agreements between the IMF and Latin America during the 1954–84 period, consists of 114 standby arrangements signed by 9 different countries.

Emphasis is placed on IMF standby arrangements for several reasons. Perhaps most important, such a focus facilitates the process of identifying a large number of stabilization programs in a variety of different countries over a 30-year period. The resulting list of programs is not necessarily inclusive, inasmuch as larger countries and those with exceptional access to other sources of credit, such as Venezuela, often have found it unnecessary to resort to IMF lending. Non-IMF stabilization programs also proliferated during the 1970s, when the widespread availability of commercial loans transformed the IMF into a lender of last resort. Nevertheless, taking the 1954–84 period as a whole, a high proportion of Latin American stabilization programs have involved IMF standby agreements.

The reason is not merely that access to IMF resources in the upper-credit tranches hinges on the introduction of stabilization policies; countries facing persistent balance-of-payments disequilibria also seek IMF approval in order to expedite debt renegotiation, attract other outside funds, reduce currency speculation, and reverse capital flight.

Because IMF stabilization programs evince a number of key similarities, restricting analysis to standby arrangements also facilitates comparison by limiting the range of variance. The IMF's institutional role creates a major commonality among standby programs—one that encourages opponents of stabilization to accuse political authorities of selling out while it allows authorities to attempt to shift blame for austerity to the Fund. The politics of stabilization are likely to be rather different where an outside villain cannot be identified so readily. The IMF's institutional role also creates pressures and incentives for countries to adhere to their stabilization programs. Standby arrangements require countries to submit to IMF scrutiny of their economic situation and policies, and since 1956, when phasing was introduced, drawings under standby arrangements have depended on the maintenance of satisfactory performance as defined by a letter of intent establishing an agreement with the Fund.

Despite the evolution of IMF programs and operating procedures over time, basic similarities in IMF prescriptions and lending policies also create a basis for comparison across time periods and national units.[23] Until very recently, the time horizons of IMF standby programs have been short term. The overwhelming majority of programs considered in this study, for example, involved only one-year commitments, although a high proportion were renewed. In contrast, other stabilization programs, particularly those initiated in connection with World Bank structural adjustment lending or the IMF's own Extended Fund Facility, have emphasized longer-term structural adjustment. The similarities among IMF stabilization programs are also marked inasmuch as standby agreements have typically emphasized demand management techniques of fiscal and monetary policy plus exchange-rate adjustments. This orthodox approach and its attendant squeeze on popular-sector living standards is at the root of arguments concerning the incompatibility of democracy and economic stabilization. Of course, the specific program targets that are incorporated into IMF conditional lending agreements vary from case to case, but countries typically resort to Fund lending in the upper-credit tranches to cope with a common set of problems (persistent balance-of-payments deficits associated with moderate to high inflation), and the economic diagnoses and medicines dispensed by the Fund also evince major commonalities. Indeed, critics frequently charge the IMF with adopting a "stereotyped approach" that ignores important economic contrasts among countries.[24]

The subsequent analysis makes no attempt to assess the wisdom of IMF lending policies or to provide a full explanation of their variable impact. It focuses instead on two explicitly political questions: (1) Are stabilization programs politically riskier for competitive than for authoritarian regimes? and (2) Are authoritarian regimes more successful at implementing stabilization programs than are competitive regimes? It should be emphasized that for the purposes of this study, success does not refer to economic outcomes such as inflation. Success and failure are defined instead in terms of policy implementation, as measured by basic indicators of fiscal and monetary policy. Although the issue of outcomes has figured prominently in previous discussions of the politics of stabilization, it cannot be assumed that short-term stabilization policies have any impact on economic performance, much less a positive impact. Even the Fund's own analyses show only a moderate correlation between the implementation of IMF prescriptions and the achievement of desired economic results.[25] Moreover, economic models of stabilization remain so highly controversial that policy outcomes cannot be analyzed in any manner not open to serious theoretical and empirical challenge. For example, according to neostructuralist analysts, orthodox stabilization programs produce perverse results: instead of reducing inflation, such programs provoke it by raising interest rates.[26] Likewise, it is possible to construct models showing that monetary restraint reduces exports and increases imports.[27] Hence, lowered inflation rates and improvements in the trade balance might plausibly be construed as signs of program breakdown or failure, rather than as indicators of success. The farther one moves from policy in the direction of outcomes and economic performance, the more tenuous the conclusions that can be drawn about the impact of regime.

Table 4.2 provides basic information about the cases under analysis. The sample is divided relatively equally between stabilization programs initiated by competitive and authoritarian regimes, which in itself suggests that Latin American democracies do not go to unusual lengths to avoid economic stabilization. Indeed, taking into consideration the relative frequency of democratic rule in the nine countries, which was less than 50 percent for the entire 1954–84 period, the data indicate that democratic regimes are even more likely to introduce stabilization policies than are authoritarian ones. The same is true even if the question of time period is taken into account. The propensity to resort to IMF lending was greatest during the 1960s, when democratic rule was unusually prevalent in Latin America. Nevertheless, in every decade except the 1980s, which accounts for only nine of the total number of cases, the percentage of standbys initiated by democracies exceeds the frequency of democratic rule.

Individual country data show similar trends, although Brazil, Ecuador, and Uruguay stand out as exceptions inasmuch as democratic sponsorship of standbys is a little low relative to years of democratic rule. In general, however, the cross-national differences emerging from table 4.2 reflect variations in the extent of democratic experience. Hence, Brazil, which has signed most of its standby arrangements under military rule, has enjoyed far fewer years of democracy than have Chile or Colombia, which have initiated a high proportion of their stabilization programs under democratic rule.

Can the frequency with which competitive regimes initiated standby programs be explained on the basis of necessity? Barry Ames has recently shown that military governments are more fiscally conservative than are democratic ones.[28] Hence, it might be hypothesized that competitive regimes are forced to undertake more stabilization programs because they are more likely to generate inflation.[29] Comparative evidence, however, fails to bear out this hypothesis. Analysis of the set of cases listed in table 4.1, which make it possible to look at military and competitive regime performance on a before and after basis as

Table 4.2
IMF Standby Arrangements in Nine Latin American Countries,
1954–84

	Competitive Regime Initiation	Authoritarian Regime Initiation	Total
Argentina	4	6	10
Bolivia	6	7	13
Brazil	2	8	10
Chile	10	3	13
Colombia	13	2	15
Ecuador	5	5	10
Honduras	8	5	13
Peru	11	6	17
Uruguay	6	7	13
Total	65	49	114

Source: International Monetary Fund, *Annual Report,* 1954–84.

well cross-nationally, indicates that there are no statistically significant differences between the annual percentage change in the rate of domestic price increases under military and competitive rule. Some military regimes, such as that headed by General Videla in Argentina, have dramatically braked an inflationary spiral; others, such as the Bolivian military regime of the 1964–79 period, have not. The performances of competitive regimes have been equally mixed.

Even if democratic regimes are not more reluctant to initiate standby programs, do they nonetheless fall victim to stabilization policies more frequently than do their authoritarian counterparts? The evidence fails to support such a conclusion. As indicated by table 4.3, regime change followed the initiation of 12 percent of the stabilization programs, but democratic regimes proved no more vulnerable than authoritarian ones. If anything, the data point in the opposite direction because the breakdown rates for authoritarian regimes are marginally higher. Moreover, with the exception of Bolivia, every nation that has experienced democratic regime collapse after signing a standby arrangement has also experienced a military regime collapse under similar circumstances. Even in the Bolivian case, the first phase of a transition from military to competitive rule occurred after a standby agreement had been reached with the IMF in early 1980, although the transition was not completed until 1982.

Table 4.3
Regime Survival Rates under IMF Standby Arrangements
(in Percentages)

	Competitive Regimes	Authoritarian Regimes
Breakdown[a]	10.8 (7)	14.0 (7)
Survival	89.2 (58)	86.0 (42)
Total	100.0 (65)	100.0 (49)

[a] Includes all cases of transition from democracy to authoritarianism or vice versa under standby arangements or during the 12-month period following the initiation of such arrangments.

The overlap between authoritarian and democratic regime breakdown suggests that some countries are more vulnerable to political instability than are others. It also points to the variable impact of stabilization policies, which can be implemented with much less economic dislocation—and presumably political risk—in some settings more than in others. In the countries considered here, the highest rate of regime breakdown was registered in Argentina, where orthodox stabilization has proved notoriously costly and difficult. Although Argentine exports respond slowly to incentives such as devaluation, stabilization policies tend to have unusually immediate and highly negative effects on food prices, real wages, and income. Such policies, therefore, provoke intense resistance from popular-sector groups, which traditionally have been both well organized and politically assertive in Argentina.

In general, however, the experience of the 9 countries considered in this study suggests that political risks of stabilization have been overdrawn. During the 1954–84 period, 46 percent of the regime changes in the 9 countries occurred in conjunction with stabilization programs. Although this figure sounds high, it is surprisingly low considering that stabilization programs were in effect 44 percent of the time. Put another way, the odds of regime collapse during years in which standby arrangements prevailed and years in which they did not were 1 out of 9.4 and 10.5, respectively (not significantly different). Moreover, an analysis of the 14 regime changes occurring while standby programs were in effect indicates that stabilization policies often had little political impact and that even when such policies did contribute to regime breakdown, as in the case of the Argentine coup of 1962, they were not the sole or even the major factor. A higher rate of regime change might have been anticipated simply on the grounds that the economic difficulties associated with standbys, such as inflation and shortages of foreign exchange, are themselves politically destabilizing. At least in Latin America, regimes are either more resilient or standby arrangements less consequential than observers have assumed. In view of the propensity of Latin American nations to resort repeatedly to IMF credit, the latter explanation seems particularly plausible. Hence, it can be hypothesized that standby arrangements have not caused more regime instability because the risky cures recommended by the IMF simply have not been administered by either military or civilian governments.

The Implementation of IMF Programs

To assess the relationship between regime and implementation, the subsequent analysis looks at a common set of indicators of credit expansion and fiscal performance. It thereby attempts to remain as close as possible to the issue of policy (as opposed to policy outcomes) without totally reducing the question of implementation to one of success versus failure. The majority of stabilization programs fall somewhere between these extremes inasmuch as governments typically administer some stabilization measures more energetically and effectively than others. Hence, policy implementation cannot be assessed adequately on the basis of such criteria as program suspension or cancellation. Even when some of the criteria specified in a letter of intent are not met and drawings of IMF credits are suspended, governments may comply with other aspects of a stabilization program. Moreover, program breakdown, whether resulting from cancellation by borrowing countries or IMF suspension, establishes no objective basis for comparison. Not all IMF standby programs are equally demanding, stringent, or realistic, nor are all countries treated equally with respect to the flexibility of conditionality.[30] Variability in program content and flexibility also makes it difficult to evaluate policy implementation on the basis of IMF performance criteria or program-specific goals. In any case, information about the targets of specific programs usually remains confidential, making it necessary for non-IMF researchers to rely on other indicators of implementation.

Indicators of credit expansion and fiscal performance were selected to assess policy implementation in this analysis chiefly because credit ceilings and fiscal targets have been emphasized more heavily and consistently by the IMF itself than have other performance criteria. This emphasis has been criticized, especially with respect to credit ceilings; nevertheless, as Tony Killick has shown, "ceilings on total domestic credit and on that part of it lent to the public sector are almost invariably components of Stand-by and EFF programmes and . . . in most cases observance of these ceilings is the most serious hurdle the government must surmount in order to retain access to the credit in question."[31]

Fiscal performance targets have been the second most common criteria of implementation since the 1960s, reflecting the IMF's traditional emphasis on fiscal restraint. Indeed, Fund programs often begin with the assumption that rapid inflation and balance-of-payments deficits are rooted in government deficits. According to a sample of 30 countries receiving upper-tranche credits in the 1964–79 period, IMF standby missions identified public-sector management as an "acute" problem more frequently than any other, except the balance of payments itself.[32] Consequently, during the 1969–78 period, nearly 80 percent of standby programs included fiscal performance clauses; many programs that did not nevertheless included statements by government authorities about their fiscal policy intentions.[33] Due to the confidentiality of IMF programs, it is impossible to know precisely what proportion of programs included fiscal targets in the pre-1969 period, but available information suggests that the emphasis on government-sector performance has not increased over time.[34] Certainly, most other performance criteria have fluctuated much more widely in importance both over time and among cases. Devaluation, for example, traditionally has been consodered a central component of IMF policy packages; yet in the 1969–79 period, less than one-third of upper-tranche lending agreements involved exchange rate action.[35]

94

Fiscal policy also warrants emphasis because failure to adhere to public-sector performance targets constitutes the single most important reason for the breakdown of IMF programs.[36] Expenditure targets have created particular difficulty and, according to an IMF staff analysis, were achieved by only 43 percent of the standbys during the 1969–78 period.[37] This rate of success is low relative to that for other targets, even domestic credit ceilings, which were attained by 55 percent of the IMF standby programs during the same period.[38] Moreover, public-sector performance is controlled more directly by the government than are most other indicators of policy implementation. Hence, to the extent that regime differences do produce variations in the ability of governments to sustain stabilization efforts, those variations should be particularly evident in public-sector behavior.

Subsequent tables compare the relative success of democratic and authoritarian regimes in controlling fiscal deficits, real expenditures, and rates of credit expansion. Table 4.4 describes the implementation of IMF programs during years in which standby agreements were at least nominally in effect for 11 months or more, regardless of whether IMF credits were actually used. Table 4.5 presents data only for those years in which the IMF actually disbursed funds under standby arrangements to the countries considered in this study. A third and broader variety of cases is considered in tables 4.6 through 4.9, which present data for all years in which standby programs were at least nominally in effect for 6 months or more. It should be emphasized that in all cases the data represent averages of individual years rather than individual standby programs, a number of which lasted more than a single year. The tables thus compare average performance during years in which democratic regimes administered standby programs with average performance during years of authoritarian or mixed regime administration. Included in the mixed category are all cases of regime change that resulted in a single regime ruling less than 11 months of the year.

Looking first at table 4.4, we find no support for the view that the political sustainability of standby programs is any greater under military rule. Although caution is necessary in comparing data across widely disparate cases and time periods,

Table 4.4
Performance during Calendar Years Fully Covered by IMF
Standby Arrangements[a] (in Percentages)

	Competitive Regimes	Authoritarian Regimes	Mixed Regimes	All Regimes
Government Deficit as % GDP[b]	1.8 (37)	3.4 (16)	1.7 (10)	2.2 (63)
% Change in Gov. Deficit as % GDP[c]	1.1 (36)	77.6 (19)	63.6 (9)	32.6 (64)
Growth of Real Gov. Expenditures[d]	5.0 (21)	13.0 (18)	6.0 (9)	8.2 (48)
Growth of Domestic Credit[e]	21.4 (40)	70.7 (20)	17.3 (10)	34.9 (70)
% Change in Rate of Growth of Domestic Credit[f]	47.7 (39)	20.3 (20)	30.4 (10)	37.3 (69)

Source: Internatonal Monetary Fund, *Monthly Financial Statistics*, 1954–1985; idem, *International Financial Statistics*, 1954–85; United Nations, *Statistical Yearbook*, 1955–69.

[a] Includes all calendar years during which IMF standby arrangements were at least nominally in effect for 11 months or more. Data exclude Uruguay and Brazil, which experienced full-year standby programs as defined for the purposes of this table under only one type of regime.

[b] Data were missing for 7 cases. Differences among categories significant at .001 level.

[c] Data were missing for 6 cases.

[d] Data were missing for 22 cases.

[e] Differences among categories significant at .05 level.

[f] Data were missing for 1 case.

competitive regimes actually outperformed authoritarian ones in four of the five comparisons shown in the table. Moreover, on the basis of a one-way analysis of variance, the only statistically significant differences between competitive and authoritarian regimes are those pointing in the direction of inferior military program implementation. The results are similar if attention is focused only on years in which credits were actually disbursed under standby arrangements.[39]

Approaching the data simply in terms of the direction of change of the various indicators also fails to produce evidence of superior military performance. As table 4.5 indicates, democratic regimes consistently outperformed authoritarian ones during years in which the IMF disbursed credits under standby arrangements, although the differences are not

96

significant. The results are virtually identical if the analysis is expanded to include all years in which standby arrangements were nominally in effect for at least six months, regardless of whether credits were canceled, suspended, or never utilized. Such findings cannot be dismissed on the grounds that the magnitude of adjustment problems increased in the post-1973 period, when military rule was particularly prevalent. Deleting the post-1973 period from the analysis presented in table 4.5 only widens the gap between competitive and authoritarian performance. The figure for competitive regime budget reductions in table 4.5, for example, rises to 64.5 percent, whereas the success rate for authoritarian regimes falls to 37.5 percent.

Table 4.5
Success Rates during Years When Credits Disbursed under IMF
Standby Arrangements[a] (in Percentages)

	Competitive Regimes	Authoritarian Regimes	Mixed Regimes	All Regimes
Reduced Gov. Deficit as % GDP[b]	62.5 (32)	46.7 (15)	83.3 (6)	60.4 (53)
Reduced Rate of Growth of Real Expenditures[c]	53.8 (26)	53.3 (15)	83.3 (6)	57.4 (47)
Reduced Rate of Growth of Domestic Credit	68.4 (37)	61.1 (18)	66.7 (6)	66.1 (62)
Reduced Two of Three Indicators	69.2 (26)	66.7 (6)	53.3 (15)	63.7 (47)
Reduced All Three Indicators	38.5 (26)	33.3 (6)	26.7 (15)	34.0 (47)

Source: As for table 4.4.
[a] Excluding data for Colombia, which only made drawings of IMF upper-tranche credits under democratic rule.
[b] Data were missing for 10 cases.
[c] Data were missing for 15 cases.

The data presented in table 4.5 also underline the high rate of failure of IMF programs. During years in which IMF credits were actually used, governments only succeeded in pushing individual performance indicators in the right direction approximately 60 percent of the time. Simultaneous reductions in all three indicators were achieved only 34 percent of the time.

The rates are even worse for years in which standby agreements were nominally in effect for at least six months. In light of previous research on the IMF, much of which emphasizes the high breakdown rate of standby arrangements, these figures are not altogether surprising; nevertheless, the data presented here do lend concrete support to the view that the average IMF program has had a limited impact in Latin America. If a high proportion of IMF standby arrangements have failed to reduce the fiscal deficit as a proportion of GDP or even to lower the rate of growth of real expenditures and domestic credit, there is little basis for thinking such arrangements have profoundly reduced domestic consumption, damaged local industry, or increased inequality either.

The weak impact of standby arrangements is further underlined if the analysis shifts away from average performance data to consider the question of implementation strictly on a before-and-after basis. For this purpose IMF programs that formed part of a continuing series of stabilization arrangements are ignored in favor of programs that actually initiated stabilization policies. Hence, the implementation of standby programs is evaluated by comparing the performance of key variables in the 12 months preceding and following program initiation, but solely in relation to years in which no prior standby arrangement was in effect with the IMF. Because such a high proportion of Latin American programs have formed part of the continuing series, this procedure sharply reduces the number of programs that can be considered, but it also provides more meaningful information about program implementation.[40]

The results of this analysis strongly reinforce the findings reported earlier. The 24 IMF programs falling within the sample that were implemented by authoritarian regimes had no statistically significant impact on indicators of expenditures, deficits, or domestic credit. The implementation record of democratic regimes was also weak, but the 20 democratic programs in the sample did effect a reduction in the rate of growth of real expenditures that was significant at the .05 level. Hence, democratic and authoritarian regimes again evince similar patterns of weak policy implementation, but democracies turn in a slightly better performance record.

An examination of the most and least successful cases in the before-and-after sample is also revealing. Nine of the 44 programs considered produced major improvements in 2 of the 3 performance indicators, and 7 of those 9 (Argentina, 1959 and 1967; Ecuador, 1961 and 1969; Brazil, 1965; Chile, 1974; Colombia, 1957) were administered by new governments that had been in power less than one year. Five were liberal democracies. At the other extreme stand 4 cases (Brazil, 1961; Bolivia, 1973; Honduras, 1968; Argentina, 1983) distinguished by virtue of their economic policy failures. Three cases were authoritarian regimes that had been in power for a period of five or more years. Particularly abysmal were the performance records of military regimes in Bolivia and Honduras during the late 1960s and early 1970s. For example, after entering into an agreement with the IMF in January 1973, the Bolivian military allowed real expenditures to increase 18 percent in a single year. Hence, although newly established regimes often compile dismal records of economic stabilization, particularly because of their propensity to consolidate a basis of political support by increasing government spending, the evidence also suggests that regime change enhances the possibilities for effective stabilization, particularly under democratic auspices.

Other evidence of the linkage between regime change and effective stabilization emerges from tables 4.4 and 4.5, which show that better-than-average performance rates have characterized years of mixed regime administration. The numbers are small, however, and the findings open to more than one interpretation. Is effective stabilization a cause or a consequence of regime change? Do new regimes find it easier to administer stabilization programs, or are the relatively high success rates for years of regime change a product of vigorous program administration and resulting regime breakdown?

The cases of unusually effective stabilization that emerge from the before-and-after sample point to the importance of regime change as a precondition for effective stabilization. Table 4.6, on the other hand, suggests that the relationship between regime change and stabilization is more complex. Data presented in this table show that whereas program administration may be unusually vigorous in the year of regime breakdown itself, success rates for years following regime change are somewhat mixed. The implementation of IMF standby programs also appears less than uniformly superior in years following democratic elections. New governments, whether resulting from regime change or elections, do not necessarily excel at economic stabilization. In terms of indicators of domestic credit and government expenditures, the average performance of new regimes, especially military ones, even falls below par. The success rates of regimes implementing IMF standby programs during years prior to regime breakdown, on the other hand, exceed average figures, except in the deficit category. Vigorous implementation of IMF programs consequently appears to enhance the risk of regime breakdown, although ineffective stabilization is not necessarily a recipe for political survival. The cases of regime change analyzed in table 4.6 include instances of unsuccessful as well as successful

Table 4.6
Success Rates of IMF Programs and Political Change[a] (in Percentages)

	Reduced Gov. Deficit as % GDP	Reduced Rate of Increase of Real Government Expenditures	Reduced Rate of Growth of Domestic Credit
Years Preceding Regime Change	41.7 (12)[b]	66.7 (9)[c]	83.3 (12)[c]
Years Following Regime Change	62.5 (16)	46.7 (15)[b]	50.0 (16)
Democratic Administration	83.3 (6)	60.0 (5)[b]	50.0 (6)
Authoritarian Administration	50.0 (10)	40.0 (10)	50.0 (10)
Years Following Democratic Elections	50.0 (14)[d]	55.6 (9)[e]	64.3 (14)[d]
All Standby Years[f]	49.1 (116)	54.0 (87)	56.1 (123)

Source: As for table 4.4.

[a] Includes all years preceding and following regime change in which IMF standby arrangements covered a period of at least six months. Data calculated on the basis of performance during the full calendar year.

[b] Data were missing for 1 case.

[c] Data were missing for 4 cases.

[d] Data were missing for 3 cases.

[e] Data were missing for 8 cases.

[f] All years IMF standby arrangements at least nominally in effect for six months or more. Data missing for 11, 40, and 4 cases, respectively.

implementation of standby programs, presumably because a deteriorating economic situation undermines political support and/or because underlying political weaknesses contribute both to implementation failures and to regime change. In this connection note that in the nine countries considered by this study, economic stabilization followed regime change more frequently than regime change followed efforts to achieve economic stabilization.

Looking at the data on a country-by-country basis provides additional confirmation of previous findings as well as further insights into the relationship between regime change and economic stabilization. Table 4.7 indicates that as far as government expenditures are concerned, military regimes have outperformed their democratic counterparts in only two countries—Chile and Peru. Moreover, in most cases the gap between authoritarian and democratic performance has been considerable.

Table 4.7
Average Annual Percentage Change in Real Government
Expenditures under Standby Arrangements[a]

	Competitive Regimes	Authoritarian Regimes	Mixed Regimes	All Regimes
Argentina	1.4 (3)	17.0 (5)	–7.6 (1)	8.0 (9)
Bolivia	2.9 (4)	13.6 (7)	10.8 (1)	7.7 (12)
Brazil	6.0 (3)	7.3 (8)	—	6.9 (11)
Chile	8.4 (10)	–3.1 (2)	—	6.5 (12)
Ecuador	11.7 (6)	17.9 (3)	4.7 (3)	7.6 (12)
Honduras	0.9 (5)	12.2 (5)	0.4 (2)	5.5 (12)
Peru	12.9 (5)	–2.4 (4)	13.4 (4)	8.3 (13)
Uruguay	2.6 (5)	6.4 (6)	10.4 (1)	5.1 (12)
Average	5.4 (41)	9.0 (40)	5.2 (12)	6.9 (93)

Source: As for table 4.4.
[a] Data for all years in which standby arrangements were at least nominally in effect for more than six months. Data missing for Colombia.

Patterns that are much more mixed emerge from tables 4.8 and 4.9, which basically suggest that the relative success of democracy and authoritarianism in implementing IMF programs has varied from place to place, without regard for level of social modernization. Again, however, Chile and Peru stand out by virtue of the effectiveness of authoritarianism in restricting the expansion of government deficits and domestic credit. The cases falling at the other extreme are Argentina, Bolivia, Ecuador, and Uruguay. In these four cases, competitive regimes have outperformed authoritarian ones in terms of all three indicators of implementation.

Table 4.8

Average Annual Percentage Change in Rate of Domestic Credit
Expansion under IMF Standby Arrangements[a]

	Competitive Regimes	Authoritarian Regimes	Mixed Regimes	All Standby Years
Argentina	−2.7 (3)	19.8 (6)	−40.2 (1)	7.1 (10)
Bolivia	−16.7 (7)	−1.7 (7)	−3.4 (1)	−8.8 (15)
Brazil	8.8 (4)	3.5 (8)	—	5.3 (12)
Chile	17.4 (10)	−120.9 (3)	—	4.1 (13)
Colombia	10.1 (14)	−33.5 (1)	−44.5 (1)	4.0 (16)
Ecuador	−26.7 (6)	164.4 (3)	−26.3 (3)	47.9 (12)
Honduras	356.9 (5)	14.4 (5)	18.0 (3)	146.9 (13)
Peru	8.6 (9)	−0.4 (4)	82.5 (4)	23.9 (17)
Uruguay	−15.0 (6)	16.2 (9)	—	3.8 (15)
Average	28.7 (64)	15.0 (46)	16.7 (13)	22.3 (123)

Source: As for table 4.4.

[a] Includes all years in which IMF standbys were at least nominally in effect for more than six months.

The country-by-country patterns consequently conform to broader trends. Few differences emerge between democratic and military implementation of stabilization programs, and those that do tend to point in the direction of greater democratic effectiveness. Marked evidence of superior authoritarian performance exists only in the cases of Chile and Peru. Moreover, both of these cases represent weak exceptions in the sense that the achievements of authoritarianism occurred in the context of exceptionally high levels of government expenditure. In the Peruvian case, severe cutbacks in real expenditures in 1978 and 1979 produced a negative figure presented in table 4.7, although they left the ratio of government spending to GDP at a figure of 23 percent. Similarly, Chilean government spending had reached unprecedented levels during the Allende period,

Table 4.9
Average Annual Percentage Change in Government Deficit as
Percentage of GDP under IMF Standby Arrangements[a]

	Competitive Regimes	Authoritarian Regimes	Mixed Regimes	All Standby Years
Argentina	-37.9 (3)	-24.1 (5)	111.8 (1)	13.6 (9)
Bolivia	-25.7 (4)	27.4 (7)	20.0 (1)	9.1 (12)
Brazil	2.4 (4)	-28.2 (8)	—	-18.0 (12)
Chile	-4.0 (10)	-62.4 (2)	—	-4.4 (12)
Colombia	75.3 (14)	-23.1 (1)	30.0 (1)	66.3 (16)
Ecuador	-12.4 (6)	-5.1 (3)	-24.9 (3)	-13.7 (12)
Honduras	3.7 (5)	188.8 (5)	-9.8 (3)	71.8 (13)
Peru	3.4 (9)	-37.6 (1)	201.7 (1)	36.8 (17)
Uruguay	-62.1 (4)	135.5 (8)	—	69.7 (12)
Average	8.0 (59)	36.3 (43)	72.2 (13)	25.2 (115)

Source: As for table 4.4.
[a] Includes all years in which IMF standbys were at least nominally in effect for more than six months. Data missing for 12 cases.

and the contrasts between authoritarian and competitive regime performance that emerge in table 4.7 reflect the deep budget cuts of 1974. The success of military regimes in Chile and Peru in cutting the rate of expansion of domestic credit and budget deficits as a percentage of GDP likewise represents developments in a brief time period characterized by exceptional financial disequilibrium, rather than a long-term pattern. In both Chile and Peru, the deficit had risen to more than 7 percent of GDP—a figure other countries considered in this study have yet to approach, with the single exception of Bolivia in the early 1980s.

Yet, if the deviant cases provide only weak counterevidence, they are nevertheless revealing in terms of the issue of regime change. In Chile a democratic regime breakdown paved the way for unusually vigorous implementation of IMF policy prescriptions under exclusionary authoritarian auspices—an experience that illustrates the political risks of deferring economic stabilization as well as the link between regime change and successful stabilization. In the Peruvian case, on the other hand, the political risks of mounting economic problems were born by an authoritarian regime, as were the costs of the subsequent stabilization. Against a background of unsuccessful non-IMF stabilization, the austerity policies of the 1976–79 period mobilized opposition and intensified divisions within the inclusionary Peruvian military government, generating a profound political crisis that culminated in a transition to democracy. The two cases are similar in that a severe economic crisis placed authorities in a predicament and thereby paved the way for regime change. The responses of Chilean and Peruvian authorities to that crisis, however, differed significantly, creating very disparate incentives and opportunities for economic stabilization after regime breakdown.

The Chilean and Peruvian cases, which were characterized by highly divergent forms of military rule, consequently shed additional light on the complex relationship between regime change and economic stabilization. Together with the other data on regime change presented earlier, they suggest that regime transitions result less from stabilization policies than from economic crisis, but that the policy responses of authorities to economic crisis are nonetheless important for understanding the outcome of regime change processes. The type of political coalition emerging after regime breakdown and the related willingness and capacity of new authorities to implement orthodox stabilization policies are conditioned by the perceived successes and failures of their predecessors. At stake here is the much neglected issue of political learning. The political sustainability of economic stabilization subsequent to regime change varies with the intensity of prior implementation efforts.

Conclusion

The most fundamental conclusion to be drawn from the preceding analysis is a negative one: there is no evidence that military regimes have a distinctive macroeconomic impact. Military regimes are not better than competitive regimes at promoting economic growth. Military regimes are not better at maintaining price stability. They are not even better at restoring economic stability over the short run. As compared with democracies, military regimes are no more likely to initiate stabilization programs or survive their political reverberations. Moreover, whether the data are pooled, approached on a country-by-country basis, considered by time period, or analyzed in terms of the before-and-after performance of key indicators, the results are the same: there is no evidence that the implementation of stabilization programs is any more rigorous under authoritarianism than under competitive rule. Indeed, to the limited extent that regime differences are significant, competitive regimes appear to have the edge.

These findings are very much at odds with the conventional view that competitive regimes are inept at coping with economic crisis and managing austerity programs. Obviously, democracies enjoy strengths that have been denigrated or overlooked, such as legitimacy and popular support; but perhaps more to the point, the rationality, efficiency, unity, expertise, political isolation, and coercive capability of authoritarian governments have been grossly exaggerated. As measured by increases in budget deficits, expenditures, and domestic credit, the most egregiously unsuccessful IMF stabilization programs in Latin America over the past 30 years have been those managed by military—not democratic— regimes. Hence, although military rulers may tout the strength, efficiency, impartiality, and effectiveness of authoritarianism, their claims appear to provide a rather distorted lens through which to view empirical reality.

Because support for military coups is buttressed by the assumption that the military is better at managing economic crises, these findings have important political implications. At the very least, they raise questions about the capacity of military rulers to cope with serious macroeconomic disequilibria. The theoretical implications of the preceding analysis are equally profound. If stabilization policies provide no basis for linking regime type with macroeconomic performance, there is no reason to suppose such a relationship can be found elsewhere. Stabilization has been repeatedly singled out as the policy area in which the economic performance of military and civilian regimes differs significantly. Moreover, to the extent that coercion, which presumably is a distinctive feature of military regimes, makes a difference, its impact should be felt most profoundly in an area of economic performance in which policy implementation is the central problem.

The appropriate conclusion is not that regime is irrelevant or only important for understanding strictly political variations over time or among cases. As the analysis of stabilization policies indicates, regime change may make a significant difference even if regime type does not. Virtually every instance of unusually successful stabilization identified on the basis of a before-and-after analysis was a product of regime change. This finding suggests that regime breakdowns occurring in conjunction with economic crisis create exceptional space for the implementation of stabilization policies, particularly when regime collapse is attributed to policy inaction rather than to austerity measures. Economic crisis and regime breakdown discredit prior political formulas, opening up room for new authorities to blame economic problems on their predecessors and otherwise manuever in the face of economic necessity. Hence, as in the case of Chile, military regimes may succeed where their democratic predecessors have failed. Likewise, regime change appears to enhance the willingness and capacity of new democratic authorities to implement stabilization policies. It seems reasonable to suppose that the possibilities for policy innovation in other areas conform to a similar pattern.

Notes

1 Government Junta of the Armed Forces and Carabineros of Chile, "The Reasons of the Junta," reprinted in *The Politics of Antipolitics: The Military in Latin America*, ed. Brian Loveman and Thomas M. Davies, Jr. (Lincoln: University of Nebraska Press, 1978), 199.

2 General Jorge Rafael Videla, "A Time for Fundamental Reorganization of the Nation," reprinted in ibid., 179.

3 In the case of Argentina, for example, the economic collapse of the mid-1970s followed the death of Perón and the resulting struggle for power within the Peronist movement. For an analysis of these events see Guido Di Tella, *Perón-Perón, 1973–1976* (Buenos Aires: Sudamericana, 1983); Gary W. Wynia, *Argentina in the Postwar Era: Politics and Economic Policy Making in a Divided Society* (Albuquerque: University of New Mexico Press, 1978); Liliana De Riz, *Retorno y derrumbe: el último gobierno peronista* (Mexico City: Folios Ediciones, 1981).

4 Statistical significance was evaluated on the basis of the Mann–Whitney test, which is considered a useful alternative to the parametric t-test, when the t-test assumptions are not met.
5 For a survey and review of this literature see Karen L. Remmer, "Evaluating the Policy Impact of Military Regimes in Latin America," *Latin American Research Review* XIII, 2 (1978): 39–55.
6 Jonathan Hartlyn and Samuel A. Morley, *Latin American Political Economy: Financial Crisis and Political Change* (Boulder, CO: Westview Press, 1986), 45.
7 Ibid., 46.
8 See, for example, *LASA Forum* 15 (Winter 1985), 1, in which the former president of the Latin American Studies Association, Helen Safa, commented at length on the tensions between economic stabilization and democratization in Latin America. See also Jorge Dominguez, "Political Change: Central America, South America, and the Caribbean," in *Understanding Political Development*, ed. Myron Weiner and Samuel P. Huntington (Boston: Little, Brown & Co., 1987), 83; Rosemary Thorp and Laurence Whitehead, "Introduction," in *Inflation and Stabilization in Latin America*, ed. Rosemary Thorp and Laurence Whitehead (New York: Holmes & Meier, 1979), 11, 18; Robert R. Kaufman, "Democratic and Authoritarian Responses to the Debt Issue: Argentina, Brazil, and Mexico," *International Organization* 39 (Summer 1985): 473–503; Barbara Stallings, "Peru and the U.S. Banks: Privatization of Financial Relations," in *Capitalism and the State in U.S.-Latin American Relations*, ed. Richard R. Fagen (Stanford: Stanford University Press, 1979), 217–53; Robert Frenkel and Guillermo O'Donnell, "The 'Stabilization Programs' of the International Monetary Fund and Their Internal Impacts," in ibid., 171–216; Thomas E. Skidmore, "The Politics of Economic Stabilization in Postwar Latin America," in *Authoritarianism and Corporatism in Latin America*, ed. James M. Malloy (Pittsburgh: University of Pittsburgh Press, 1977), 149–90; John Sheahan, "Market-Oriented Economic Policies and Political Repression in Latin America," *Economic Development and Cultural Change* 28 (January 1980): 267–91; Alejandro Foxley, *Latin American Experiments in Neo-conservative Economics* (Berkeley: University of California Press, 1983); Christian Anglade and Carlos Fortín, eds., *The States and Capital Accumulation in Latin America*, Vol. 1 (Pittsburgh: University of Pittsburgh Press, 1985), 8; Riordan Roett, "The Foreign Debt Crisis and the Process of Redemocratization in Latin America," in *A Dance along the Precipice: The Political and Economic Dimensions of the International Debt Problem*, ed. William N. Eskridge, Jr. (Lexington, MA: Lexington Books, 1985), 207–30.
9 Joan M. Nelson, "The Politics of Stabilization," in *Adjustment Crisis in the Third World*, ed. Richard E. Feinberg and Valeriana Kallab (New Brunswick, NJ: Transaction Books, 1984), 99.

10 Ibid., 4.
11 Kaufman, "Democratic and Authoritarian Responses," 478. See also Skidmore, "The Politics of Economic Stabilization," 179.
12 Kaufman, "Democratic and Authoritarian Responses," 479. See also Mancur Olson, *The Rise and Decline of Nations: Economic Growth, Stagflation, and Social Rigidities* (New Haven: Yale University Press, 1982).
13 Carlos Díaz-Alejandro, "Southern Cone Stabilization Plans," in *Economic Stabilization in Developing Countries*, ed. William R. Cline and Sidney Weintraub (Washington, DC: Brookings Institution, 1981), 120.
14 Ibid., 123.
15 Stephan Haggard and Robert Kaufman, "The Politics of Stabilization and Structural Adjustment," paper prepared for the NBER Project on Developing Country Debt, 1987, 5–6.
16 Skidmore, "The Politics of Economic Stabilization," 181.
17 Kaufman, "Democratic and Authoritarian Responses," 482.
18 Stephan Haggard, "The Politics of Adjustment: Lessons from the IMF's Extended Fund Facility," *International Organization* 39, 3 (Summer 1985): 512; "The Politics of Stabilization: Lessons from the IMF's Extended Fund Facility," paper presented at the 1984 meeting of the American Political Science Association, Washington, DC, August 3–September 2, 1984, 12.
19 Haggard, "The Politics of Adjustment," 529–32.
20 Nelson, "The Politics of Stabilization."
21 As cited in Tony Killick, "The Impact of Fund Stabilisation Programmes," in *The Quest for Economic Stabilization: The IMF and the Third World*, ed. Tony Killick (New York: St. Martin's, 1984), 261. See also C. David Finch, "Adjustment Policies and Conditionality," in *IMF Conditionality*, ed. John Williamson (Washington, DC: Institute for International Economics, 1983), 79; Omotunde Johnson and Joanne Salop, "Distributional Aspects of Stabilization Programs in Developing Countries," *IMF Staff Papers* 27 (March 1980): 23.
22 Because these changes create major problems of comparability across time periods, attention is limited to pre-1984 stabilization programs. After 1984, the debt crisis produced important changes in the international context of economic stabilization. These changes were reflected in the IMF's own policies, which were liberalized enough to accept rather unorthodox stabilization programs. The Plan Austral, for example, made its debut in Argentina in 1985.
23 For an analysis of the evolution of IMF programs and practices over time see Sidney Dell, *On Being Grandmotherly: The Evolution of IMF Conditionality*, Princeton Essays in International Finance, 144 (Princeton: Department of Economics, October 1981). See also E. M. Ainley, *The IMF: Past, Present and Future*, Bangor Occasional Papers in Economics, 15 (Bangor: University

of Wales Press, 1979); J. Keith Horsefield, ed., *The International Monetary Fund, 1945–1965: Twenty Years of International Monetary Cooperation*, 3 vols. (Washington, DC: International Monetary Fund, 1969); Margaret Garritsen de Vries, ed., *The International Monetary Fund, 1966–1971: The System under Stress*, 2 vols. (Washington, DC: International Monetary Fund, 1976); idem, *Balance of Payments Adjustment, 1945–1986: The IMF Experience* (Washington, DC: International Monetary Fund, 1987).

24 Sidney Dell, "Stabilization: The Political Economy of Overkill," in *IMF Conditionality*, ed. Williamson, 17–45.

25 For a summary of this evidence, see Killick, "The Impact of Fund Stabilisation Programmes."

26 Lance Taylor, "IS/LM in the Tropics: Diagrammatics of the New Structuralist Macro Critique," in *Economic Stabilization in Developing Countries*, ed. Cline and Weintraub, 465–503; William R. Cline, "Economic Stabilization in Developing Countries: Theory and Stylized Facts," in *IMF Conditionality*, ed. Williamson, 182–86.

27 Milton Charlton and Deborah Riner, "Political Dimensions of Economic Stabilization Programs in Latin America: A Rapporteur's Report," Working Paper No. 50, Latin American Program, Woodrow Wilson International Center for Scholars (Washington, DC), 3. In this connection it can be noted that much depends on whether emphasis is placed on the short-run or long-run impact. See Rudiger Dornbusch, "Stabilization Policies in Developing Countries: What Have We Learned?" *World Development* 10 (September 1982), 701–08.

28 Barry Ames, *Political Survival: Politicians and Public Policy in Latin America* (Berkeley: University of California Press, 1987).

29 I am indebted to Stephan Haggard for this suggestion.

30 Tony Killick, "IMF Stabilisation Programmes," in *The Quest for Economic Stabilisation*, ed. Killick, 183–226.

31 Ibid., 213.

32 Ibid., 224. See also Claudio M. Loser, "The Role of Economy-Wide Prices in the Adjustment Process," in *Adjustment, Conditionality, and International Financing*, ed. Joaquin Muns (Washington, DC: International Monetary Fund, 1984), 94.

33 W. A. Beveridge and Margaret R. Kelly, "Fiscal Content of Financial Programs Supported by Stand-By Arrangements in the Upper Credit Tranches, 1969–78," *IMF Staff Papers*, 27 (June 1980): 220.

34 Killick, "IMF Stabilisation Programmes," 192, 224–26.

35 Ibid., 195.

36 Killick, "The Impact of Fund Stabilisation Programmes," 252–53. See also Thomas Reichmann and Richard Stillson, "How Successful Are Programs Supported by Stand-by Arrangements?" *Finance and Development* 14 (March 1977): 25.

37 Beveridge and Kelly, "Fiscal Content of Financial Programs," 227.
38 See Killick, "The Impact of Fund Stabilisation Programmes," 252–55, for a summary of this evidence.
39 For a fuller report of these findings, see Karen L. Remmer, "The Politics of Economic Stabilization: IMF Standby Programs in Latin America, 1954–1984," *Comparative Politics* 18 (October 1986): 1–24.
40 To assess the impact of standby arrangements on expenditures, deficits, and domestic credit, the data on program implementation were calculated as weighted averages, with the weights determined by the month of program initiation and the differences between the before and after samples evaluated on the basis of a nonparametric test for differences in frequency distributions. For a more detailed discussion of the procedures followed, which are similar to those used by other IMF researchers, see the methodological appendix of Killick, "The Impact of Fund Stabilisation Programmes," 266–68.

PART II

Military Rule in Chile

CHAPTER 5

The Consolidation of the Pinochet Regime

More than three dozen military regimes have ruled in Latin America since World War II. The dictatorship of General Augusto Pinochet Ugarte in Chile stands out among them on several counts. Pinochet's 1973 seizure of power destroyed one of the oldest constitutional democracies in the world; terminated the presidency of Salvador Allende, who had attracted world attention by attempting to pursue a constitutional path to socialism; and unleased a counterrevolutionary process fully as unprecedented as the socialist experiment of the 1970–73 period.

In terms of its origins, the Pinochet dictatorship resembled its exclusionary authoritarian counterparts in Argentina and Uruguay. The three Southern Cone military regimes seized power at approximately the same time and for roughly similar reasons. Rooted in accelerating class conflict and mounting economic disequilibrium, all three represented a political reaction against increasing popular-sector political activity and pressure. The three regimes were also similar in terms of their repressive character, base of social support, and ideology. Looking to business and financial sectors for support, they harshly repressed trade unions and political parties and attempted to justify their rule in terms of national security threats. In addition, the Southern Cone military regimes of the 1970s endorsed strikingly similar solutions to long-standing problems of inflation and low growth, articulating from the outset a commitment to free markets, private enterprise, trade liberalization, monetary discipline, and other elements of a

113

development strategy variously labeled *neoconservatism* or *neoliberalism*.

Despite these and other commonalities, which have been explored at some length in the literature on bureaucratic authoritarianism, the Chilean military regime exhibited three distinctive characteristics. First, as indicated in chapter 2, political power in the Chilean case became concentrated in the hands of an individual at the expense of rule by the military as an institution. As President of the Republic, Generalissimo of the Chilean Armed Forces, Captain General, and Commander-in-Chief of the Chilean Army,[1] Pinochet achieved a position of preeminence unrivaled by any of his recent counterparts in the more modernized countries of Latin America. As a result, his regime cannot be regarded as simply another example of bureaucratic authoritarianism but rather must be seen as posing a theoretical challenge in its own right. The idea of impersonal control by the military institution as a whole is central to the bureaucratic-authoritarian model.[2]

Second, by the standards of other countries with well-developed popular-sector organizations, Chilean authoritarianism demonstrated extraordinary durability after 1973. It stood up against a broad array of obstacles and pressures, including two of the deepest economic crises in Chilean history, mass protests, widespread internal opposition, and a constant barrage of international criticism. During the late 1970s and early 1980s, the regime also weathered a continent-wide wave of democratization, outliving its counterparts in Argentina, Bolivia, Brazil, Ecuador, El Salvador, Guatemala, Haiti, Honduras, Nicaragua, Peru, and Uruguay with which it had once been contemporaneous. With the exception of General Alfredo Stoessner, no South American military officer has ruled for a longer period of time in the postwar era than has General Pinochet, nor indeed has any president in Chilean history.

The persistence of the regime appears even more remarkable when one takes into account the political context in which it was established. With the possible exception of Uruguay, no Latin American military regime has confronted a political tradition more overtly hostile to the consolidation of military rule. Between 1830 and 1973, Chile had experienced only one period of direct military rule, establishing an impressive record of constitutional stability. As Régis Debray once remarked, "European liberal democracies, France for example, with its changing regimes and revolving republics, look like banana republics in comparison with Chile."[3]

The third exceptional feature of Chilean authoritarianism was its policy performance over the course of the 1973–89 period. The success with which the Pinochet dictatorship addressed acute problems of economic stabilization and the fervor with which it embraced neoliberal economic solutions were highly distinctive. To date no Latin American military regime has pursued an orthodox program of structural reform with greater determination or effectiveness. Hence, although all recent Southern Cone military regimes have shared a formal commitment to market-oriented development policies, the Pinochet regime stands out by virtue of how it translated that commitment into reality.

The distinctive internal structure, durability, and policy performance of the Pinochet dictatorship in comparison to other military regimes in the region pose a number of theoretically significant questions. Why did a country with a strong democratic political tradition give rise to such a durable authoritarian regime? Why did military rule disintegrate in response to internal divisions and mounting opposition in Argentina and Uruguay during the early 1980s but not in Chile? How did exclusionary authoritarianism in Chile come to assume such a personal face? Why didn't the regime exhibiting the greatest degree of personal rulership also prove the most inconsistent in its pursuit of neoliberal economic policies? What accounts for the unusual coherence and orthodox rigor of Chilean economic policy? To what extent do the contrasts between military rule in Chile and authoritarianism in other Southern Cone nations reflect Pinochet's extreme concentration of personal power?

The answers to such questions are significant not only for understanding the Chilean case but also for the comparative study of authoritarian rule. Building on the framework presented in chapter 2, Part II of this book analyzes how social class forces and institutional structures interacted in Chile to produce a highly personal and durable authoritarian regime with a profound social impact. This chapter traces the consolidation of the Pinochet dictatorship. It argues that personal rulership must be seen as a central rather than incidental feature of Chilean authoritarianism. Both the durability and distinctive policy performance of military rule in the 1973–89 period were rooted in the concentration of power achieved by Pinochet. The bureaucratic-authoritarian label, implying impersonal and bureaucratic control, obscures this critical point and thus provides no basis for understanding the important contrasts between authoritarianism in Chile and other Southern Cone countries. The relevance of institutional structures for understanding the functioning and impact of military rule are underlined further in the next chapter, which explores the impact of military rule on Chilean society. The concluding chapter discusses the consequences of institutional structures for the process of regime transition and the role of the armed forces under civilian rule.

The Origins of Chilean Authoritarianism

A deep social crisis, which was manifested in acute economic instability and the polarization of political forces along social class lines, created the basis for the establishment of the Pinochet dictatorship. As class conflict accelerated between 1970 and 1973, it engulfed virtually every facet of Chilean society, from the music played in Santiago to the organization of production in the countryside. Chile is not unique; every recent Southern Cone military regime has seized power in response to acute and mounting class tensions. But nowhere in the Southern Cone has the perception of crisis been more widely generalized or the "threat from below" more palpable than in Chile.[4]

The reason is that Chilean leftist forces were not merely challenging dominant class interests from outside the state. With the election of Salvador Allende to the presidency in 1970, the Marxist Unidad Popular coalition gained control over the executive branch and proceeded to effect major structural changes in Chilean society. It carried out a vigorous program of land reform, redistributed income in a downward direction, and nationalized virtually all major industries and banks.

Hence, in Chile a break with capitalism was more than a threat. A transition to socialism had already begun, and Chile's capitalist class felt itself on the verge of extinction. No comparable threat to dominant class interests emerged prior to military seizures of power in Uruguay or Argentina. There, the basic parameters of capitalist society remained relatively intact, with the threat to dominant class interests coming from the trade union movement and guerrilla groups rather than from within the state apparatus itself.

The precoup situation in Chile thus created an unusually favorable set of conditions for the installation of a highly repressive and autonomous military regime.[5] Its consolidation was a different matter. The strength of the popular sector provoked the profound political reaction leading up to the 1973 coup, but the partisan allegiances, organizational networks, working-class consciousness, and stability of competitive institutions underlying that strength also undercut the military's capacity to institutionalize authoritarian rule and carry forward a program of fundamental structural change. The country's constitutional tradition was hostile to the consolidation of a military regime; moreover, no country in Latin America matched Chile's lengthy tradition of lower-class organization and militancy At the time of the 1973 coup, the Chilean labor movement was probably the largest and strongest labor movement in Latin America.[6] This movement had developed comparatively early, was historically led by Marxist elements, and was quite unified and autonomous vis-à-vis the state, particularly by the standards of such countries as Mexico, Argentina, and Brazil. The Chilean left was also strong in electoral terms. In no country in Latin America had Marxist parties demonstrated the vote-gathering capacity of the Socialists, Communists, and other Unidad Popular parties in Chile. Indeed, the electoral success of the Chilean left was impressive even by the standards of non-Marxist, lower-class political movements, such as Peronism in Argentina, one of the most durable and powerful, lower-class political forces on the continent. Add to these traditions and capabilities the non-union and nonelectoral forms of political activity that burgeoned after 1964, and one has a picture of a politically inexperienced military confronting what was in 1973 the most organized and politically involved popular sector in Latin America, with the possible exception of Cuba.

High levels of political mobilization provoked the harsh repression that followed the coup, but political defeat left many of the popular-sector's resources unscathed. Continuing repression was necessary to achieve a fundamental restructuring of society, and in the Chilean context repression had to be severe to achieve its objectives. The difficulty is that extreme levels of repression carry high costs. In the Chilean case, these costs included the withdrawal of both international and domestic political support for the Pinochet regime: a tendency that began immediately after the coup and became increasingly accentuated over time. The impact of the precoup threat consequently cut in more than one direction. It created strong incentives for the installation of exclusionary authoritarianism, but the political strength of the popular sector raised the costs and limited the opportunities for regime consolidation. The military was not insensitive to these costs and limitations, which is one reason the initial phase of military rule was not characterized by a frontal assault on the popular sector.

The military cohesion necessary to consolidate authoritarian rule was anything but a given in September 1973. The crisis that had engulfed Chilean society also left its mark on the military, undermining institutional unity and respect for hierarchy. Like the process of popular-sector political mobilization, the breakdown of military discipline began before 1970 and consequently cannot be understood simply in terms of the policies of the Allende government. The *tacnazo* of 1969, which involved an uprising led by General Roberto Viaux against the government of Eduardo Frei, was one symptom of this development,[7] but there were also many other signs that politicization of the armed forces was undercutting professional norms and democratic institutions.[8] Frei's lack of confidence in the top ranks was exhibited in 1969, when he bypassed six more senior generals to name General René Schneider commander-in-chief of the army. Following the kidnapping and murder of Schneider a year later, four more generals were forced into retirement by the appointment of General Carlos Prats. In a corps of generals numbering only twenty-five in 1973, the resulting turnover rate of the army top command was extraordinarily high.[9]

The growing incapacity of democratic institutions to resolve political conflicts after 1970 accelerated the trend toward military career instability, politicization, and the breakdown of discipline.[10] Within the army the most senior officers were not even involved in the coup plotting; rather, it was thrust on them from below, forcing General Prats to retire and involving Pinochet only at the last moment. The pattern was similar in the carabineros, whose representative on the junta was only the seventh in command at the time of the coup.[11]

The legacy of precoup crisis for the consolidation of military rule in Chile was thus doubly ambiguous. To the extent that the crisis created incentives for a drastic reorganization of state power, it also worked against the consolidation of authoritarian rule because the breakdown of Chilean democracy was associated with a loss of military cohesion and the emergence of a highly mobilized and politicized popular sector.

The conditions surrounding the emergence of Chilean authoritarianism provide an even weaker basis for understanding the distinctive features of the Pinochet dictatorship relative to other Southern Cone military regimes: namely, its highly personalistic form, policy impact, and durability. As indicated in chapter 2, the operating procedures, patterns of appointment, and decision-making processes that characterize neopatrimonial as distinct from bureaucratic organizational structures emerge under conditions of both limited and extreme social polarization. Likewise, bureaucratic regime structures can be associated with both inclusionary and exclusionary military rule.

Comparative evidence also suggests that originating conditions provide a limited basis for understanding the Pinochet regime's determined pursuit of economic orthodoxy. A minimal condition for the implementation of a coherent program of policy change is regime cohesion, and regime cohesion does not vary directly with the magnitude of precoup crises. In the Argentine case, for example, two military regimes emerging one decade apart under widely varying social conditions disintegrated in precisely the same number of years. The terrorist violence and economic disintegration associated with the 1976 Argentine coup simply failed to provide the basis for any more regime unity than did the conditions of moderate politico-economic conflict associated with the 1966 coup. As a result, efforts to implement a neoliberal program in Argentina during the 1970s ended in catastrophe. Rivalries within the military and the related fragmentation of political authority even prevented the head of the economic team, José Martínez de Hoz, from making much headway in his efforts to control the budget deficit and privatize selected state industries. His program repeatedly encountered resistance from the Ministries of Labor and Social Welfare and from Fabricaciones Militares, the military's industrial complex.[12] Especially after the posts of president and commander-in-chief of the army were separated in the late 1970s, a feudal division of political power among rival services created enormous opportunities for blocking and delaying major initiatives. This structure of power did not reflect the crisis associated with the regime's origins; it was a product of intra- and interservice rivalries and of the related determination of military leaders to prevent a repetition of the Onganía period. The result was a military regime with no more cohesion than its predecessor in the 1960s, which had originated under conditions of relatively mild social conflict.

The links that may be drawn between the durability of the Chilean authoritarianism and the depth of the crisis associated with its origins are equally tenuous. The reason is that the capacity of exclusionary authoritarian regimes to weather challenges to their authority is less a function of the alignment of social forces than of coercive capability. Nowhere is this more obvious than in the Chilean case. In 1983, the Pinochet regime appeared as close to collapse as its counterparts in Argentina, Uruguay, and Brazil. The breakdown of the regime's free market economic model had left the private financial system bankrupt, one-third of the labor force unemployed, and the majority of private firms under state control. In political terms, the crisis was marked by the departure of leading government technocrats, policy vacillation and incoherence, the fragmentation of the right, mass mobilization against the regime, and the related unraveling of Pinochet's base of support. The persistence of the regime under these circumstances cannot be explained in terms of the depth of the crisis associated with its emergence or the related alignment of social class forces.

From 1983 on, the issue of threat, which has figured so prominently in discussions of exclusionary authoritarianism, ceased to rally support around the regime and became instead a major source of tension among conservative forces, both within and outside of the state apparatus. Symptomatic of this development was the National Accord of August 1985 calling for a transition to full democracy. The Accord was promoted by such figures as Fernando Léniz Cerda, Pinochet's first civilian Minister of the Economy and a director of one of the country's largest private corporations; signed by a former member of the junta, the two political parties most representative of the right, as well as by centrist and leftist groups; and even welcomed in cautious terms by the head of the Chilean Air Force, General Fernando Matthei, who described it as "interesting."[13] The evidence of middle-class desertion of the regime is also unambiguous. By 1986, only 13.2 percent of Santiago residents felt that the continuation of the Pinochet regime represented the best political alternative for Chile.[14]

Notwithstanding this profound realignment of political forces, optimism regarding the possibility of a democratic transition before 1989, when Pinochet's presidential term was to expire, proved unfounded. Pinochet was determined to serve out his presidency, and he retained the repressive capability to do so, despite serious divisions within the governing coalition, the erosion of his regime's social base, and growing fears that his continuation in office enhanced rather than reduced the threat from below. This development can only be understood in terms of the structure of the Pinochet regime and its relationship to the armed forces.[15]

The Chilean Military Tradition

The obvious starting point for any analysis of the role of the Chilean military under authoritarian rule is the highly professional character of the Chilean armed forces and their tradition of nondeliberation, constitutionalism, and subordination to civilian authority. No other South American military can boast of a comparable tradition, which before 1973 was breached only once in the twentieth century—with disastrous results for the military *qua* institution. That breach, which occurred in the 1924–32 period, gave rise to the dictatorship of Carlos Ibáñez and ended with a total breakdown of military discipline, morale, and prestige. According to Frederick M. Nunn,

> for several years after the restoration of civilian control of government, a soldier wearing his uniform in public was likely to find himself scurrying to home or barracks, his blouse, cap, or pants stained with spittle, garbage, or worse.[16]

For the generation of officers trained during the period of civilian reaction that followed, the lessons were clear: the institutional interests of the military and its professional capabilities are undermined by political involvement. The resulting corporate ethic of constitutionalism was not particularly democratic. The Prussian influence on the Childean armed forces precluded such an orientation, at least as far as the army was concerned.[17] Nevertheless, the military's commitment to the constitution reinforced longer-standing civilian traditions, permitting four decades of political stability and formal democracy. The commitment to constitutionalism, however, also had another consequence. It produced an inflexible institution that was unusually isolated from the rest of society and out of touch with ongoing sociopolitical debates. Under these conditions, anti-Marxist sentiments, which the Chilean military shares with all of its Southern Cone counterparts, assumed a particularly virulent form. When Chilean democracy unraveled in the 1970s, these sentiments came to the fore, establishing a basis for a highly repressive and durable exclusionary regime.

This tendency was accentuated by a generational phenomenon characteristic of relatively isolated institutions. As the constitutionalist Commander-in-Chief General Carlos Prats noted in his memoirs,[18] the officers assuming top ranks in the early 1970s had not experienced the antimilitary reaction of the 1930s nor the drastic professional losses associated with it. Prats himself, who was commissioned in 1934, was the last of this generation. The officer corps was increasingly drawn instead from a generation formed during World War II and the Cold War epoch that followed. As a result, the convergence between the regime's anti-Marxist rhetoric and antistatist policies, on the one hand, and the ideological proclivities of the officer corps, on the other, increased over time. By 1984, every general in the regular line of command had received his military commission between 1949 and 1956.

The isolation of the armed forces enhanced the salience of a less obvious generational phenomenon as well. As in other parts of Latin America, the Chilean armed forces have traditionally recruited a high proportion of their officers from military families.[19] Systematic data are not available, but the officer corps that has stood behind the Pinochet regime does not seem unusual in this regard. If anything, the proportion of officers drawn from military families is greater than in the late 1960s inasmuch as the attractiveness of a military career declined in the years before 1973, enhancing the importance of family traditions for military recruitment. Roy Allen Hansen pointed to the dangers of this development in 1967, suggesting that "professional military culture may be expected to become increasingly isolated from the perspectives and needs of the general public and hostile to civilian political institutions."[20] What is particularly distinctive about the officer corps supporting authoritarian rule, however, is less the prevalence of family military traditions than the nature of those traditions. A surprising number of prominent officers have fathers or other male relatives who participated in the Honorable Mission of the 1924–32 period.[21] Not coincidentally, this was a generation of officers that received a heavy dose of Prussian military training, and many even served within the ranks of the German army.

The list of officers with family links to military men participating in the events of the 1924–32 period includes a member of the original military junta, Admiral José Toribio Merino, plus a number of army generals. The uncle of General Luis Danús, Santiago Danús Peña, was one of the 57 junior officers who participated in the military intervention of 1924, as was Javier Palacios Hurtado, the father of General Javier Palacios Ruhmann, who in turn was a key figure in the 1973 coup. The father of another prominent coup maker, Pedro Ewing

123

LIBRARY ST. MARY'S COLLEGE

Hodar, was Alfredo Ewing Acuña, a leader of the 1924 intervention and a member of the military junta formed in September 1924.

Striking parallels also can be drawn between the military careers of members of the Viaux family. General Roberto Viaux led the abortive coup attempt of 1970. His father, General Ambrosio Viaux Aguilar, who was one of the officers of his generation to have served in the German army, similarly participated in a "premature" coup plot in 1919. Of the officers supporting the Pinochet regime, at least twenty-two other army generals and three admirals also had fathers who served in the armed forces during the 1924–33 period and participated in the events surrounding the emergence of the Ibáñez dictatorship.

The connection with the interventionist officers of the 1920s even extends to the civilian advisors of the Pinochet regime. The Minister of Economic Coordination appointed in mid-1974, Raúl Sáez Sáez, was the son of General Carlos Sáez Morales, a member of the military junta of 1924. The first civilian to serve as Minister of Foreign Relations was Hernán Cubillos, a retired navy officer whose father was a former commander-in-chief of the navy. Cubillos's grandfather, father, and uncle all served in the navy during the interventionist period of 1924–33. In short, the officers supporting Pinochet in 1973 appear to have been carrying on a military tradition that was very much at odds with the broader institutional commitment to constitutionalism. Yet, paradoxically, that commitment and the resulting isolation of the armed forces facilitated the development of contrapuntal military subcultures and traditions supportive to military rule.

The institutional isolation of the military also had important consequences for the process of staffing the Pinochet administration. Especially in the early stages of the regime, personal links to military officers and their families often counted for more than experience, expertise, or policy orientation. This tendency was just as evident at top levels of the regime as at the bottom. For example, as a former vice president of Corporación de Fomento de la Producción (CORFO—the state development corporation), one of the original "wisemen" of the Alliance for Progress, and Minister of Finance under President Eduardo Frei, Raúl Sáez had impressive qualifications for appointment to the post of Minister of Economic Coordination; but, as noted earlier, Sáez was also the son of General Sáez and close to the head of the Chilean Air Force, General Gustavo Leigh. Similarly, the first civilian Minister of the Economy, Fernando Léniz, was not only a man of energy and management skill who had earned impeccable political credentials during the Allende years as director of *El Mercurio*; he also had personal links to top navy officers, had married the daughter of a former commander-in-chief of the army, and was recommended for his post by Raúl Sáez. Another of the earliest civilians to serve in the cabinet was Gonzalo Prieto Gándara, the son of a retired Auditor General of the navy and himself an advisor in international law to the navy. In some instances, such as the appointment of General Leigh's brother to the Constitutional Commission, the importance of personal connections to military officers was even more blatant.

Even the appointment of the professional economic team known as the Chicago Boys, which appeared to symbolize the triumph of expertise over particularism, partially reflected the political isolation of the military and the related importance of personal links. The entry of the Chicago Boys into the government owed much to the influence of Léniz, who brought in Sergio de Castro; but it was facilitated by other personal connections as well. The military Subsecretary of the Economy was the father of Tomás Lackington, who had worked with Sergio de Castro, Pablo Baraona, and Sergio de la Cuadra in drawing up the economic program for Alessandri's 1970 presidential campaign.[22] All three men eventually served as cabinet ministers under Pinochet.

The incorporation of the Chicago Boys into the government was also promoted by Roberto Kelly, a retired naval officer who headed the state planning agency (ODEPLAN) after the coup and later served as Minister of the Economy. Kelly is credited with initiating the development of an economic plan on behalf of the navy prior to the coup and thereby establishing the crucial link between the Chicago Boys and the military.[23] Among the Chicago-trained economists participating in the development of this economic plan were José Luis Zabala, who joined the Central Bank staff in 1973; Alvaro Bardón, who was later appointed president of the Central Bank; Pablo Baraona, who came to serve both as president of the Central Bank and Minister of the Economy; and Sergio de Castro, who was appointed Minister of the Economy in 1975 and Minister of Finance in 1976. The initial group of technocrats, in turn, brought their students into the government, creating an economic team of unusual depth and cohesion that allowed for policy continuity even after the first group of Chicago Boys had left their posts. A case in point is Hernán Alberto Büchi, who joined Sergio de Castro's economic team in 1975 and was appointed Minister of Finance a decade later.

The constitutional tradition of the Chilean military and its related political isolation also contributed to the exceptional autonomy enjoyed by civilian technocrats under Pinochet. Coming to power without prior immersion in policy debates and without the benefit of a development ideology, the military was forced to rely heavily on civilian expertise. This tendency was evident in the planning processes that took place before the coup, and it subsequently facilitated the implementation of free market policies that have run up against the nationalist and developmentalist orientations of more politically experienced and economically entrenched militaries in other parts of South America.

The relative isolation of the military further enhanced the power of technocrats by limiting the capacity of organized groups to penetrate the policy-making process. In marked contrast to neighboring Argentina, political parties did not have a well-developed network of connections within the military. Officers with identifiable political contacts, such as General Oscar Bonilla, were easily isolated and purged from the institution. Personal links between the military and civilian spheres were also limited, exacerbating the isolation of the institution as a whole and inhibiting the development of ties between military officers and the business community, which private firms have used to such good advantage elsewhere. The data collected by Hansen in the late 1960s speak to this point. The retired officers he interviewed were asked to name their five best friends during their last years of active service. Eighty-one percent of those named were other military officers.[24]

After more than a decade in power, this social isolation still persisted, helping to insulate the regime from rising dissatisfaction and the deepening political crisis. As late as 1986, not

1 of the largest 20 private corporations in Chile included a military officer on its board, although the traditional pattern was clearly changing. The willingness of army officers to parlay their skills and government connections for business purposes was one symptom of such change. The career trajectories of the nearly 20 air force officers who resigned in solidarity with General Leigh in July 1978 are also revealing. As of late October 1978, 10 had already developed a second career in industry, commerce, or consulting work.[25] By the early 1980s, there were also instances of army officers, such as General Agustín Toro Dávila, moving into the business world.[26] Such activities stand out, however, precisely because they remained atypical of retired army generals. Certainly by Argentine standards, the civilian and military realms remained relatively distinct and the process of integrating retired generals into the private business world rather slow.

The Chilean military tradition consequently provides a basis for understanding the unusual coherence of economic policy making under Pinochet as well as the durability of his regime, which was insulated from the growing pressure of civilian opposition by the separation of the military institution from the rest of society. Perhaps most important, however, the professionalism, constitutionalism, and related institutional isolation of the Chilean military explain the pivotal contrast between authoritarianism in Chile and in other Southern Cone countries, namely, the emergence of a highly personal but nonetheless institutionalized system of military rule with a patrimonial rather than bureaucratic character. As head of the army, Pinochet drew on national military traditions after the coup to restore the cohesion of an increasingly politicized and fragmented military and, subsequently, to enhance the autonomy of his government vis-à-vis the armed forces. Any military efforts to check his government's increasing concentration of power could be labeled political, hence unprofessional. Likewise, after introducing the constitution of 1980, Pinochet used the constitutionalist tradition to justify continuing military support for authoritarian rule and thereby weather the crisis of the early 1980s. The resulting perversion of Chilean military traditions disguised the eminently political role being played by the military as well as the tension between that role and more narrowly defined professional concerns.

The Consolidation of Military Control

The conditions that promote regime change do not necessarily facilitate the consolidation of political control. The tension is particularly obvious in the Chilean case. On the one hand, the crisis promoting military intervention assured the new regime of significant ideological, economic, and political support, both from international and domestic sources. On the other hand, the overthrow of Allende was achieved through the breakdown of the military discipline and hierarchy so vital to the consolidation of authoritarian rule.

Another difficulty for Pinochet was that the political initiative in 1973 was very much in the hands of the other service chiefs. To emerge as leader of the military government, he therefore not only had to reestablish discipline and oust possible rivals in the army, but also to assert the predominance of the army over the navy and air force. Consequently, Pinochet's consolidation of control in the aftermath of the coup cannot be attributed simply to the "highly disciplined and vertical nature of the Chilean military."[27] The restoration of military cohesion and respect for hierarchy represented a very real—and critical—challenge. As Manuel Antonio Garretón has argued, the "process of consolidation and discipline enforcement within the army and other branches of the armed forces was as important as that of consolidating the leadership at the state level."[28]

After revising the rules governing military promotions and retirements, which made it possible to clear out dissenters within the military, Pinochet's first step was the mid-1974 Statute of the Government Junta (D.L. 527). This measure elevated Pinochet to the position of President of the Junta and Supreme Chief of the Nation and thereby set aside previous conceptions of a rotating presidency and relative parity among the three major services. As General Leigh later complained, Pinochet soon began ignoring other junta members in appointing ministers, ambassadors, and other top officials.[29] The junta also began meeting only once or twice a month rather than weekly; outsiders were brought into the meetings, diluting their significance; and the ministerial councils, through which the navy and the air force had controlled economic and social policy, were dissolved.[30] Together these steps established the basis for a more hierarchical and less collegial decision-making process.

Even more important to the consolidation of Pinochet's control over the military was the creation in mid-1974 of a centralized military intelligence agency, the Dirección Nacional de Inteligencia (DINA). Although DINA originally drew personnel from all three services and was designed to achieve greater intelligence coordination among them, under the leadership of Manuel Contreras it reported directly to Pinochet rather than to the junta.[31] DINA's powers were enormous. It operated virtually without restraint, both inside and outside of Chile, repressing dissenters and eliminating leading opposition figures, including General Prats. DINA thereby played a vital role in the consolidation of Pinochet's control over the army and predominance over the other service chiefs. The myth of military unity, which discouraged outsiders from seeking allies within the military, helped to preserve the autonomy of decision makers, and bolstered Pinochet's authority, also owed much to DINA.

By the end of 1974, Pinochet was designated President of the Republic (D.L. 806), and a steady accumulation of new titles and powers followed. Other junta members were relegated to the margins of the policy process and assigned purely legislative functions. The pinnacle of this achievement was the 1980 constitution, which placed Pinochet definitively above the junta and extended his presidential term until 1989.

The shifting composition of the cabinet provides a key indication of the progressive concentration of power. In the immediate aftermath of the coup, the four military services shared control over the cabinet, which included only two civilians. The navy's role at this time was nearly as important as that of the army, with admirals heading four different ministries: Defense, Education, Finance, and Foreign Relations. The first major cabinet reorganization in July 1974 preserved the predominance of the military, but as indicated by table 5.1, the situation began to change in 1975. By June of that year, civilian participation had risen to 41 percent, and an army general had assumed command of the Ministry of Defense. Three years later, military participation in the cabinet had fallen even lower,

Table 5.1

Military Participation in the Chilean Cabinet, 1973–87[a] (in Percent)

Date	Military	Civilian
Sept. 1973	87.0 (13)	13.0 (2)
Jan. 1974	87.0 (13)	13.0 (2)
Jan. 1975	82.0 (14)	18.0 (3)
Jan. 1976	56.3 (9)	43.8 (7)
Jan. 1977	56.3 (9)	43.8 (7)
Jan. 1978	56.3 (9)	43.8 (7)
Jan. 1979	31.3 (5)	68.8 (11)
Jan. 1980	43.8 (7)	56.3 (9)
Jan. 1981	56.3 (9)	43.8 (7)
Jan. 1982	56.3 (9)	43.8 (7)
Jan. 1983	43.8 (7)	56.3 (9)
Jan. 1984	33.3 (5)	68.8 (11)
Jan. 1985	29.4 (5)	70.6 (12)
Jan. 1986	29.4 (5)	70.6 (12)
Jan. 1987	29.4 (5)	70.6 (12)
Total Ministers, 1973–87[b]	49.0 (51)	51.0 (53)

Source: Directorate of Intelligence, Central Intelligence Agency, *Chiefs of State and Cabinet Members of Foreign Governments,* 1973–87.

[a] Military percentage includes both retired and active-duty officers; figures exclude the head of ODEPLAN.

[b] Based on total number of individuals serving in cabinet during the period as a whole, including those not in office during the month of January.

leaving only one representative from each service other than the army in the cabinet. Replacing military men in the other posts were technocrats with ties to the financial sector, men linked with the right, and individuals personally connected with Pinochet. A particularly striking example of the latter category is Pinochet's niece, Mónica Madariaga, who was appointed to the cabinet as Minister of Justice in April 1977 but later broke with the regime. Taking the 1973–87 period as a whole, it appears that military participation in the government fluctuated inversely with Pinochet's personal power, reaching its peak levels in the early days of the regime and in the immediate wake of the crisis of mid-1982. Conversely, at moments of strength, as in the aftermath of Pinochet's personal triumph in the 1978 plebiscite and the related ouster of Leigh, military participation was limited.[32]

Without support from within the military, opposition to the consolidation of the Pinochet regime was ineffective and overcome by widening the scope of repression to include centrist forces. This is not to imply that the consolidation of the regime went entirely unchallenged. As civilian opposition to the regime mounted in 1975, a group of generals sent Pinochet a letter criticizing the economic "shock" policies and the role of DINA. The chief result was a series of early retirements. A more serious challenge to the consolidation of personal rulership came from the air force in 1978. By then, however, Pinochet's position was so strong that he simply surrounded air force bases with army troops and dismissed Leigh, whose permanence had theoretically been guaranteed by the Statute of the Government Junta. The resignation of eight more senior air force officials paved the way for the appointment of General Matthei. These events established a precedent that was repeated in August 1985 to remove General César Mendoza, the head of the carabineros. The threat of a second intervention of the air force was also apparently used in 1986 to intimidate General Matthei into continuing compliance with the regime.[33] No other Southern Cone military regime has been characterized by such an extraordinary concentration of military control. Even when the head of the army has also served as president, as in Argentina between 1976 and 1978, other services have enjoyed autonomy, with each service chief naming his own successor.

A combination of political shrewdness and favorable circumstances allowed Pinochet to take full advantage of Chilean military traditions and outmaneuver his rivals. In 1975, when resistance to Pinochet's control was mounting within the army itself, border tensions developed with Peru. In mid-1978, when Pinochet removed Leigh, Chile was facing the prospect of war with Argentina. Professional considerations entered the equation as well. By the mid-1970s, all of the services were benefiting from Pinochet's government. Military expenditures soared immediately after the coup, reaching a figure in 1974 that was nearly 50 percent above the 1973 level.[34] Defense expenditures apparently declined the following year due to economic austerity, but they increased steadily in subsequent years, more than doubling in real terms between 1975 and 1980.[35]

Career opportunities and competition for recruitment into the officer corps expanded apace. The number of army generals increased from 25 in 1973 to 54 in 1984, reducing the average number of years necessary for promotion to the rank of general from 31 to 28.[36] This trend reflected the growth in military responsibilities, particularly on the part of the army. To preserve professional traditions, a distinction was drawn between the government and the military, but active-duty officers came to serve in many areas of public administration. As indicated by table 5.1, nearly 50 percent of cabinet officials between 1973 and 1987 were military officers. Active-duty officers also served as subsecretaries, university rectors, diplomats, administrators of state corporations, regional intendants, mayors, governors, and members of the junta's four legislative commissions.[37] One indicator of the pervasiveness of this practice is that 35 percent of the army generals on active duty in 1985 held some sort of government post. When the issue of political transition began to overshadow all other concerns in 1987, this proportion increased, reaching a figure of 44 percent by May 1988.[38] Moreover, until Pinochet's defeat in the October 1988 presidential plebiscite, professional and government posts were inextricably linked. The heads of military divisions also served as the intendants for their region. Likewise, the governors, who were predominantly military, headed military command posts. The resulting dual role demands were dealt with through the delegation of responsibilities. Pinochet, for example, appointed an army vice commander-in-chief to assume some of his purely military responsibilities, and the same system was followed down the line.

Military wives were also drawn into the political system, gaining new authority and responsibility. The principal vehicle was the National Association of Mothers' Centers (CEMA), which was designed to rally support behind the regime by administering patronage programs at the local level. The hierarchy of the organization paralleled that of the military. Pinochet's wife was made the national head, and the wives of high-ranking officers played leadership roles at the provincial and regional levels.

For the military as an institution, a major consequence of the expansion of career opportunities was a steady process of politicization totally at odds with traditions of professionalism and nondeliberation. As indicated by the career trajectories of the young officers who served on the junta's advisory committee (COAJ) in 1973, nonmilitary skills, training, and experience came to count heavily in the promotion process. Beginning with the passage of Decree Law 1639 at the end of 1976, retirement norms were repeatedly violated, creating a corps of superannuated generals. In one prominent instance, retirement from the line of command was even reversed for political reasons. Likewise, early promotions were earned by officers who collaborated closely with the government, such as General Ernesto Videla. Officers identified as not fully in accord with government policy, on the other hand, were assigned to remote areas and retired prematurely.

The expansion of career opportunities and related politicization of the military institution unquestionably helped Pinochet maintain the support of the officer corps after 1973. At the same time, however, the incorporation of military officers into government inevitably entailed professional costs—costs that became particularly obvious in the wake of the 1988 plebiscite. Long before that date, however, professionally oriented carabineros had begun to chafe against their role in political repression on the grounds that it undermined the image of their institution as well as its capacity to combat crime.[39] The reputation of the army appears to have deteriorated even more. Whereas in the 1960s the public rated the military higher than the police in terms of such characteristics as loyalty and honesty, by 1986 the relative rankings had been reversed.[40] Other professional costs can be noted as well. In the late 1970s, international opposition to the Pinochet regime cut off the military from its traditional sources of supply, preventing the purchase of equipment, such as Rolls Royce engines for Chile's Hawker Hunters or parts for its U.S.-made F–5s, a cost for which the strengthening of the local defense industry failed to compensate. As more than one regional commander complained in 1986, the concentration of troops in Santiago and their use in shantytown raids also detracted from the military's ability to defend the nation's borders.[41] The expression of such dissent, however, came comparatively late in the regime's history and was anything but surprising. Tension between the military as government and the military as a professional organization is a common feature of military regimes. What is curious about the Chilean case is that the tension took so long to surface. To understand this issue it is necessary to look beyond military traditions and institutions and examine the broader structure of political power that emerged in Chile during the mid-1970s.

The Personalization of Political Power

Between 1973 and 1976, Pinochet used a wide variety of different resources to reestablish military cohesion and eclipse rival service chiefs. He also managed to distance himself from the military institution itself, creating a government that was eminently personal in nature and not immediately responsive to pressures from the officer corps. In terms of recent Southern Cone experience, the only military government to have achieved a comparable distance from the military as an institution was that of General Onganía in Argentina. Like Pinochet, Onganía guarded his power and brooked no military interference in the policy-making process, except when military advice was formally solicited.[42] But Onganía's position was much more fragile than Pinochet's. As a retired officer, he exercised only limited control over the military yet remained totally dependent on it for political support. Pinochet's military base was much more solid due to his control over military retirements and promotions. Even more significant for understanding the consolidation of Chilean authoritarianism, the Pinochet regime enjoyed a much broader and more diversified base of support outside of the military. This support reflected the long-standing strength of conservative forces in Chile as well as their ideological and organizational offensive of the early 1970s.

In contrast to Argentina and Uruguay, where the right has never represented a discrete and viable electoral alternative, Chilean conservatives regularly received 20 to 30 percent of the vote before 1973. They backed the winning candidate in two of the three presidential elections prior to the coup. In the election of 1958, the right gained control of the executive branch on its own, and it nearly repeated the feat in 1970 when its candidate, Jorge Alessandri, was only narrowly defeated by Allende.

Precisely because of this electoral capacity the military played a modest role in Chilean politics before 1973.

The traditional political right by no means constituted the Pinochet regime's only or even most important source of talent in the aftermath of the coup. Conservative forces in Chile have also been well organized outside of electoral channels through economic associations, such as the Sociedad de Fomento Fabril (SOFOFA); hard-core Catholic groups, such as Opus Dei; organizations of the ultraright, such as Patria y Libertad; right-wing think tanks, such as the Centro de Estudios Políticos or the Corporación de Estudios Nacionales; and in the *gremialista* movement.[43] Taken together, these organizations provided the Pinochet government with sources of experienced and committed personnel, ideological support, and legitimation unknown by any other Southern Cone authoritarian regime.

The constitution of 1980, which played such a key role in the regime's survival after 1983, underlines the importance of nonmilitary political resources. The staffing of the constitutional commission, the elaboration of ideological bases for authoritarian democracy, the drafting of the constitution, and the mobilization of popular support behind the plebiscite of 1980 all depended on the existence of a developed political right. Comparisons with Argentina and Uruguay emphasize this point. In the former case, the lack of outside ideological support has prevented any exclusionary authoritarian regime from moving beyond the economic phase to articulate a political project that would provide the basis for more than short-term survival. In Uruguay, a constitutional proposal was developed but failed to obtain the necessary support in the national plebiscite of 1980.[44]

The collaboration of the right also provided Pinochet with a source of experienced personnel from outside the military realm. Although the regime came to rely mainly on individuals without strong party or organizational attachments, former activists in the National party and *gremialista* movement filled top government posts, staffed such support organizations as the Secretaría Nacional de la Juventud, and rescued the regime in moments of crisis, most notably in 1983 when the former head of the National party, Sergio Onofre Jarpa, assumed the post of Minister of the Interior. Ex-presidents Alessandri and

Gabriel González Videla and other well-known political figures also lent the regime legitimacy in its earlier stages by serving on the Council of State. The collaboration of the economic right was even more important to the consolidation of the regime. Chile's large conglomerates provided a source of expertise in such cabinet ministers as José Piñera, a leading figure in the Cruzat financial empire who later masterminded the privatization of Chile's social security system and the development of its new labor code. In addition, the economic right provided the link between Pinochet and the Chicago Boys, who dominated the management of the economy after 1973.

The availability of a sizable pool of conservative economists willing to serve an authoritarian regime is in itself an indication of the strength of right-wing forces in Chile. In this connection it must be emphasized that the Pinochet regime did not create the Chicago Boys. Due to U.S. penetration of Chilean society, they had become entrenched in the economics program of one of the country's top universities long before 1973, establishing themselves as the chief font of economic wisdom for conservatives seeking alternatives to the reformism of the Christian Democrats or the socialism of the left. Many of the Chicago Boys, including Sergio de Castro, who was the former Dean of Economics at the Catholic University and Pinochet's Minister of Finance from 1976 until 1982, had actually studied at the University of Chicago; others had absorbed Chicago doctrine secondhand at the Catholic University, whose ties with the Chicago department date back to an exchange agreement of the 1950s that was sponsored by the Agency for International Development (AID).

Prior to the 1973 coup, the Chicago Boys had played a comparatively minor role in Chilean politics. Nevertheless, a number served in the Frei administration of the 1960s, including Juan Villarzú, José Luis Zabala, Alvaro Bardón, Andrés Sanfuentes, and Sergio de la Cuadra. As indicated earlier, the Chicago Boys had also participated in the 1970 presidential campaign by helping to draft the program of the right-wing candidate, Alessandri. In addition, the Chicago Boys had developed important bastions in the media, most notably through columns in *El Mercurio*, the newspaper that received extensive CIA funding to maintain the opposition offensive against the Allende government.[45] Their role in the post-1973 period provides an important illustration of how the development of conservative bastions before the coup subsequently buttressed the emergence of a highly personalistic form of government.

The relationship between Pinochet and the Chicago Boys was mutually reinforcing. The Chicago Boys provided Pinochet with an economic program, a source of nonmilitary expertise, and valuable international financial contacts. The nearly unfettered influence achieved by the Chicago Boys, in turn, reflected Pinochet's relative autonomy from the military institution rather than, as is often supposed, an unusual lack of military resistance to market-oriented policies. There were many symptoms of such resistance in Chile, including Decree Law 640 of October 1974, which attempted to limit labor dismissals; the prolonged debate over the mining code; and delays and exceptions to the denationalization process. Interviews with former policy makers also leave little doubt as to the existence of conflict between the policy orientation of the military and the economic team. For example, according to Pinochet's first civilian Minister of the Economy, convincing the armed forces of the need to pursue such policies as the privatization of state industries required intensive effort. Léniz initially devoted roughly half of his time to traveling around the country, addressing military officers and their wives, and otherwise attempting to rally support for his economic program.[46] His success cannot be attributed solely to his powers of persuasion, nor even to the lack of expertise within the military itself. A key difference between authoritarianism in Chile and other Southern Cone countries is that policy makers became progressively insulated from military pressures due to the centralization of decision-making power—a trend that Léniz deliberately encouraged and the Chicago Boys abetted and reinforced.

The resources of the right consequently worked together with Chilean military traditions to create a system of highly personal rulership. This system came to evince most of the traits typically associated with tyranny, including the classic policy of *divide et impera*. *Blandos* were played off against *duros*, *Alessandristas* against *gremialistas*, and so on. Even the organization of repression conformed to this tendency, involving the Central Nacional de Informaciones (formerly DINA), the army, and rival police organizations. At various times certain elements of the governing coalition appeared to have won out at the expense of others; but Pinochet remained above the fray, where he was able to take advantage of divisions and conflicts. When the economic boom of the late 1970s collapsed, for example, Pinochet won the applause of fascist elements by turning on the large economic groups with which his regime had collaborated so closely, pitting one set of supporters against another to surmount the crisis and channel popular dissent in directions not immediately threatening to the regime itself. The ruling style became reminiscent of the Stalinist era in the Soviet Union, with its scapegoating of targeted groups, extreme centralization of power, career uncertainty, and rivalry among regime supporters. Moreover, as the personalization of the regime intensified, a crypto-politics of gossip, rumor, rival factions, and personal connections came to coexist with a formal politics of parades, official celebrations, lunches, meetings, and regional tours. Both kinds of politics revolved around Pinochet. Pinochet himself emphasized this point:

> Many speak of the economic team as if the President of the Republic were an isolated entity and they worked on one side and I on the other. No, gentlemen, they are wrong. Not a leaf moves in this country if I am not moving it! I wish to make this clear. All the economic plans, all the laws pass through the presidency, because to govern, gentlemen, you have to stay on your toes.[47]

If anything, this tendency increased during the 1980s with the emergence of an opposition movement, the growing prospect of a regime transition, and the related defection of members of the traditional political right, including such prominent regime collaborators as Francisco Bulnes, a former National party senator who had served on Pinochet's Council of State.

The rapid rotation of top officials provides a concrete indication of the ruling style. After the posts of president and junta member were separated by the 1980 constitution, three different generals served as the army's representative on the junta. Other politically sensitive military posts also changed hands frequently. Ten different generals served as commander of the metropolitan region between 1977 and 1987. Similarly, cabinet officials averaged only 20 months in their posts, and the figure is virtually the same for both military and civilian appointees. *Inter alia*, these frequent personnel changes enabled Pinochet to distance himself from unpopular policies, to create the impression of action and initiative, and to prevent independent loci of power from developing within his administration. Between 1973 and 1987, only a few individuals, such as General César Raúl Benavides and Sergio de Castro, survived more than one major cabinet reorganization.

From the mid-1970s on, Pinochet also guarded his power by treating the cabinet as a set of individuals responsible for specific tasks rather than as a collegial decision-making body. Major decisions were reached without prior discussion with the cabinet as a whole and often even without consultation with relevant ministers. A striking example is the decision to pursue a policy of "economic shock," which was reached in early 1975 without the involvement of the minister responsible for economic coordination, Raúl Sáez, and which was implemented over his objections.[48] Likewise, the June 1982 decision to devalue was made without the active participation of the Minister of the Economy or head of ODEPLAN.[49] Minor decisions also conformed to this pattern. For example, Pinochet apparently decided to bale out sugar beet growers in Panguipulli in 1982 without even consulting his economic team.[50]

To protect his power Pinochet also assigned overlapping functions to various administrative agencies. In the early 1980s, for example, the president received advice from three different bodies: the cabinet, Comité Asesor Presidencial, and Estado Mayor Presidencial. Periodic bureaucratic reorganizations further prevented the development of independent power loci and accentuated career uncertainties. Hence, in early 1983, the Secretaría General de la Presidencia emerged as a fusion of two separate presidential advisory organs, together employing approximately 150 civilians and 130 military officers.[51]

Pinochet also developed his personal control over the government after 1973 by using subsecretaries as a check on top government officials. Departmental proposals and other communications between ministries and the president's office were routinely passed through the office of the relevant subsecretary. Excluding subsecretaries with responsibilities for military affairs, such as the Subsecretary of the Navy, 66.3 percent of subsecretaries serving between 1973 and 1986 were civilians.[52] But perhaps not surprisingly, active-duty army officers, whose careers depended on Pinochet rather than on their supervising minister, predominated in the most sensitive and important subsecretarial posts (Defense, Foreign Relations, Economy, Finance, Telecommunications, and Secretary General of Government) and provided public administration with an element of continuity not found at ministerial levels. A case in point is former Colonel Enrique Seguel, who outlasted several Ministers of Finance in the early 1980s before being promoted to general and head of the Central Bank. Such relative permanence obviously undercut ministerial power, especially in the case of military subsecretaries who gained the confidence of Pinochet. In late 1983, for example, when Pinochet named the third Minister of Foreign Relations in a single year, it became known that the subsecretary, Colonel Humberto Julio Reyes, had been exercising responsibilities, such as naming ambassadors, that formally belonged to the minister.[53] Such instances were atypical of the subsecretarial level as a whole, however, because on average subsecretarial posts turned over nearly as rapidly as ministerial ones. The tendency toward what Oscar Ozlak[54] has called "political castling," or the reciprocal substitution of functionaries, could also be observed at the subsecretarial level.[55]

The failure of the Pinochet government to develop an organized mass base, even at the height of its popularity, provides a final indication of its fear of independent loci of political power. The Movimiento de Unidad Nacional (MUN), which was formed under the leadership of Leon Villarín, Manuel Valdés, and Guillermo Medina in 1975, rapidly disappeared. The proposed Movimiento Pinochetista of 1978 never moved beyond the conceptual stage due to a lack of official support. The Movimiento Cívico Militar, which theoretically was to coordinate political activity at the municipal level, also failed to develop any momentum. Subsequent to Pinochet's announcement of the movement in 1980, only 665 citizens joined in the entire city of Santiago.[56] With the number of military retirees approximating 200,000 at this time,[57] the lack of enthusiastic support from above is evident. The approach of the constitutionally scheduled plebiscite of 1988 did not significantly change this situation. Instead of building an organizational base of support outside of the state apparatus, the regime turned increasingly to traditional patronage policies to construct a popular following.

The structure of government associated with such a pattern of appointment, decision making, and political organization cannot be described as bureaucratic. Far from evincing the pyramidal organization of authority associated with bureaucracy, authority patterns became radial in nature, with Pinochet occupying the center of the political scene. Likewise, whereas bureaucracies are defined as impersonal organizations that function on the basis of fixed rules, personalistic control and a discretional pattern of decision making characterize Chilean authoritarianism. At various points Pinochet even invoked divine rather than rational authority to justify his position.[58] The term *patrimonialism* captures these basic regime features much more effectively than the concept of bureaucratic authoritarianism.[59]

Consider, for example, the following quotations from the work of Oscar Ozlak, which draws heavily on Max Weber's typology of *Herrschaft:*

Patrimonialism means domination by one man, who needs functionaries for executing his authority . . . ; the authority structure is shaped in a radial format . . . ; the president occupies the center of the political scene . . . ; an informal and relatively cohesive structure is formed, which is controlled by a personal *clique* of *hombres de confianza* (trustworthy men) responsible for the functioning of certain key administrative and military units.[60]

Techniques of political control that figured prominently in Pinochet's Chile, such as the recriprocal substitution of functionaries, *divide et impere*, and the deliberate overlapping of responsibilities and functions, also enter into Ozlak's account of patrimonialism. Interestingly enough, however,

Ozlak follows existing conventions and cites Chile as an instance of bureaucratic authoritarianism.[61]

Why has the patrimonial rather than bureaucratic character of the Pinochet regime received so little emphasis, even by a scholar such as Ozlak who considers patrimonialism one of two basic forms of Latin American authoritarianism? Part of the answer can be found in the empirical focus of research on military rule, which has neglected the importance of structural differences among regimes. The applicability of the patrimonial label has been further obscured by the continuing influence of Weberian concepts, which build the dichotomy between traditional and modern societies into regime typologies. The resultant propensity to neglect important political similarities and differences among nations in favor of broad societal characteristics has posed major conceptual problems for the comparative analysis of Latin American politics. Nevertheless, O'Donnell, Ozlak, and others have followed Weber and defined patrimonialism as a form of traditional rule; bureaucratic authoritarianism, on the other hand, has been seen as a product of modern society. The result is a vocabulary that has obscured not only the distinctive features of Chilean authoritarianism, but also the broader theoretical significance of institutional arrangements for understanding variations in the functioning, durability, and performance of military regimes.

Conclusion

Under the leadership of Pinochet, the role played by the armed forces under Chilean authoritarianism became characterized by a relatively high level of institutional participation within the framework of an extremely concentrated authority structure. The resulting sultanistic regime structure cannot be regarded as a merely incidental or secondary characteristic of Chilean authoritarianism. The preeminence achieved by Pinochet became at once the source of his regime's durability and unusual policy performance.

Military traditions and the long-standing strength of the right are both important for understanding the structure of Chilean authoritarianism. The constitutionalist tradition opened the door to the concentration of political power by creating an isolated military with a Prussian-style reverence for hierarchy, professionalism, and discipline. The political inexperience of the military resulting from the constitutionalist tradition also played into Pinochet's hands. Whereas interventionist militaries in such countries as Argentina have developed explicit power-sharing arrangements to counteract tendencies toward personal dictatorship, the Chilean military seized control without clearly defined plans for postcoup decision-making structures. The personal concentration of power was further facilitated by the historical strength of the Chilean right, which placed significant political resources at Pinochet's disposal and lessened his dependence on the military.

Perhaps the most important theoretical lesson that can be drawn from the Chilean case is the potential flexibility and durability of personalistic authoritarian rule. Contrary to the views of Samuel P. Huntington,[62] who regards personal rulership as inherently precarious, stable and personalistic forms of authority do not represent opposite ends of a single continuum. Such a misconception has produced futile U.S. policies as well as flawed analyses of authoritarian rule. For example, because of its personalistic character, Pinochet's regime was repeatedly characterized as fragile and therefore susceptible to outside pressure, when by comparative standards it proved anything but. Moreover, it was precisely during those periods when the patrimonial character of Chilean authoritarianism was most muted that the regime appeared most vulnerable and uncertain of its policy course. What this experience suggests is that the processes of personalization and institutionalization may prove complementary rather than contradictory. Just as comparatively faceless regimes do not necessarily rest on strong institutional foundations or prove very durable, personalism is not a synonym for weakness.

But the issue is not simply one of compatibility of strong institutions and personal rulership or of personalization and institutionalization. For the analysis of authoritarian regimes, whose opaqueness disguises critical frailties and whose breakdown is therefore difficult to predict, it is essential to recognize that strong personal leadership is a possible source of regime resilience. Indeed, the Chilean case emphasizes that in confronting the dilemmas and contradictions of military rule, sultanistic regimes enjoy some distinct advantages over more impersonal and bureaucratic ones. The reason is not merely that sultanistic rule promotes and preserves the institutional unity of the armed forces. The central predicament of military regimes is that they alter the conditions favoring their emergence. Recent Southern Cone regimes, for example, have assumed control with a relatively broad base of social support but ruled in the interest of a minority; depended on a relatively professional military but sacrificed professionalism to political goals; and pursued internationally oriented policies that conflict with the nationalistic outlook of their major institutional pillar. Consequently, over time class polarization has diminished, the social base of support for military rule has evaporated, divisions have emerged within the governing coalition, and policy consistency has become increasingly problematic.

Weathering such fundamental political realignments requires a flexibility uncharacteristic of bureaucracies as well as a capacity to obviate, surmount, or at least mitigate key sources of tension. Because of its neopatrimonial character, the Pinochet regime evinced just such a capacity in the 1973–89 period. By the standards of comparable regimes, the clash between the professional and political roles of the armed forces remained muted; the autonomy of decision makers, marked; the conflict between internationally oriented economic policies and the nationalism of the military, strictly delimited; opportunities for linking up opposition agenda to cracks within the state apparatus, meager; and the success of the regime in rallying popular support at critical points in the late 1970s, pronounced. Neopatrimonialism may make equally vital contributions to inclusionary military rule. Indeed, the recent history of Latin America suggests that personalistic leadership is a precondition for even the tentative consolidation of such rule.

Is the personalization of power a fatal flaw in the long run? The death or removal of the leader of a highly personalized regime obviously poses problems of political succession as well as the threat of regime breakdown. The more closely a regime is identified with an individual, the greater that threat. Yet, as

144

the extended reigns of such dictators as Franco and Stroessner remind us, the long run can be very long indeed, especially by the standards of the average Latin American military regime, whose life span has averaged only six years in the postwar era. For such regimes, the real issue is the consolidation of authoritarian rule beyond the very short run. Given such time horizons, the personalization of power may represent less the Achilles' heel of authoritarianism than its keystone.

Notes

1 The term *comandante en jefe* has been translated literally here rather than as "chief of staff" to avoid two sources of confusion: (1) the top ranks of the Chilean army also include a chief of general staff (*jefe del estado mayor*), and (2) the operational responsibilities of the commander-in-chief of the Chilean army are much greater than those of a U.S. chief of staff.

2 According to David Collier, for example, bureaucratic authoritarianism can be defined as "a type of authoritarianism characterized by a self-avowedly technocratic, bureaucratic, non-personalistic approach to policy making and problem solving" (Collier, ed., *New Authoritarianism*, 399). Likewise, Fernando Henrique Cardoso has emphasized the importance of the contrast between the old forms of *caudillo* domination and control of power by the military institution as such. In his view, "the characteristic feature of the types of regimes implanted in Latin America in more recent years has been precisely the fact that in these regimes it is not a single general or a colonel who, like the *caudillos* of the nineteenth century, imposes a personal order by decrees. Rather, it is the military institution as such which assumes the power in order to restructure society and the state." "On the Characterization of Authoritarian Regimes in Latin America," in ibid., 35.

3 Régis Debray, *The Chilean Revolution: Conversations with Allende* (New York: Vintage Books, 1971), 30. For further information about the pre-1973 political system, see Alan Angell, *Politics and the Labour Movement in Chile* (London: Oxford University Press, 1972); Michael Fleet, *The Rise and Fall of Chilean Christian Democracy* (Princeton, NJ: Princeton University Press, 1985); Manuel Antonio Garretón, *The Chilean Political Process*, trans. Sharon Kellum (Boston: Unwin Hyman, 1989); Federico Gil, *The Political System of Chile* (Boston: Houghton Mifflin, 1966); Brian Loveman, *Chile: The Legacy of Hispanic Capitalism* (New York: Oxford University Press, 1979); Frederick M. Nunn, *The Military in Chilean History: Essays on Civil-Military Relations, 1810–1973* (Albuquerque: University of New Mexico Press, 1976);

145

James Petras, *Politics and Social Forces in Chilean Development* (Berkeley: University of California Press, 1969); Barbara Stallings, *Class Conflict and Economic Development in Chile, 1958–1973* (Stanford, CA: Stanford University Press, 1978); Arturo Valenzuela and Julio Samuel Valenzuela, eds., *Chile: Politics and Society* (New Bunswick, NJ: Transaction Books, 1976).

4   The literature on the 1970–73 period is extensive. For scholarly accounts that provide a variety of different perspectives on the events leading up to the breakdown of Chilean democracy, see *inter alia* Sergio Bitar, *Chile: Experiment in Democracy* (Philadelphia: Institute for the Study of Human Issues, 1986); Edward Boorstein, *Allende's Chile: An Inside View* (New York: International Publishers, 1977); Nathaniel Davis, *The Last Two Years of Salvador Allende* (Ithaca, NY: Cornell University Press, 1985); Stefan de Vylder, *Allende's Chile: The Political Economy of the Rise and Fall of the Unidad Popular* (Cambridge: Cambridge University Press, 1974); Carmelo Furci, *The Chilean Communist Party and the Road to Socialism* (London: Zed Books, 1984); Joan Garcés, *Allende y la experiencia chilena* (Barcelona: Editorial Ariel, 1976); Pio Garcia, ed., *Fuerzas armadas y el golpe de estado en Chile* (Mexico City: Siglo XXI, 1974); Federico G. Gil, Richard Lagos E., and Henry A. Landsberger, eds., *Chile at the Turning Point: Lessons of the Socialist Years, 1970–1973* (Philadelphia: Institute for the Study of Human Issues, 1979); Edy Kaufman, *Crisis in Allende's Chile: New Perspectives* (New York: Praeger, 1988); James Petras and Morris Morley, *The United States and Chile: Imperialism and the Overthrow of the Allende Government* (New York: Monthly Review Press, 1975); Ian Roxborough, Philip O'Brien, and Jackie Roddick, *Chile: The State and Revolution* (New York: Holmes and Meier, 1977); Paul Sigmund, *The Overthrow of Allende and the Politics of Chile, 1964–1976* (Pittsburgh: Pittsburgh University Press, 1977); Alain Touraine, *Vie et mort du Chili populaire: Juillet/Septembre 1973* (Paris: Editions du Seuil, 1973); Arturo Valenzuela, *The Breakdown of Democratic Regimes: Chile* (Baltimore: Johns Hopkins University Press, 1978); Pedro Vuscovic et al., *El golpe de estado en Chile* (Mexico City: Fondo de Cultura Económico, 1975).

5   As Ralph Miliband has argued: "The degree of autonomy which the state enjoys for most purposes in relation to social forces in capitalist society depends above all on the extent to which class struggle and pressure from below challenge the hegemony of the class which is dominant in such a society. . . . Where . . . the hegemony of a dominant class is persistently and strongly challenged, the autonomy of the state is likely to be substantial, to the point where, in conditions of intense class struggle and political instability, it may assume 'Bonapartist' and authoritarian forms, and emancipate itself from constraining constitutional checks and controls." "State Power and Class Interests," *New*

Left Review 138 (1983): 61. As indicated in chapter 2, the same line of theoretical argument has been elaborated in the literature on bureaucratic authoritarianism with specific reference to Latin American military regimes. See O'Donnell, *Modernization and Bureaucratic-Authoritarianism*; idem, "Reflections," *Latin American Research Review*, 3–38; idem, "Tensions in the Bureaucratic-Authoritarian State," in *New Authoritarianism*, ed. Collier, 285–318; Stepan, *The State and Society*; idem, "State Power and the Strength of Civil Society in the Southern Cone," in *Bringing the State Back In*, ed. Evans, Rueschemeyer, and Skocpol, 317–43.

6 See Karen L. Remmer, "Political Demobilization in Chile, 1973–1978," *Comparative Politics* 12 (April 1980): 275–301.

7 Florencia Varas, *Conversaciones con Viaux* (Santiago: n.p., 1972).

8 Genaro Arriagada H., *Pinochet: The Politics of Power*, trans. Nancy Morris (Boston: Unwin Hyman, 1988), 81–86; Carlos Prats González, *Memorias: testimonio de un soldado* (Santiago: Pehuén, 1985), 109–37.

9 Arriagada, *Pinochet*, 86.

10 See Prats, *Memorias*.

11 Phil O'Brien and Jackie Roddick, *The Pinochet Decade* (London: Latin American Bureau, 1983), 46.

12 Interview with José Martínez de Hoz, Buenos Aires, May 1986.

13 *Cauce* 2, 47 (5–11 noviembre 1985), 5.

14 Carlos Huneeus, *Cambios en la opinión pública. Una aproximación al estudio de la cultura política en Chile* (Santiago: Centro de Estudios de la Realidad Contemporánea, 1986), 39. See also the results of the poll taken by the Centro de Estudios del Desarrollo and Facultad Latinoamericana de Ciencias Sociales, *Informe de Encuesta: Opinión pública y cultura política* (Santiago, 1987).

15 In a similar vein, J. Samuel Valenzuela and Arturo Valenzuela have stressed "Pinochet's proven capacity to command the armed forces." "Introduction," in *Military Rule in Chile: Dictatorship and Oppositions*, eds. J. Samuel Valenzuela and Arturo Valenzuela (Baltimore: Johns Hopkins University Press, 1986), 10.

16 Nunn, *The Military in Chilean History*, 186. See also idem, *Chilean Politics, 1920–1931: The Honorable Mission of the Armed Forces* (Albuquerque: University of New Mexico Press, 1970), which provides an excellent overview of the 1924–32 period.

17 Nunn, *The Military in Chilean History*; see also idem, *Yesterday's Soldiers: European Military Professionalism in South America, 1890–1940* (Lincoln: University of Nebraska Press, 1983).

18 Carlos Prats González, *Memorias*.

19 Roy Allen Hansen, "Military Culture and Organizational Decline: A Study of the Chilean Army" (Ph.D. dissertation, UCLA, 1967), 172.

20 Ibid., 319.

21   This and all subsequent assertions concerning the family back-grounds of Chilean military officers have been gleaned from three sets of sources: (1) personal interviews conducted in Santiago in 1985 and 1986; (2) press reports and interviews appearing in *El Mercurio, Qué Pasa*, and *Ercilla* between 1973 and 1988; and (3) the following historical materials: Raúl Aldunate Phillips, *La revolución de los tenientes; tres años de la historia de Chile* (Santiago, [1971?]); Emilio Bello Codesido, *Recuerdos políticos: La junta de gobierno de 1925* (Santiago: Nascimento, 1954); Estado Mayor General del Ejército, *Historia del ejército de Chile*, vol. 8: *La primera guerra mundial y su influencia en el ejército* (Santiago, 1980); *Diccionario biográfico de Chile*, 1st–18th editions (Santiago: Empresa periodística Chile, 1936–86); Luis Valencia Avaria, *Anales de la República*, vol. 1 (Santiago: Imprenta Universitaria, 1951); Virgilio Figueroa, *Diccionario historico, biográfico y bibliográfico de Chile*, 5 vols. (Santiago: Barcells & Co., 1925–31); *Chilean Who's Who* (Santiago: Empresa Chilena Who's Who Ltda., 1937).

22   "Logros y fracasos de los Chicago boys," *Qué Pasa*, no. 650 (22–28 septiembre 1983), 33–37.

23   O'Brien and Roddick, *Chile: The Pinochet Decade*, 38.

24   Hansen, "Military Culture and Organizational Decline," 178.

25   "¿Qué hacen Leigh y sus Generales?" *Qué pasa*, no. 393 (26 octubre–1 noviembre 1978), 10–11.

26   "General (R) Agustín Toro Dávila: 'No les pedí que confiaran en mí . . . Esa confianza me la gané'," *Qué pasa*, no. 534 (2–8 julio 1981), 66.

27   Valenzuela and Valenzuela, "Introduction," in *Military Rule in Chile*, 6.

28   Manuel Antonio Garretón, "Political Processes in an Authori-tarian Regime," in ibid., 163.

29   Florencia Varas, *Gustavo Leigh: El general disidente* (Santiago: Editorial Aconcagua, 1979), 55.

30   Ibid., 32–33, 51–62.

31   Ibid., 78.

32   Note that the lowest level of military participation was achieved in November 1978, when 75 percent of cabinet officials were civilian.

33   "Los conflictos en la moneda," *Apsi*, no. 179 (19 mayo–1 junio 1986), 6–7.

34   *SIPRI Yearbook 1983: World Armaments and Disarmament* (Stockholm: Stockholm International Peace Research Institute, 1983), 166. See also Augusto Varas, *Militarization and the International Arms Race in Latin America* (Boulder: Westview Press, 1985).

35   *SIPRI Yearbook 1983*, 166.

36   Arriagada, *Pinochet*, 157.

37   For a detailed analysis of this participation, see Carlos Huneeus

and Jorge Olave, "Autoritarismo, militares y transición a la democracia: Chile en una perspectiva comparada," paper presented at the first congress of the Asociación de Ciencia Política, Santiago, 8–9 September 1986.

38 This figure is based on the government assignments listed in the *Directorio de instituciones de Chile* (Santiago: Silber, 1988).

39 *Latin America Weekly Report*, no. 28 (24 July 1986), 4; "Los conflictos en la moneda," *Apsi*, no. 179 (19 mayo–1 junio 1986), 6–9.

40 Hansen, "Military Culture and Organizational Decline," 108; Huneeus, *Cambios en la opinión pública*, 60.

41 "Los conflictos en la moneda," *Apsi*, no. 179 (19 mayo–1 junio 1986), 6–9; *Latin America Weekly Report*, no. 19 (16 May 1986), 8.

42 Interview with Nicanor Costa Méndez, Buenos Aires, May 1986.

43 On the gremialist movement, see "La historia de los gremialistas," *Qué pasa*, no. 652 (6–12 octubre 1983), 14–18. Other sectors of the right are discussed in "Los secretos del nacionalismo," ibid., no. 626 (7–13 abril 1983), 12–17; "Pablo Rodríguez: los 'duros' y sus divisiones," ibid., no. 556 (3–9 diciembre 1981), 23–27.

44 On this point see the interesting analysis provided by Luis E. González, "Transición y partidos en Chile y Uruguay," *Serie Documentos de Trabajo*, no. 93, Centro de Informaciones y Estudios del Uruguay (Montevideo, 1985).

45 See "Logros y fracasos de los Chicago boys," *Qué pasa*, no. 650 (22–28 septiembre 1983): 33–37; "Chicago Boys: Cómo llegaron al gobierno," *Qué pasa*, no. 548 (8–14 octubre 1981): 22–29; O'Brien and Roddick, *Chile: The Pinochet Decade*.

46 Interview with Fernando Léniz, Santiago, May 1986.

47 "Qué pasa en la moneda," *Qué pasa*, no. 548 (8–14 octubre 1981), 9.

48 Interview with Raúl Sáez, Santiago, May 1986.

49 "La devaluación y el conjunto de medidas," *Qué pasa*, no. 584 (17–23 junio 1982), 12–13.

50 "¿Está cambiando el esquema económico?" *Qué pasa*, no. 578 (6–12 mayo 1982), 18.

51 "¿Gabinete para la emergencia?" *Qué pasa*, no. 577 (29 abril–5 mayo 1982), 8–11; "Nuevo ministro para el Gabinete," ibid., no. 617 (3–9 febrero 1983), 18–20.

52 Huneeus and Olave, "Autoritarismo, militares y transición," 16.

53 "Cambio de Gabinete," *Qué pasa*, no. 663 (22–28 diciembre 1983), 10.

54 Oscar Ozlak, "Public Policies and Political Regimes in Latin America," *Working Papers of the Latin American Program*, no. 139, Wilson Center, Washington, DC, 1984, 10.

55 See "¿Gabinete para la emergencia?" *Qué pasa*, no. 577 (29 abril–5 mayo 1982), 10.

56 "Movimiento Cívico Militar: A la espera de una definición," *Qué pasa*, no. 495 (2–8 octubre 1980), 9.

57 "¿Cierre . . . o apertura?" *Qué pasa*, no. 634 (2–8 junio 1983), 8–10.
58 In 1987, for example, Pinochet publicly claimed that God put him in his post: "Yo lo estoy viendo desde arriba, porque Dios me puso ahí." "El retorno del brujo," *Apsi* (13–19 July 1987), 4.
59 This is not to suggest that patrimonialism and bureaucracy are opposite or mutually incompatible forms of authority. The two forms may be combined such that the exercise of patrimonial authority depends on bureaucratic structures. Likewise, important parallels can be drawn between patrimonialism and bureaucracy, as the following quote from Max Weber illustrates: "Solidarity of interest with a chief is maximized at the point where both the legitimacy of the status of the members and the provision for their economic needs is dependent on the chief retaining his position. For any given individual, the possibility of escaping this solidarity varies greatly according to the structure. It is most difficult where there is complete separation from the means of administration, thus in purely traditional patriarchal structures, under pure patrimonialism and in bureaucratic organizations resting on formal rules." Talcott Parsons, ed. *The Theory of Social and Economic Organization* (New York: Free Press, 1947), 383–84.
60 Ozlak, "Public Policies and Political Regimes," 24.
61 Ibid., 23–28.
62 *Political Order in Changing Societies.* For Huntington, stability is a function of institutionalization, which is defined in terms of adaptability, complexity, autonomy, and coherence. Even by these criteria, personal rulership is not incompatible with institutionalization or stability. Indeed, as argued throughout this chapter, personal rulership may enhance adaptability, complexity, autonomy, and coherence. Yet Huntington repeatedly characterizes dictatorships and personalistic leaders as "unstable" and "uninstitutionalized" (e.g., p. 3). He even applies these labels to the Duvalier regime in Haiti, which endured longer than most Latin American democracies in the postwar era, and to the Stroessner regime, which ranks among the most durable regimes in Latin American history (p. 398). Particularly telling is the contrast Huntington draws between the instability of the Stroessner regime and the stability of Chilean democracy (p. 80), because the latter collapsed only five years after the publication of his book.

CHAPTER 6

The Policy Impact of Chilean Authoritarianism

In January 1976, the Ecuadoran military postponed its overthrow of General Guillermo Rodríguez Lara's government to allow the president's daughter Nancy to celebrate her wedding in the presidential palace. A photograph appearing in the *New York Times* on January 13, 1976, shows Rodríguez Lara dancing in the street the day after the coup at a party welcoming him back to his native village of Pujilí. Political power is not always transferred so peacefully and amicably. During the military uprising against the Popular Unity government of Salvador Allende, the Chilean air force bombed the presidential palace. The president and thousands of his supporters died during the ensuing conflict. Tens of thousands of other Chileans were arrested or fled into exile.

The contrast between events in Ecuador and Chile is not just a matter of national style. The stakes of the political conflicts surrounding the Chilean military coup were much greater than in the Ecuadoran case. The consequences of the two coups varied accordingly. Whereas the ouster of Rodríguez Lara paved the way for a gradual return to competitive rule and modest shifts in public policy, the Chilean coup produced an immediate and drastic change in the rules of the political game, the transfer of power from one set of class forces to another, and a profound reorientation of state activity in accordance with doctrines of national security and economic neoliberalism. Hence, military coups made a difference in both nations. But coups and regime changes are far from equal in their impact.

By the standards of other Latin American countries, the

151

consequences of the 1973 Chilean coup were unusually far-reaching. Indeed, apart from the revolutionary experiences of Cuba and Nicaragua, no regime change in recent Latin American history has unleashed a more abrupt or extensive process of social transformation. Between 1973 and 1989, the military dictatorship of General Augusto Pinochet pursued a program of structural change that went well beyond a mere reversal of the initiatives of its Socialist predecessor. Beginning with a program of economic adjustment and stabilization, the regime progressively widened the scope of its reforms to encompass virtually all aspects of society. In the process, it significantly altered the relationship between the Chilean economy and the international system, redefined the role of the state in accordance with a combination of neoliberal economic doctrine and national security ideology, and created a new set of political institutions designed to act as a bulwark against any future resurgence of socialism.

The Chilean experience is unusual not only by Latin American standards but also by broader comparative ones. First, drastic policy change, including state transformation, usually results from war, military conquest, decolonization, social revolution, or other major changes in international status rather than simple regime change. Chile provides a rare example of profound sociopolitical change occurring in the absence of any major change in international position. The election of the Allende government may have posed the threat of international realignment, but that threat never approached realization. Second, dramatic instances of policy change characteristically involve the expansion of the state's socio-economic role. In Chile we have a rare instance of state retrenchment. Third, and perhaps most interesting, the transformation of the Chilean state and the dramatic break with preexisting models of capital accumulation were not simply a function of shifts in the strength, orientation, and alignment of social class forces. State transformation in the post-Allende period shaped and defined social class interests at least as much as the other way around. Between 1973 and 1989, the Pinochet regime successively constructed, destroyed, and reconstructed the nation's private sector.

The experience of Chile consequently raises important

questions about the conditions under which military takeovers promote extensive sociopolitical change. The answers to such questions shed light on the impact of regime change more generally. Precisely because Chile represents an extreme and atypical case, it provides a basis for understanding the factors that have limited the consequences of military takeovers in other situations. Even when the rhetoric has been shrill, the violence of the repressive apparatus unconstrained, and the shift in the class composition of the governing coalition dramatic, Latin American military coups have not always had as much effect as their promoters intended. In Chile, on the other hand, the impact of regime change went far beyond that envisioned by most coup supporters. How social class forces and institutional structures interacted to produce this outcome is the subject of this chapter.

Phase I: Dismantling the Peaceful Road

The sheer magnitude of the crisis surrounding the emergence of military rule in Chile established the basis for fundamental policy change and the reorganization of state power. The economic situation alone provided a powerful rationale for state actors to seize the initiative and take strong measures. With the popular sector in a state of disarray and the capitalist class enfeebled by socialist measures and the mounting economic crisis, there were also few forces outside of the state capable of dominating the decision-making process. Yet the impetus to policy innovation was not most pronounced during the early reactive stages of the regime, when the fear of socialism was felt most keenly and the constraints on state action were most limited. Vigorous policy reform and the transformation of the Chilean state followed and reflected the consolidation of personal control in the hands of General Pinochet. Hence, the possibility for state change was created by the trauma of the Allende years, but its actualization depended on the consolidation of a particular structure of political power.

During the first phase of military rule, which lasted from September 11, 1973, until April 1975, the chief preoccupation of government authorities was "normalization." In political terms this meant repressing all of the trade unions and parties affiliated with Unidad Popular and placing other political organizations in a state of suspended animation.[1] At this stage important distinctions were drawn between pro- and anti-Allende forces, allowing popular-sector forces to retain some access to government authorities. Individuals drawn from the conservative wing of the Christian Democratic party were appointed to government positions, while leaders of major unions, including peasant confederations of Christian Democratic orientation, met with government ministers and members of the military junta. Prominent military officers even spoke in a populist vein of defending the conquests of workers. For example, in October 1973, General Sergio Nuño, a leading coup maker and head of the state development agency (CORFO), stated, "The condition of the worker ought to be considered of equal importance within the enterprise."[2] Similar pronouncements were made by General Oscar Bonilla, the Minister of the Interior; General Sergio Arellano Stark, the head of the Santiago garrison; Colonel Pedro Ewing, the Secretary General of the Government; and General Augusto Lutz, who served as secretary to the junta.[3] General Javier Palacios went so far as to speak of his admiration for the Swedish system, declaring, "All my life I have been a socialist."[4] Every one of these officers played a key role in the coup, although not one retained a command position in the second phase of military rule.[5]

Despite the extremism and violence triggered by the coup, moderation and pragmatism also played a role in the formation of economic policy. During the first phase of military rule, the emphasis was placed on economic stabilization, the restoration of market mechanisms, and the regularization of property relationships.[6] The policies that formed part of this effort included tax reform, reductions in government employment, the removal of price controls, the lowering of import tariffs and other restrictions on foreign trade and investment, the restoration of illegally seized businesses and lands to former owners, the payment of compensation to the North American copper companies that had been expropriated by the Allende government, the parcelization of property in the reformed sector, and the sale of government assets inherited from the Allende period. At this stage, however, no priority was placed on austerity, much less on emasculating the Chilean state, which remained the preponderant force in the economy relative to the private sector. Despite good copper prices, new taxes, and the sale of government assets, the fiscal deficit in 1974 exceeded 5 and perhaps even 10 percent of GDP, while the government sector absorbed more than 80 percent of the credit provided by the banking system.[7] The major reason was the continued expansion of expenditures.[8] Military spending alone grew 33 percent or more between 1973 and 1974.[9] Success in overcoming inflation, which had escalated beyond the 300 percent level in 1973, was accordingly slow.

A variety of factors account for the failure of the government to move more rapidly to gain control over the economic situation: inexperience, political disunity, the complete absence of foreign exchange reserves, and a reluctance to compromise national sovereignty by turning to international agencies for financial help.[10] The tendency for new governments, including military ones, to consolidate support through increased spending during their first year in office might be cited as well.[11] Whatever the reason, the failure to take advantage of high copper prices and rapidly stabilize the economy paved the way for a transition to the second phase of military rule in April 1975.

Phase II: Neoliberalism and National Security

By the end of the first quarter of 1975, it had become apparent that existing policies were not sustainable. Copper prices had dropped precipitously, undermining Chile's already precarious balance of payments position; inflation was accelerating; and criticism of the junta's record on human rights was mounting, both domestically and internationally. Under these inauspicious conditions, the marriage between the Chilean military and the group of neoliberal technocrats known as the Chicago Boys was consummated—a marriage whose progeny include the personalistic dictatorship of General Augusto Pinochet, the structural transformation of the Chilean economy, and the redefinition of the social role of the state.

The link between the Chicago Boys and the Chilean military

was forged before the coup. Under the leadership of De Castro, the Chicago Boys had participated in drawing up an economic plan for a post-Allende government. The plan circulated among military officers before Allende's ouster, and it established the basis for the entry of conservative technocrats into advisory positions afterwards. As indicated in the previous chapter, the Chicago Boys' way was also eased by a variety of personal connections. Until 1975, however, the top civilian advisors in the government were men of practical experience, such as Raúl Sáez who had been appointed the Minister of Economic Coordination.

The "shock treatment" announced in April 1975 signaled the rise to prominence of the Chicago Boys and the rupture with the gradualist policies of the first phase of military rule. Faced with an increasingly untenable economic situation, Pinochet, who had assumed the presidency of the military junta, decided in early 1975 to embrace the draconian set of policy remedies advocated by the Chicago Boys and their most distinguished mentor, University of Chicago economist Milton Friedman. The basic package consisted of sharp cuts in fiscal expenditures, new taxes, a tight monetary policy, and increased rates for public enterprises. Gradualism, it was argued, offered no solution to Chile's problems. A dose of stiff medicine was needed to break inflationary expectations and clear the way for a new model of capitalist development.

In adopting the recommendations of the Chicago Boys, Pinochet ignored the advice of Sáez and other more moderate and pragmatic elements within the government.[12] Pinochet thereby asserted his authority over the entire government, distancing himself from policy advisors linked with rival service chiefs while also avoiding the dangers of becoming dependent on experts within his own service or on individuals with an independent power base. De Castro, who was to serve in the government until 1982, soon replaced Léniz as Minister of the Economy, and Pablo Baraona took control of the Central Bank. Concomitantly, advisors with links to the centrist Christian Democratic party, such as Sáez and Vallarzú, left the government.

Predictably, the immediate economic impact of the shock treatment was a deep recession. According to official data, industrial production declined more than 28 percent in 1975,[13] and the GDP fell by nearly 13 percent.[14] By the first quarter of 1976, open unemployment in the greater Santiago area had reached a level of 17 percent, despite the creation of a Program of Minimal Employment (PEM). Real wages, which had already suffered major declines in 1973 and 1974, also plummeted.[15] High unemployment and related inequalities in the distribution of both personal and family income were to remain features of the economy under Chicago management through the late 1980s.[16]

The political costs of the shock treatment were equally high. The regime found itself increasingly isolated and thrown back on its military base of support for survival. The church, the Christian Democratic party, centrist trade unions, moderate army officers, and even SOFOFA, the industrialists' association, joined the growing chorus of criticism.[17] The result was anything but a retreat. By 1975, Pinochet had outmaneuvered the heads of rival services and established dominance over the executive branch of government. He had built a centralized military intelligence agency (DINA) that reported to him personally. By revising the rules governing military promotions and retirements, he had also gained an unprecedented degree of control over the military institution itself, preventing any assertion of corporate interests distinct from those of the government. As a result, the breakdown of the broad coalition that had swept the military to power was not translated into a regime crisis. Pinochet used his considerable resources to clear out remaining dissenters within the military, widen the scope of political repression, and further consolidate his political position. This process culminated with D.L. 1697 of March 1977, which placed the Christian Democratic and National parties in the same category as the previously outlawed Popular Unity parties. The hardening of the regime was reflected in its political discourse, which progressively emphasized the exigencies of national security.[18]

The concentration of power achieved by Pinochet and the related triumph of neoorthodoxy over pragmatism paved the way for a deepening of structural reforms and a frontal attack on the protectionist and interventionist activities of the Chilean state. The military's initial economic program had called for a gradual opening up of the economy. Import barriers and restrictions on foreign investment were to be eliminated and international competition encouraged through the reduction of import tariffs.[19] This process was accelerated in 1975, when the Chicago team announced that tariffs would be cut to a maximum nominal rate of 35 percent. The break with three decades of state-supported import substitution industrialization (ISI) was finalized in late 1977. The new goal was a uniform nominal tariff rate of only 10 percent by mid-1979—a goal that was duly achieved with but a few exceptions.[20]

The process of international opening was pursued in other ways as well. In late 1976, Chile withdrew from the Andean Pact. Pact membership, which entailed restrictions on foreign investment and a common framework for tariffs, was considered inconsistent with the new emphasis on the efficiency of the private sector, unfettered competition, export-oriented development, comparative advantage, and the free movement of capital. Soon after, in March 1977, a new statute on foreign investment was adopted (D.L. 1748) offering foreign capital a variety of guarantees and incentives to invest in Chile.

The process of denationalization also gained impetus in 1975. Over the course of more than 30 years, the Chilean state had assumed a major entrepreneurial role, mainly through the vehicle of the state development corporation (CORFO) that was founded in 1939. Starting with investments in such vital industries as steel, CORFO's activities had steadily expanded. By 1970, it controlled 46 firms.[21] Under Allende, CORFO took on an even more important role. It came to include almost all of the companies that were bought, requisitioned, intervened, and nationalized by the Unidad Popular government—some 460 enterprises and 19 banks.[22] A major question confronting decision makers in the aftermath of the coup was what to do with these firms, many of which were operating at a loss and imposing a severe strain on the national treasury.

During the initial phase of military rule, emphasis was placed on returning the 259 confiscated firms to their owners. By September 1975, most of them had been or were in the process of being "normalized."[23] Disposing of the assets the state had acquired in more than 200 other enterprises posed greater difficulties, but by September 1975, more than half, including

158

most of the large banks, had been auctioned off to the private sector.[24] By 1980, CORFO controlled only 24 firms, a figure roughly half that for 1970.[25] The process of privatization thus went far beyond a rollback to the pre-Allende status quo.

The most conspicuous exception to the accelerated process of privatization was copper. Under Allende all of the large copper mines, traditionally described as "Gran Minería" in Chile, had been expropriated and placed under the control of a new state corporation, CODELCO. Despite the combined pressure of Chicago technocrats and private-sector interests, public ownership of the large mines continued after 1973, giving the state control over 82 to 84 percent of annual copper output and approximately half of all national exports.[26] This development can only be understood in terms of the question of military power.[27] Where military interests collided directly with laissez-faire doctrines, the latter often buckled. Gran Minería represents only one instance, albeit a highly significant one.

Neoliberal economics also ran up against other obstacles. Whether one is analyzing Thatcher's Britain or Pinochet's Chile, the fit between neoliberal economics and conservative or reactionary politics has never been entirely comfortable.[28] In Chile neoliberalism clashed not only with national security doctrine, through which the military came to define its interests, but also with Catholic traditionalism, corporatism, nationalism, and all of the other antidemocratic ideological currents that found expression in the government.[29] The bureaucracy that had grown up around three decades of state interventionism also posed a problem. In attempting to deregulate transportation, for example, the economic team met resistance from bureaucrats in the Ministry of Transportation and their established clienteles. Daniel Wisecarver has provided a fascinating account of how the finance ministry used its power to approve periodic changes in public-sector tariffs to blackmail the transportation bureaucracy into a slow and piecemeal deregulation of urban transportation.[30] In the early 1980s, however, bus fares were still controlled by the state, as were many other activities falling under the purview of the transportation bureaucracy. Yet the defeats and disappointments of the Chicago team are much less remarkable than its successes. By comparative standards the magnitude of the reforms undertaken and the speed with which they were implemented seem positively breathtaking.

Phase III: The Chicago Road to Socialism

The policies adopted after April 1975 created the basis for a transition to a more institutionalized system of military rule in the late 1970s. Whatever its social cost, the shock program and its attendant program of structural reform had helped to stabilize prices, promote nontraditional exports, and, perhaps most important, validate the military regime's commitment to an orthodox policy course. These results were helpful in attracting the international bank loans on which the economic boom of the late 1970s was floated. Economic success and the related emergence of a politically supportive capitalist class in turn created conditions favorable to the consolidation of changes in the state during the third phase of military rule, which lasted from 1978 until 1983.

In political terms, the hallmarks of the third phase of military rule were the progressive personalization and institutionalization of military power. The two processes went hand in hand and were fueled by a series of major challenges to the regime's survival. These challenges included the prospect of war with Argentina; mounting international criticism of Chilean violations of human rights; the U.S. Justice Department's investigation of the assassination of Orlando Letelier; and air force resistance to the perpetuation of Pinochet's rule, which may also have involved U.S. authorities.

The plebiscite of January 1978 inaugurated the transition to the third phase. Faced with an official U.N. condemnation for violating human rights, Pinochet turned to the Chilean public, asking for a vote of confidence. His victory, which was highly personal in nature, had significant consequences. It led indirectly to the ouster of the head of the air force, General Leigh, who had objected to the personalization of power represented by the plebiscite, thereby providing Pinochet with an opportunity to assert his control over the armed forces as a whole. The plebiscite also paved the way for a greater separation of military and political power. In April, Pinochet named his first civilian Minister of the Interior, Sergio Fernández, and the participation of the armed forces in the cabinet plummeted to a new low. Neoliberal conceptions proceeded to dominate virtually all areas of policy. In a program of Seven Moderniza- tions, the government announced that the process of reshaping the role of the Chilean state would be extended to social security, education, health, regional decentralization, agriculture, justice, and labor.

The first project to be implemented was the Labor Plan, which was pushed forward in response to growing labor unrest, pressures from the Carter administration, and the threat of an international boycott. The plan, which emerged in final form in mid-1979, established a new legal framework for labor organizations and collective bargaining.[31] After six years, trade unions finally regained the right to represent their members, but on terms highly disadvantageous to organized labor. Among other innovations, the new legislation limited collective bargaining to the plant level, eliminated closed shops, impeded agricultural unionization, provided for employer lockouts, and strictly regulated strikes on terms favorable to employers. For organized labor, the one palatable feature of the new legislation was that it guaranteed workers pay increases commensurate with prior inflation. Even this concession was eliminated, however, in mid-1982, when the costs of backward indexation became apparent.[32]

In 1980, an equally sweeping reform of the social security system was introduced, which was designed to lower labor costs.[33] Social security reform had long been a part of the political agenda in Chile, but the military's reforms went far beyond those discussed by prior governments. It partially privatized as well as rationalized a highly complex system, creating a pay-as-you-go scheme revolving around individual retirement accounts. The administration of the system was placed in the hands of private companies. Significantly, the one key exception to this state-shrinking move was the military's retirement program, which remained outside the new system. Further changes in the direction of decentralization and privatization were also achieved through the other moderniza- tions. For example, private insurance companies gained a new role in health care; and in the area of education, state subsidies were reduced and schools turned over to local governments.[34]

The process of creating a new institutional framework for the Chilean state culminated with the constitution of 1980, which perpetuated Pinochet's presidency until 1989, with an option for renewal. *Inter alia*, the constitution coupled strong guarantees of property rights with extensive limitations on political rights, sanctifying the union of national security doctrine and Chicago economics. Its flavor can be gleaned from Article 8, outlawing parties "propagating doctrines that threaten the family, promote violence, or a conception of society . . . based on class struggle." Likewise, Article 11 provided for the loss of Chilean citizenship "for crimes against the dignity of the fatherland or the essential and permanent interests of the State."[35] After limited debate, the constitution was ratified by a national plebiscite on September 11, 1980, and apparently received the support of the majority of Chileans.[36] At the time of the plebiscite, inflation had declined below the 30 percent level for the first time in more than ten years, the economy was growing at an annual rate of more than 7 percent, foreign capital was flowing into the country, and middle-class consumers were enjoying unprecedented access to foreign cars, Scotch whiskey, and other luxury imports. Pinochet's faith in the Chicago Boys appeared to have been vindicated. Within two years, however, the economy was in ruins, making it obvious that the boom had been built on a foundation of financial speculation and international indebtedness.

The collapse of the "Chilean miracle" and the related breakdown of the governing coalition began in early 1978 with an exchange rate policy known as the *tablita*. Under this policy, the government sought to combat continuing inflation by preannouncing a declining rate of devaluation. With significant tariff barriers removed, the theory was that a preannounced rate would break inflationary expectations and push the domestic rate of inflation down toward the level of world inflation. In June 1979, the policy was modified to establish a fixed exchange rate of 39 pesos to the dollar, which the government later committed itself to defending indefinitely. That commitment proved costly. With domestic inflation failing to converge with world inflation and the dollar appreciating, Chilean exports became increasingly uncompetitive on world markets. Imports, on the other hand, became enormously attractive. The problem became apparent in 1980, when firms began lobbying for a change in policy, but economic authorities stubbornly resisted making any adjustments to the exchange rate. The resulting trade deficit was financed by international banks. Loans were flooding into all of Latin America at the time, but by removing a major element of risk, the *tablita* made foreign borrowing particularly attractive. Optimism about Chile's economic future, the liberalization of financial markets, and high local interest rates also helped. Financial services rapidly became the fastest growing component of the GDP. Bank lending as a percentage of GDP nearly doubled between 1978 and 1982, while total foreign indebtedness nearly tripled.[37] According to the economic team, this debt posed no real problem because it corresponded to private rather than public borrowing. As confidence in the banking system eroded, the artificiality of this distinction became apparent. In December 1981, the economic team was forced to set aside its compunctions about state interference and rescue eight financial institutions.

By the first quarter of 1982, the exchange rate had appreciated more than 30 percent relative to early 1979. Massive speculation against the peso began, pushing real interest rates above the 40 percent level. With labor costs also rising due to wage indexation, firms throughout the economy faced bankruptcy. External conditions did not help. International interest rates were rising, and copper prices falling. Still the government continued to rely on automatic adjustment mechanisms to resolve the crisis. When devaluation finally came in mid-1982, it was a case of "too little, and too late."[38] If anything, economic uncertainty increased, fueling divisions at the very center of the Pinochet regime. Within a 12-month period, four different economic teams tried to resolve the crisis, including one with a large military cast. The results were not impressive. The GDP fell more than 14 percent in 1982 and continued to fall the following year, while unemployment reached 30 percent of the work force, including those employed in emergency public programs. In 1983, the deepening crisis provoked the government into liquidating or assuming control over ten banks and financial institutions, accounting together for 45 percent of the total capital and reserves of the financial system.[39] Given the high level of indebtedness into which private firms had fallen, the public sector thereby reassumed control over much of the productive structure of the country, reversing a decade of free market policies. The nationalization of most of the private debt followed. Local wags began to talk about "the Chicago road to socialism." Thoroughly discredited, Chicago Boys began leaving posts throughout the government and by late 1983 appeared to have lost all influence.[40]

The speed with which the economy collapsed and the scope of the resulting damage reflected the structure of the capitalist system that developed after the coup. The system was characterized by two closely related fragilities. First, believing in a minimum of state regulation, the Chicago Boys had exercised only limited supervision over the financial system. The costs of this policy became evident as early as 1976, when bankruptcy struck a major bank and several of the private financial institutions (*financieras*) that had grown up after the coup. Until the crisis, the *financieras* had been exempted from virtually all banking regulations, including minimum capital requirements. Although a few new regulations were subsequently introduced, a policy of lax state control continued to characterize the financial system until mid-1981.

The problems created by inadequate state supervision of the financial system were compounded by the process through which Chilean capitalism was reconstituted. Industrial firms and banks were privatized with enormous speed and without regard for the question of ownership concentration. Hence, in 1975 alone, 86 percent of the share capital of banks that had been in the hands of CORFO was returned to the private sector.[41] Moreover, no effort was made to enforce the law governing bank privatization, which theoretically limited individual citizens and firms, respectively, to the purchase of 1.5 and 3.0 percent of the stock of a particular bank.[42] In the case of business enterprises, the sin was not merely one of omission. The government actually encouraged ownership concentration by auctioning off the shares of firms held by CORFO as a block to be purchased by an individual buyer. Under conditions of deep recession and high interest rates, the process favored those with liquid assets or access to foreign funds.[43] As a result, a small number of conglomerates or *grupos* controlling banks and large companies managed to buy up denationalized firms at bargain basement prices, creating a private sector with an unprecedented degree of ownership concentration. The banks became mere appendages to the conglomerates, leading to the suspension of prudent banking practices and the accumulation of bad loans.

Economic recession and tariff reforms, which drove less efficient producers out of the market, intensified the tendency toward property concentration, as did the wide spread between domestic and international interest rates, which allowed those with access to foreign funds to garner huge profits.[44] The process of property concentration was also furthered by the social security reform, which transferred the administration of social security funds totalling approximately 20 percent of GDP to private companies called AFPs. Most of the AFPs were owned by the big groups.[45] Last, but not least, large conglomerates enjoyed privileged access to government decision makers. Top government officials, such as José Piñera, the architect of the Labor Plan, and Rolf Lüders, the Minister of Finance who directed the bank takeovers of 1983, were drawn from the ranks of conglomerate management; others, such as the first civilian Minister of the Economy, Fernando Léniz, joined the large groups after retiring from public office. At the very least, these close connections facilitated the transfer of inside information, which became a critical resource under the conditions of acute economic uncertainty prevailing in Chile.[46]

According to Fernando Dahse's study, by 1978, nearly 70 percent of corporations registered on the stock exchange were linked with one of the large financial groups. The ten biggest groups alone controlled 112 of the 250 largest private companies, 66 percent of foreign credit, 45 percent of all bank assets, and 60 percent of all bank system lending.[47] Property concentration was not new to Chile, but it went much further after 1973. The big groups that emerged in the wake of the military takeover also differed from their predecessors in several respects. Unlike past groups, which were fiscally conservative, built around family connections, decentralized, and involved primarily in industrial activities, the new conglomerates were technocratic, aggressive, oriented toward financial and primary-sector export activities, and managed in a comparatively centralized fashion by trained professionals, many of whom had studied in foreign business schools.[48] The change is symbolized by the rise of the Cruzat-Larraín group, whose holdings increased from 10 firms in 1969 to more than 100 in 1978.[49]

Large economic groups also played a much more powerful role in postcoup Chile than in the past due to the lack of significant challenges or competition from either the state or foreign capital. The state was playing an increasingly minimal economic role, while transnationals remained reluctant to enter the local market. Under these conditions, a relatively cohesive local bourgeoisie achieved a position of extraordinary power. Instead of serving as the junior partner in a tripartite alliance with state and transnational capital, as in classic portrayals of dependency,[50] the local bourgeoisie became the driving force in the economy. Precisely because of this change, the relative autonomy enjoyed by state actors during the first few years of military rule began to diminish. In its 1980 report on the Chilean economy, the World Bank warned against the dangers of this trend, pointing out that "large concentrations of economic power seldom remain divorced forever from political influence and may ultimately undermine the economic strategy itself."[51] Its warning went unheeded, paving the way for the 1982 crash.

The power of the groups was evident in the government's rigid adherence to the *tablita* long after its costs had become evident. Insulation from public opinion created the opportunity for this disastrous policy error. The concentration of power in the hands of a few large groups created the incentive. Given their high levels of foreign indebtedness, devaluation represented a costly policy option for the *grupos*. The two largest conglomerates alone had accumulated a foreign debt exceeding that of the entire public sector.[52] The groups consequently threw their weight behind the fixed exchange rate, encouraging the economic team to maintain its faith in automatic adjustment mechanisms, even though influential sectors of the public were clamoring for some form of positive action.[53] The magnitude of the crisis that developed in Chile was a direct consequence. As one recent study concluded, the maintenance of a passive policy stance "helped transform what would have been a serious crisis into a catastrophic recession."[54] Moreover, when devaluation finally did take place, the government created a preferential exchange rate for debtors with foreign liabilities, thereby extending a major subsidy to the groups. Additional support came from the Central Bank, which propped up failing financial institutions to the tune of 200,000 million pesos—a sum roughly equivalent to 15 percent of the 1982 GDP.[55] Precisely because the groups were so powerful, the economic team came to equate their well-being with that of Chilean capitalism, threatening the very foundations of the state. In the end, this mistake became apparent, leading to a reassertion of military power over the government.

Phase IV: Pragmatic Neoliberalism

Two contradictory sets of forces shaped government policy during the fourth phase of military rule, which began in 1983. To overcome the economic and political damage associated with the financial collapse, the Pinochet regime was under intense local pressure to reverse the policy initiatives of the previous decade. Industrialists were demanding a more expansionist monetary policy, cheaper credit, and protection against foreign imports. The opposition movement was also gathering unprecedented momentum, pushing for political liberalization, and altering the basic contours of Chilean authoritarianism in the process. Concomitantly, the regime's prior basis of political support was dissolving. Business leaders, parties of the right, and even former regime officials defected and extended support to alliances pressuring for a transition to democracy. The incentives for the regime to adopt a more popular set of policies consequently increased. The approach of the October 1988 presidential plebiscite, which was designed to extend Pinochet's term in office into the 1990s, only intensified this dynamic.

The international situation pushed in the opposite direction and imposed severe constraints on policy makers. Relative to GDP, Chile's debt outstripped that of most other Latin American countries. Its room for maneuver was also limited by virtue of its size. Unlike Mexico and other large Latin American countries, Chile was not in a position to wring major concessions from the international banking community. To make matters worse, much of the debt contracted under military rule had gone to finance housing and consumption rather than to productive investments capable of generating income for servicing loans. Chile was therefore under intense pressure to meet its international obligations but in a poor position to do so. This, in turn, meant strict fiscal austerity, a continuing squeeze on consumption, and, in general terms, the adoption of policies compatible with IMF orthodoxy.

The regime wavered in response to these cross-cutting pressures, raising tariffs, fixing agricultural prices, embarking on new public-housing projects, subsidizing specific producer groups, and otherwise taking steps to buttress its faltering base of support. The tendency toward populist policies, however, was undercut by international pressures, which strictly limited the government's freedom of maneuver. By early 1985, a Chicago Boy was back in control of the finance ministry. Fiscal austerity, export promotion, renewed privatization, and denationalization via debt-for-equity swaps became the order of the day. Compromises with free market principles were frequent and many, but the economic role of the state continued to decline. In 1986, the government even started selling off shares in the state steel company, which had been one of CORFO's earliest projects.[56]

The process of state shrinking was consequently resumed during the fourth stage of military rule, but less in response to the extraordinary autonomy achieved by technocrats in the second stage of military rule or the political weight of local conglomerates, which had buttressed technocratic authority in the third, than to pressures from the international banking community. By bolstering sympathetic elements within the regime, external forces thus helped restore some of the momentum that had been lost through the financial crash. The large *grupos* that had been built during the second phase of military rule had not disappeared. Those oriented primarily toward export rather than financial activities had survived the disasters of the 1982–83 period and remained very much a part of the scenery. The Angelini empire, which became the largest group in the mid-1980s, is a case in point. The power of the groups, however, was diluted by the increased economic weight of foreign investors and bankers. The change is symbolized by the fate of the nation's social security funds. Until the state takeover of the banks in early 1983, most of the funds had been administered by companies affiliated with the Cruzat and Vial groups. With reprivatization in the mid-1980s, a significant share of the funds came to be administered by foreign corporations, such as Bankers Trust.

The Evolution of the State Sector

The process of state shrinking left Chile with a robust public sector. During the 1980s, the revenues of state corporations involved in mining, electricity, steel, and other productive activities still amounted to some 20 to 25 percent of the GDP,[57] while total public-sector expenditures accounted for more than 30 percent. Simply in terms of its economic weight, the state thus remained extremely powerful. Nevertheless, military rule did significantly alter the contours of the state. Its productive apparatus declined, its repressive and administrative arms grew, and the overall thrust of state intervention shifted dramatically against labor in the interest of capital.

Data on the distribution of government spending by area of activity provide startlingly clear evidence of these trends. Table 6.1, which establishes a basis for comparing the pre- and post-Allende situations, breaks down public spending into four general areas, two of which grew rapidly under military rule while two did not. Corresponding to the expansion of the state's coercive arm, the fastest growing category of state expenditure was defense. Military spending more than doubled between 1969 and 1979, increasing from approximately 7 percent of total spending in both 1969 and 1970 to 13 percent or more in every subsequent year. Also growing, but at a lesser rate, was the area of general administration, including public administration, finance, justice, foreign relations, and the military police. The expenditures falling into this second category accounted for approximately 7 percent of total public-sector spending before the election of Allende as compared to

Table 6.1
Distribution of Public Spending, 1969–79
(Index Based on Millions of 1978 Pesos)

	1969	1970	1974	1975	1976	1977	1978	1979
Defense	100	124	263	202	185	202	204	202
General Administration	100	127	176	152	159	140 ·	149	160
Social Services	100	111	109	91	88	99	101	107
Economic Services	100	116	133	66	57	53	75	72
Total	100	114	131	96	91	96	104	107

Source: Jorge Marshall, "El gasto público en Chile, 1969–1979," *Colección estudios CIEPLAN* 5 (July 1981): 73.

10 percent in 1979. In contrast, spending on social services, including education, health, social security, labor, and housing, remained relatively constant between the pre- and postcoup periods, both in absolute and relative terms. Social expenditures accounted for the lion's share of state spending under both democracy and military rule. The precise percentage figure, 58.5 percent, was identical in 1969 and 1979. Because of population growth, however, the amount of social spending declined roughly 10 percent on a per capita basis.[58]

The impact of the military's state-shrinking program is most obvious when one looks at the fourth category, which includes a whole variety of programs affecting agriculture, mining, industry, commerce, energy, transportation, and communication. These programs included subsidies, public works programs, research activities, transfers to state enterprises, irrigation projects, technical assistance, and support for agrarian reform. Nearly all were drastically cut after 1975, producing a 30 percent drop in spending on economic services between 1969 and 1979. Precisely because of this drop overall public-sector spending declined between 1970 and 1979.

Trends in public-sector employment followed a similar pattern. Prior to 1973, public-sector employment opportunities had expanded steadily. The shock treatment reversed this trend. Between 1974 and 1979, approximately 90,000 jobs were eliminated from the state sector.[59] The major exception to this trend was military employment, which grew nearly 120 percent during this same period, not counting the military police, whose numbers also expanded rapidly after 1973. Mainly because of this trend, public-sector salary expenditures increased 28.6 percent in real terms between 1970 and 1979. The bulk of this increase corresponded to spending on defense personnel, whose share of public-sector salary payments rose from 16 to 27 percent, again with the exception of the military police.[60]

Taken together, these trends correspond rather closely with the theory of the state that was articulated in the military junta's Declaration of Principles of early 1974. Combining elements of national security doctrine, traditional Catholic social thought, and neoconservative economics, the appropriate role for the state was seen to be that of fighting Marxism while respecting the principle of "subsidiarity." What this implied was a strengthening of the state's repressive apparatus coupled with a limitation of the state's role in setting the rules of the game, financing administrative expenditures, and assisting impoverished groups through social programs. It was expected that the application of these principles would entail a progressively smaller economic role for the state—an expectation that was met until the financial crash of 1982–83.

Unfortunately, a detailed breakdown of public-sector spending for the post-1979 period is not available. Table 6.2, however, presents data drawn from three different sources that provide a general picture of the evolution of the public sector relative to the economy over the 1973–87 period. Even though the absolute figures differ, the data show that after 1975 public-sector spending fell sharply relative to GDP. This trend was briefly reversed with the crash, restoring spending as a percentage of GDP to levels prevailing before the Allende government. A major reason was increased military spending, which soared to the unprecedented level of 9.5 percent of GDP in 1982—the highest ratio in South America.[61] The overall trend toward increased spending was subsequently reversed, however, as the economic and political situation began to stabilize.

The Changing Structure of the Chilean Economy

The transformation of the state had far-reaching implications for the structure and functioning of the whole economy. The growth of the economy, its relationship to the international

Table 6.2
The Evolution of Public Spending in Chile (Percentage of GDP)

	Total Public Sector (Marshall)	Government Expenditures (Edwards)	General Government (IADB)	Defense Spending
1969	34.0	–	–	2.0
1970	38.0	28.1	40.8	2.5
1971	–	32.4	–	2.3
1972	–	32.2	–	2.6
1973	–	44.7	–	3.7
1974	36.1	32.4	–	6.7
1975	33.1	27.4	–	5.7
1976	27.9	25.8	–	5.3
1977	28.7	24.9	–	6.9
1978	28.2	23.8	–	7.0
1979	26.7	23.1	–	6.9
1980	–	25.0	31.1	6.7
1981	–	23.7	32.0	7.4
1982	–	29.0	39.0	9.5
1983	–	28.4	34.2	8.0
1984	–	–	34.6	9.6
1985	–	–	33.4	7.6
1986	–	–	33.3	8.3[a]
1987	–	–	31.0	–

Source: Marshall, "El gasto público en Chile," 55; Edwards and Edwards, *Monetarism and Liberalization*, 32; Inter-American Development Bank, *Economic and Social Progress in Latin America: 1988 Report* (Washington, DC: IADB, 1988), 551; ibid., *1987 Report*, 437; ibid., *1986 Report*, 405; ibid., *1985 Report*, 339; Stockholm International Peace Research Institute, *World Armaments and Disarmament: SIPRI Yearbook* (Stockholm: SIPRI, 1977–1988).
[a] Estimate.

system, the relative weight of the industrial sector, patterns of employment, and socioeconomic inequalities all shifted in response to the implementation of orthodox policies.

As suggested by table 6.3, the removal of state controls on international trade and capital movements led to the opening of the economy to international forces. One result was a tremendous expansion of the national debt, which grew more than 300 percent between 1974 and 1986, imposing major constraints on economic management and future growth.[62] The process of opening the economy also produced a tremendous expansion of international trade. Whereas exports and imports together in 1970 were roughly equivalent to 30 percent of GDP,

172

Table 6.3
The Performance of the Chilean Economy, 1970–87

	Real GDP (1980 Prices)[a]	GDP Growth Rate	Manuf. Exports % GDP	Production (1980 = 100)	Imports % GDP	Open Unemployment	Total Debt[b]
1970	837.6	1.4	16.0	90	15.7	5.9	(n.a.)
1974	859.6	1.0	21.0	98	21.4	9.1	4,435
1975	748.6	–12.9	25.5	70	28.4	15.7	4,854
1976	775.0	3.5	24.5	74	20.1	16.7	4,720
1977	851.4	9.9	19.5	81	21.5	13.3	5,201
1978	921.3	8.2	19.1	87	23.5	13.8	6,664
1979	997.6	8.3	22.3	94	25.2	13.5	8,484
1980	1,075.3	7.8	21.6	100	25.5	11.7	11,084
1981	1,134.7	5.5	15.3	100	25.3	10.4	15,542
1982	974.9	–14.1	19.1	85	20.6	19.6	17,153
1983	968.0	–0.7	23.4	89	20.5	18.7	17,431
1984	1,029.4	6.3	23.4	98	23.9	16.1	18,877
1985	1,054.6	2.4	27.9	98	24.5	13.8	19,318
1986	1,114.3	5.7	29.9	106	25.4	(n.a.)	19,388

Source: Banco de Chile, *Boletín mensual*, v. 59, no. 706 (1986): 3286; ibid., v. 61, no. 722 (1988). 1020; Edwards and Edwards, *Monetarism and Liberalization*, 71; International Monetary Fund, *Monthly Financial Statistics*, 1970–88; idem, *International Financial Statistics Yearbook*, 1987; Esteban Jadresic, "Evolución de empleo y desempleo," *Colección estudios CIEPLAN*, 20 (December 1986): 151.
[a] Billions of 1980 pesos.
[b] Millions of U.S. dollars.

after 13 years of military rule the proportion approximated 55 percent. Considerable export diversification also occurred, reducing copper as a percentage of total exports from 67.3 percent in 1970 to only 41.9 percent in 1986.[63] The domestic economy was restructured in response to these trends. While nontraditional exports (e.g., fresh fruit, fishmeal, and paper products) expanded in response to their new profitability, the manufacturing sector stagnated, leading to a decline in the relative contribution of manufacturing to GDP, an absolute drop in manufacturing employment, and significant restructuring within the industrial sector.

Patterns of income distribution and property ownership also shifted after 1973. The opening of the economy to international competition and the related loss of jobs in the industrial sector contributed to the high level of open unemployment shown in table 6.3. Unemployment, in turn, was reflected in growing social inequality, especially as measured in terms of family income. All types of measures of income inequality, however, increased under military rule. GINI indices of income distribution for the greater Santiago area, for example, suggest that inequalities in the distribution of both personal and family income increased sharply in the mid-1970s and again during the early 1980s, producing a greater degree of social inequality than in 1970 or even in 1958 and 1964.[64] As indicated earlier, government policies also produced an unprecedented level of asset concentration—a tendency that continued into the late 1980s.

These trends were accompanied by little real economic growth. Because dramatic declines in economic activity in 1975 and 1982 offset periods of relatively rapid expansion, per capita income was virtually the same in 1986 as in 1970. The average rate of GDP growth for the 1974–86 period was only 2.4 percent, which was considerably below the average of 3.9 percent achieved during the 1950–72 period.[65] The military's record was also dismal by the standards of other countries in the region. Hence, although Chile had the fourth highest per capita income in the region in 1970, it had sunk to seventh place by 1986.[66]

Chile in Comparative Perspective

What sets the Chilean case apart from other instances of exclusionary military rule in the Southern Cone is less the nature of its policy program than the relative zeal, consistency, and speed with which it was implemented. All three of the Southern Cone military regimes that seized power in the 1970s sought to reduce the economic role of the state, eliminate fiscal deficits, deregulate the economy, and reduce barriers to international trade. As emphasized by table 6.4, however, their success varied considerably.

Within two years of the coup, the Chilean economic team had gained control of the fiscal budget, turning an emormous deficit into a surplus. The Uruguayan record of success in the area of fiscal policy was more modest; nevertheless, it was much better than that of Argentina. The Argentine fiscal deficit was actually higher in 1981 than in the year the military seized power.

Table 6.4
Economic Policy Performance of Southern Cone Military Regimes

	Argentina, 1977–82	Uruguay, 1974–82	Chile, 1974–82
Average Fiscal Deficit as % GDP	–4.6	–2.6	0.8
Deregulation	Inconsistent	Limited	Extensive
Tariff Reform	Moderate	Limited	Extensive
Annual % Change in State Expenditures as % GDP	3.5	3.6	–1.2
Privatization	Inconsistent	Limited	Extensive
Basic Development Strategy	Inconsistent	Expansion of export-oriented industry	Expansion of export-oriented mining and agriculture

Source: International Monetary Fund, *Government Finance Statistics Yearbook* (Washington, DC: 1986); idem, *International Financial Statistics Yearbook, 1987* (Washington, DC: 1987), 157; Marc Rimez, "Las experiencias de apertura externa y desprotección industrial en América Latina," *Economía de América Latina* 2 (Marzo 1979): 103–24; Joseph Ramos, *Neoconservative Economics in the Southern Cone of Latin America, 1973–1983* (Baltimore: Johns Hopkins, 1986).

The Chilean regime also moved most rapidly and consistently to implement a new model of capital accumulation. Within four months of the coup, the military government announced plans to proceed with a profound tariff reform, and by 1976, it had achieved a tariff of 35 percent. Three years later the maximum tariff on virtually all imports had been reduced to a uniform level of 10 percent. The Uruguayan regime, on the other hand, did not even announce plans for a tariff reform until 5½ years after assuming power and only achieved the 35 percent level in 1985, some 12 years after the military takeover. Argentina fell somewhere between these two extremes with a tariff reform program that was slower, more moderate, and less consistent than the Chilean but nevertheless more vigorous than the Uruguayan. By 1981, Argentina had reduced nominal tariffs to the 35 percent level.[67]

In terms of state shrinking, Chile again stands out. As indicated earlier, the energy and determination with which the military regime introduced neoconservative policies took the

LIBRARY ST. MARY'S COLLEGE

process of privatization far beyond a mere reversal of the Allende nationalizations; firms that had formed part of the state sector before 1970 were also restored to private ownership. As the figure for the average annual change in state expenditures as a percentage of GDP suggests (table 6.4), Chile was also the only Southern Cone regime that actually reduced state participation in the economy. In both Uruguay and Argentina, state expenditures as a percentage of GDP grew more than 3 percent per year. The verbal commitment to privatization also accomplished little in either country. Uruguay privatized only one firm—a municipal bus company.[68] The participation of public sector enterprises in GDP consequently remained unchanged relative to the past.[69] The Argentine record was even less impressive. Although the economic team succeeded in subcontracting state activities and selling firms that had entered the state sector in the early 1970s, state policy can at best be described as inconsistent. At least as much priority was placed on expanding the economic role of the state as on reducing it. Indeed, in terms of the value of transfers between the private and public sectors, nationalization proceeded twice as fast as privatization, largely due to the purchase of the electricity firm Italo, which was completed under military rule. As a result, the role of public enterprises in the economy increased.[70] With respect to changes in the economic role of the state, Uruguayan policy thus occupied the middle ground and Chile and Argentina the two extremes.

The process of deregulation followed a similar pattern. The Chilean military regime moved rapidly and consistently to restore price mechanisms. With the exception of 33 goods and services, all price controls were lifted the month following the coup. Over time the exceptions were also steadily eliminated, leaving only a few utility and transport prices subject to government control in 1980.[71] Five years after the military seized power in Uruguay, on the other hand, the state was still setting the prices of half of the items in a typical "consumer basket."[72] Argentine policy conformed to a third pattern. As in the area of privatization, policy was again highly inconsistent, combining energetic deregulation at certain times with a government-imposed wage and price freeze at another.

The analysis of Southern Cone regimes consequently

reveals three rather distinct patterns of policy implementation. In Chile, neoconservative policies were implemented with vigor, speed, and consistency, creating a close correspondence between rhetoric and reality. The Chilean case was the only one in which state participation in the GDP declined in accordance with neoconservative principles. Likewise, only Chile eliminated fiscal deficits and went on to attain budget surpluses; only Chile achieved a uniform tariff rate of 10 percent and a clear reorientation of development policy away from state-supported import substitution industrialization; only Chile proceeded energetically and consistently to dismantle government price controls; and only Chile embarked on a significant program of privatization. Uruguayan policy was moderate in comparison, albeit consistent; Argentine policy was totally inconsistent and marked by egregious departures from neoconservative rhetoric. What is more, only the Chilean military regime succeeded in redefining the relationship between state and society and through a new constitution and a comprehensive set of institutional reforms.

What accounts for the exceptional success of the Pinochet regime in implementing a neoconservative economic program? Why was it able to turn a change of regime into a sweeping reorganization of state power? The answers to these questions are related to the high levels of social conflict and economic dislocation associated with the Chilean military takeover, which established the basis for a reactionary program of policy change. Yet the level of crisis or class polarization associated with the origins of the three Southern Cone regimes provides a limited basis for explaining the differences among them. Although the level of crisis and class polarization was higher in Argentina than in Uruguay, the policy performance of the former was anything but consistently more orthodox or compatible with neoconservative principles. Nor can the depth of the crisis surrounding regime origins provide a basis for understanding policy evolution through time. As Robert R. Kaufman has put it, " 'declining fear' is a secular feature of bureaucratic-authoritarian rule."[73] Yet the implementation of neoconservative economic policies in the three cases was not uniformly more vigorous during the initial stages of military rule.

Institutional structures provide a much more persuasive explanation for longitudinal and cross-sectional policy variations in the Southern Cone. Whereas the organization of power in Chile assumed a sultanistic form, Argentina conformed to the feudal model and Uruguay the oligarchic. Indicators of these differences are outlined in table 6.5. The first two indicators in the table pertain to the fusion of government and military power. As suggested by the relationship between the president and army chief and the figures for military participation in cabinets, the process of fusion of military government roles went much farther in Argentina and Chile than in Uruguay. The latter country even retained a civilian president after the 1973 takeover. Argentina stands at the other extreme. Until its defeat in the Malvinas, the overwhelming majority of cabinet posts were held by military officers, as were most important positions at regional and local levels of political authority. Active-duty officers also headed all large state-owned corporations. Chile falls somewhere between the other two cases, depending on the time period under consideration. During the first two years of military rule, nearly 80 percent of the cabinet posts were held by military officers: a figure similar to that in Argentina. By 1978, however, military participation had fallen to a level of 25 percent. It climbed back up to a figure of more than 70 percent in the aftermath of the economic crisis of 1982 but subsequently dropped again to a 30 percent figure.

The other four indicators in table 6.5 refer to the distinction between bureaucratic and neopatrimonial rule. As indicated by

Table 6.5
Institutional Structures of Military Rule in the Southern Cone

	Argentina	Uruguay	Chile
Military Participation in Cabinet (% Cabinet Appointments prior to initiation of Democratic Transition)	45–90	0–20	25–90
Strict Separation of Roles of President and Army Chief	No	Yes	No
Military Officers Elect Own Chief	No	Yes	No
Centralized Military Intelligence Service	No	No	Yes
Rotation of Presidency	Yes	Yes	No
Rotation of Army Chief	Yes	Yes	No

Source: Directorate of Intelligence, Central Intelligence Agency, *Chiefs of State and Cabinet Members of Foreign Governments*, 1973–1987.

the lack of a centralized military intelligence service, the rotation of presidential and military posts, and the election of the head of the army by high-ranking officers, the collegial or bureaucratic dimension of institutional arrangements was most pronounced in Uruguay. Power was shared between the military junta, which was made up of the heads of the three services, and a body of more than 20 top-ranking generals, known as the Junta de Oficiales Generales. Chile represents the other extreme with no individual other than Pinochet holding the posts of president or army chief after the 1973 coup. The degree to which power was concentrated varied over time in Argentina, but it never approached the extreme collegiality of the Uruguayan case or the extreme neopatrimonialism of the Chilean. Even when the posts of army chief and president were fused, as in the immediate wake of the coup, power was shared among the three service chiefs. Through a formula described as the *veto compartido* (shared veto), each retained a veto over policy, and all important initiatives had to be submitted to a Legislative Advisory Commission whose nine members were apportioned equally among the three services.[74]

How did these varying institutional structures affect the economic policy performance of the Southern Cone regimes? Because of the feudal organization of political power in Argentina, the military as an institution was able to thwart the implementation of neoconservative policies that were perceived as contrary to its corporate interests. The persistence of budgetary deficits, the failures to make headway in the area of privatization, and departures from the policy of deregulation reflected this political reality, as did inconsistencies in other areas of policy.[75] Fearful of radicalizing workers behind guerrilla activities, the military ruled out major increases in unemployment.[76] Preoccupied with defending its economic bastions within the state sector, especially Fabricaciones Militares, it also resisted cuts in government investment and the privatization of public-sector enterprises.[77] Efforts to reduce the fiscal deficit likewise ran up against energetic military lobbying on behalf of the defense budget. The number of decision-making channels combined with the high level of military participation in the government precluded the possibility of policy coherence.

179

The limited but more consistent implementation of neo-conservative economic policies in Uruguay reflected a very different power structure. Due to the relatively collegial structure of military rule, power was more widely dispersed than in Argentina or Chile, contributing to the dilution of neoconservative economic recipes. In Uruguay, however, dilution occurred principally when policy was being formulated, not implemented, allowing for greater policy coherence than in Argentina. In particular, the Uruguayan economic team gained a much higher degree of control over the fiscal deficit, which was totally eliminated for a brief period in the late 1970s. Uruguay thereby avoided the incompatibility between fiscal and exchange policy that so drastically undermined Argentine economic performance.[78] The nature of the departures from neoconservative doctrine also differed in Argentina and Uruguay. Whereas in Argentina neoconservative rhetoric and reality only coincided when military interests were not threatened, in Uruguay the coincidence depended more on the impact of policy on entrepreneurial interests. In this connection, the importance of civilian participation in the formation of economic plans should be emphasized. The economic program pursued under military rule in Uruguay had not only been drawn up but also partially implemented before the military takeover. Subsequent modifications to the program were ironed out at conferences that integrated both civilian and military participants, leaving the technocratic economic team substantial discretion and independence in policy implementation.[79]

The pattern of policy implementation in Chile corresponded to a third type of power structure. Because of the extreme concentration of political power, neither the military institution nor social interests succeeded in derailing the implementation of neoconservative policies. The resulting "purity" of Chilean economic policy should not be exaggerated. Where military interests collided with laissez-faire ideology, the latter was not invariably triumphant. Nevertheless, the opportunities for interfering with the formation and implementation of economic policy were much more limited than elsewhere. A neo-patrimonial rather than collegial institutional structure created fewer points of access to the decision-making process and fewer opportunities for the military to pursue its institutional interests at the expense of government programs.

The dynamics of the Chilean case are also extremely revealing with respect to the impact of institutional structures on policy. The incentives and opportunities for implementing neo-conservative policies were presumably greatest during the initial period of military rule, when the specter of revolution loomed the largest and the capitalist class had yet to be reconstituted. Yet policy orthodoxy was less marked in the immediate wake of the coup than during the late 1970s. In the earlier period, political authority was organized on a relatively collegial basis, and, significantly, the contours of government policy resembled those of Argentina. Moderate structural reforms, including tariff reductions, coexisted with high levels of government spending. With the progressive concentration of political power in the hands of Pinochet, state technocrats gained greater autonomy vis-à-vis both social class forces and the military institution, creating conditions favorable to the progressive deepening of structural reforms. Significantly, the one break in this process came in the aftermath of the 1982 crash, which temporarily undermined Pinochet's leadership po-sition, paving the way for greater military participation in decision making. The dominant political dynamic in Argentina was virtually the opposite. Over time, power became increasingly fragmented, and departures from neoconserva-tive wisdom progressively marked.

Comparative perspectives consequently underline the importance of the organization of state power, which allowed state technocrats in Chile to persist in a program of drastic policy change long after the class alignments and structural conditions associated with the emergence of military rule had vanished. Their activities not only transformed the Chilean state but also shaped and then reshaped the basic structure of the nation's capitalist system. The experience is one that underlines the capacity of state actors to exercise their independence. The crucial issue, however, is less that of the autonomy of the Chilean state, which waxed and waned over the course of the 1973–89 period in response to shifting class and international forces, than it is that of institutional arrangements and the resulting unity and cohesion of policy makers. The basic

181

pattern of causality was one in which state actors initiated profound policy changes in the aftermath of the coup. These changes subsequently produced concentrations of economic power favorable to the deepening and institutionalization of the process of state change, which in turn established a basis for the survival of military power after its economic and political underpinnings had eroded. With the exception of two brief albeit telling periods, the constants in this dynamic process were a highly centralized structure of military leadership and a committed, talented, and cohesive cohort of state technocrats.

Notes

1   One of the junta's first decrees, Decree Law (D.L.) 12 of September 24, 1973, outlawed the trade union central, the Central Única de Trabajadores (CUT). A month later, under D.L. 77, the junta dissolved all of the Unidad Popular parties. D.L. 78 placed all other political parties in a state of recess. On December 15, 1973, the trade union movement was virtually recessed as well. D.L. 198 required prior authorization for union meetings, whose purposes were strictly delimited, and prohibited the election of union leaders. If leadership vacancies occurred, they were to be filled on the basis of worker seniority. Chile, Junta de Gobierno, *Decretos leyes dictados por la Junta de Gobierno de la República de Chile* (Santiago: Editorial Jurídica de Chile, 1973–1974).

2   *Ercilla*, October 17, 1973, as quoted in Arriagada, *Pinochet*, 103.

3   Ibid., 103–4.

4   *Qué Pasa*, October 25, 1973, as quoted in ibid., 104.

5   General Bonilla died in an accident in early 1975; the others retired early.

6   For an overview of these policies, see Arnold C. Harberger, "The Chilean Economy in the 1970s: Crisis, Stabilization, Liberalization, Reform," *Economic Policy in a World of Change*, eds. Karl Brunner and Allan H. Meltzer, Carnegie-Rochester Conferences Series on Public Policy, vol. 17 (Amsterdam: North Holland Publishing Company, 1982), 115–97; World Bank, *Chile: An Economy in Transition*, 3 vols. (Washington, DC: 1979); Vittorio Corbo, "The Use of the Exchange Rate for Stabilization Purposes: The Case of Chile," in *Economic Reform and Stabilization in Latin America*, eds. Michael Connolly and Claudio González-Vega (New York: Praeger, 1987), 111–37; Laurence Whitehead, "Inflation and Stabilisation in Chile 1970–77," in *Inflation and Stabilisation in Latin America*, eds. Rosemary Thorp and Laurence Whitehead (New York: Holmes & Meier, 1979), 65–109; Alejandro Foxley,

Latin American Experiments in Neo-Conservative Economics (Berkeley: University of California Press, 1983); Sebastian Edwards and Alejandro Cox Edwards, *Monetarism and Liberalization: The Chilean Experiment* (Cambridge, MA: Ballinger Publishing Company, 1987).

7   International Monetary Fund, *International Financial Statistics Yearbook, 1987* (Washington, DC: 1987); Harberger, "The Chilean Economy in the 1970s," 116–17. The uncertainty regarding the precise magnitude of these figures is a function of the rapid changes in price levels, relative prices, economic structure, and accounting procedures that occurred between 1973 and 1974. These changes raise questions about the adequacy of all time series covering the 1973–74 period, especially those involving the conversion of data from nominal to real terms. For a discussion of these difficulties, see World Bank, *Chile: An Economy in Transition*, 281–300.

8   According to the World Bank, *Chile: An Economy in Transition*, 118, expenditures grew 16.5 percent in real terms between 1973 and 1974. Harberger has presented data pointing in the same direction. According to his figures, current expenditures rose from 20.6 to 25.1 percent of GDP between 1973 and 1974 ("The Chilean Economy in the 1970s," 166). Data submitted to the International Monetary Fund (*Monthly Financial Statistics*, September 1976, 99) also show an increase, albeit of lesser magnitude. Note, however, that overall public sector spending probably declined substantially between 1973 and 1974 due to cuts in transfers to public enterprises. See Whitehead, "Inflation and Stabilisation," 82; Foxley, *Latin American Experiments*, 62; and Edwards and Edwards, *Monetarism and Liberalization*, 32.

9   Stockholm International Peace Research Institute, *World Armaments and Disarmament: SIPRI Yearbook 1983* (Stockholm: SIPRI, 1983), 166; Augusto Varas, "Militarización y defensa nacional en Chile," *Mensaje* 329 (June 1984): 249.

10 See Whitehead, "Inflation and Stabilisation," for a discussion of these issues.

11 Ames, *Political Survival*.

12 Interview with Raúl Sáez, Santiago, May 1986.

13 "Síntesis estadística," *Colección estudios CIEPLAN* 18 (December 1985): 211.

14 International Monetary Fund, *International Financial Statistics Yearbook, 1984* (Washington, DC: International Monetary Fund, 1984), 123. Note that these and virtually all other official figures on the performance of the Chilean economy since 1973 are the subject of ongoing debate. See René Cortázar and Patricio Meller, "Los dos Chiles o la importancia de revisar las estadísticas oficiales," *Colección estudios CIEPLAN* 21 (June 1987): 5–21; Patricio Meller and Patricio Arrau, "Revisión metodológica y cuantificación de las cuentas nacionales chilenas," ibid. 18 (December 1985): 95–184; Patricio Meller, Ernesto Livacich, and

Patricio Arrau, "Una revisión del milagro económico chilena," ibid. 15 (December 1984): 5–109; René Cortázar, "Distributive Results in Chile, 1973–1982," in *The National Economic Policies of Chile*, 79–105.

15 "Síntesis estadística," *Colección estudios CIEPLAN*, 215, 217.

16 For an objective treatment of this issue, see Edwards and Edwards, *Monetarism and Liberalization*, 135–73.

17 For an overview of this development, see Karen L. Remmer, "Public Policy and Regime Consolidation: The First Five Years of the Chilean Junta," *Journal of Developing Areas* 13 (July 1979): 441–61. See also Eduardo Frei Montalva, "El mandato de la historia y las exigencias del porvenir," *Chile-América*, nos. 14–15 (1976): 91–110; "El partido Demócrata Cristiano y la dictadura militar," which was published in three parts in ibid., no 4 (1975): 42–54; no. 5 (1975): 48–55; and nos. 6–7 (1975): 52–70; Brian H. Smith, "Old Allies, New Enemies: The Catholic Church as Opposition to Military Rule in Chile, 1973–1979," in *Military Rule in Chile: Dictatorship and Oppositions*, ed. J. Samuel Valenzuela and Arturo Valenzuela (Baltimore: Johns Hopkins University Press, 1986), 270–303; Manuel Barrera and J. Samuel Valenzuela, "The Development of Labor Movement Opposition to the Military Regime," in ibid., 230–69; Guillermo Campero and José A. Valenzuela, *El movimiento sindical en el regimen militar chileno, 1973–1981* (Santiago: ILET, 1984).

18 For an overview of this discourse, see Pilar Vergara, *Auge y caída del neoliberalismo en Chile* (Santiago: FLACSO, 1985). On the specific question of national security doctrine, see Genaro Arriagada H. and Manuel Antonio Garretón M., "Doctrina de seguridad nacional y régimen militar," *Estudios sociales centroamericanos* 20 (1978): 129–53.

19 Between September 1973 and July 1975, maximum tariffs fell from 750 percent to 140 percent, while average unweighted tariff rates were reduced from 105 to 65 percent. For an overview of this process, see Vittorio Corbo, "Chilean Economic Policy and International Economic Relations since 1970," in *The National Economic Policies of Chile*, 107–44. See also Ricardo Ffrench-Davis, "Import Liberalization: The Chilean Experience, 1973–1982," in *Military Rule in Chile*, 51–84.

20 The most notable one was the automobile industry.

21 Daniel L. Wisecarver, "Economic Regulation and Deregulation in Chile, 1973–1983," in *The National Economic Policies of Chile*, 150.

22 Vergara, *Auge y caída del neoliberalismo*, 83n. Note that figures on the number of firms controlled by CORFO in 1973 vary considerably. Wisecarver ("Economic Regulation and Deregulation," 150) presents a figure of 463. Foxley (*Latin American Experiments*, 62), Edwards and Edwards (*Monetarism and Liberalism*, 96), and certain official sources (e.g., Presidente de la República, *Mensaje presidencial* [Santiago: 1975], 239–40) present figures as high as 510. Some of the confusion is due to the fact that not all of the

public-sector firms were incorporated in CORFO. In addition, CORFO and its affiliates already held capital shares in more than two dozen of the firms that were taken over by the Allende government.

23 Presidente de la República, *Mensaje presidencial* (Santiago: 1975), 239.
24 Ibid.
25 Pilar Vergara, "Changes in the Economic Function of the Chilean State under the Military Regime," in *Military Rule in Chile*, eds. Valenzuela and Valenzuela, 90.
26 World Bank, *Chile: An Economy in Transition*, 208.
27 Apart from broad questions of nationalism and the strategic value of copper to national security, an unpublished decree law assigned a percentage of CODELCO's profits to the military. As a result, the armed forces jealously guarded their control over Gran Minería. After 1976, military officers played a prominent role in CODELCO's management, and under D.L. 1350 of January 30, 1976, they were entitled to one of the seven positions on CODELCO's board of directors. See "¿Defenderán el cobre los militares?" *Chile-América*, nos. 72–73 (1981): 94; "El futuro del cobre está en juega," *Chile-América*, nos. 74–75 (1981): 5–7; Fernando Cordero, "Antecedentes para una evaluación del gasto militar y del gasto fiscal social en Chile, 1973–1984," *Chile 1973–1984*, ed. Rigoberto Garcia (Stockholm: Nalkas-Gruppen, 1985), 147.
28 See Desmond S. King, *The New Right: Politics, Markets and Citizenship* (Chicago: Dorsey Press, 1987).
29 See Vergara, *Auge y caída del neoliberalismo*.
30 Wisecarver, "Economic Regulation and Deregulation," 162.
31 See D.L.s 2756, 2757, 2758, and 2759 of June 29, 1979. See also Guillermo Campero and José A. Valenzuela, *El movimiento sindical en el régimen militar chileno 1973–1981* (Santiago: Instituto Latinoamericano de Estudios Transnacionales, 1984).
32 See D.L. 18,134 of June 19, 1982.
33 D.L.s 3500, 3501, and 3502 of November 4, 1980. See Ministerio del Trabajo y Previsión Social, *La reforma previsional* (Santiago: Editorial Jurídica de Chile, 1981). See also Sergio Baeza V., ed., *Análisis de la previsión en Chile* (Santiago: Centro de Estudios Públicos, 1986), which reprints speeches and other material related to the reform.
34 See Programa Interdisciplinario de Investigaciones en Educación, *Las transformaciones educacionales bajo el régimen militar*, 2 vols. (Santiago: PIIE, 1986); Antonio Rodríguez Alvarado, *Legislación del trabajo y de seguridad social*, 3 vols. (Santiago: Editorial Jurídica, 1986). See also Dagmar Raczynski, "La regionalización y la política económico-social del régimen militar: el impacto regional," *Notas técnicas CIEPLAN* 84 (July 1986); Blas Tomic and Raúl González, "Municipio y estado: dimensiones de

una relación clave," Oficina Internacional del Trabajo, Programa Regional del Empleo en América Latina y El Caribe, Working Paper No. 27 (Santiago: PREALC, 1983); Rodrigo Contreras et al., "Salud pública, privada y solidaria en el Chile actual," *Documento de trabajo*, Programa de Economía del Trabajo, no. 44 (Santiago: PET, 1986); Mauricio Culagovski, "Reforma municipal, modernización y participación local," *Documento de trabajo*, Centro de Estudios del Desarrollo, no. 31 (Santiago: CED, 1986).

35 See *Textos comparados de la constitución política de la República de Chile sometido a plebiscito por la H. Junta de Gobierno por D.L. No. 3.464 de fecha 11 de agosto de 1980 y de la constitución política de la República de Chile de 1925* (Santiago: Instituto de Estudios Generales, 1980), 19, 21.

36 See Luis E. González, "Transición y partidos en Chile y Uruguay," *Serie documentos de trabajo* 93 (Montevideo: Centro de Informaciones y Estudios del Uruguay, 1985).

37 Nowak, "Financial Liberalization Revisited," 33; Edwards and Edwards, *Monetarism and Liberalization*, 71.

38 Ibid., 48.

39 Nicolás Flaño and Raúl E. Sáez, "El modelo económico neoliberal frente a la crisis, Chile 1981–1985," *Notas técnicas de CIEPLAN* 93 (December 1986): 31. See also José Pablo Arellano, "De la liberalización a la intervención: el mercado de capitales en Chile: 1974–83," *Colección estudios CIEPLAN* (December 1983): 5–49.

40 "Los mandos medios," *Qué pasa* 657 (November 10–16, 1983): 12–14. For a more detailed analysis of the evolution of the financial crisis, see ibid. See also Edgardo Barandiarán, "La crisis financiera chilena," *Documento de Trabajo* 6 (Santiago: Centro de Estudios Públicos, 1983).

41 Felicitas Nowak, "Financial Liberalization Revisited: The Case of Chile (1973–83)," *Diskussionsbeitrage* 40 (Gottingen: Universitat Gottingen, Ibero-Amerika Institut fur Wirtschaftsforschung, 1986): 26.

42 D.L. 818 of December 27, 1974.

43 Foxley, *Latin American Experiments*, 67.

44 Roberto Zahler, "The Monetary and Real Effects of the Financial Opening up of National Economies to the Exterior: The Case of Chile 1975–1978," *CEPAL Review* 10 (April 1980): 127–53.

45 Edwards and Edwards, *Monetarism and Liberalization*, 105; Foxley, *Latin American Experiments*, 106. See also "Los grupos económicos privados entran al asalto de los fondos de la previsión a partir del 2 de mayo," *Chile-América*, nos. 70–71 (April, May, June 1981): 30–36.

46 On this point, see Andrés Sanfuentes V., "Los grupos económicos: control y políticas," *Colección Estudios CIEPLAN* 15 (December 1984), 141. The close association between the large groups and government officials may have entailed other advantages as well, as in the case of the Crav group, whose former director, Sergio de

Castro, headed the economic team from 1975 until 1982. See "Dos políticos de Sergio de Castro," *Chile-América*, nos. 72–73 (July, August, September 1981): 72–73.

47 Fernando Dahse, *Mapa de la extrema riqueza* (Santiago: Editorial Aconcagua, 1979).

48 Ricardo Lagos, "La burguesía emergente," *Chile-América*, nos. 72–73 (1981): 83–93; Edwards and Edwards, *Monetarism and Liberalization*, 98–99. For a portrait of Chilean groups before 1970, see Maurice Zeitlin and Richard E. Ratcliff, *Landlords and Capitalists* (Princeton: Princeton University Press, forthcoming); Ricardo Lagos Escobar, *La concentración del poder económico. Su teoria. Realidad chilena* (Santiago: Editorial del Pacífico, 1961).

49 Dahse, *Mapa de la extrema riqueza*, 27–35.

50 See, in particular, Peter B. Evans, *Dependent Development: The Alliance of Multinational, State, and Local Capital in Brazil* (Princeton: Princeton University Press, 1979).

51 World Bank, *Chile: An Economy in Transition*, 279.

52 Jorge Leiva Lavalle, "Las etapas de la política económica frente a la crisis: 1981–1984," *Mensaje* 329 (June 1984): 256. See also Dahse, *Mapa de la extrema riqueza*, 154–55.

53 These included the businessmen closely associated with former president Alessandri and such groups as the Association of Agricultural Producers, headed by Carlos Podlech. See "El fracaso del modelo y las críticas del empresariado alessandrista," *Chile-América*, nos. 80–81 (July, August, September 1982): 18–19; "Remate de predios agrícolas," *Chile-América*, nos. 74–75 (1981): 17.

54 Edwards and Edwards, *Monetarism and Liberalization*, 198.

55 Leiva, "Las etapas," 255. See also José Pablo Arellano, "De la liberalización a la intervención: el mercado de capitales en Chile: 1974–83," *Colección estudios CIEPLAN* (December 1983): 5–49.

56 See Flaño and Sáez, "El modelo económico neoliberal"; "La era de los Chicago 'boys,' " *Hoy*, ed. extraordinaria (May 1987): 39–42; "Los nuevos rumbos de las economías chilena y mundial," *Informe económico* 13 (April (1986); "La jugosa vía de los pagarés," *Hoy* 529 (7–13 September 1987): 27–29.

57 Carlos Fortín, "The Political Economy of Repressive Monetarism: the State and Capital Accumulation in Post-1973 Chile," *The State and Capital Accumulation in Latin America*, vol. I: *Brazil, Chile, Mexico*, eds. Christian Anglade and Carlos Fortín (Pittsburgh: University of Pittsburgh Press, 1985), 174.

58 See Jorge Marshall, "Gasto público en Chile, 1969–1979," *Colección estudios CIEPLAN* 5 (July 1981): 76.

59 Ibid., 56. Edwards and Edwards, *Monetarism and Liberalization*, 146, suggest an even sharper decline. They cite figures for government employment of 196,000 for 1960, 308,000 for 1973, and 130,000 for 1982.

60 Marshall, "Gasto público," 69.

61 Stockholm International Peace Research Institute, *World Armaments and Disarmament, 1988* (Stockholm: SIPRI, 1988), 172.

62 For an analysis of the reasons for this growth, see Patricio Meller, "La enfoque analítico-empírico de las causas del actual endeudamiento externo chileno," *Colección estudios CIEPLAN* 20 (December 1986): 19–60.

63 International Monetary Fund, *International Financial Statistics Yearbook* (Washington, DC: IMF, 1987), 279.

64 Edwards and Edwards, *Monetarism and Liberalization*, 167–68. See also Ricardo Ffrench-Davis, "Import Liberalization: The Chilean Experience, 1973–1982," in *Military Rule in Chile*, eds. Valenzuela and Valenzuela, 61–62; René Cortázar, "Distributive Results in Chile, 1973–1982," in *The National Economic Policies of Chile*, ed. Walton, 79–105.

65 Edwards and Edwards, *Monetarism and Liberalization*, 3.

66 Inter-American Development Bank, *Economic and Social Progress in Latin America: 1987 Report* (Washington, DC: IADB, 1987), 426.

67 For further analysis of these contrasts, see Marc Rimez, "Las experiencias de apertura externa y desprotección industrial en América Latina," *Economía de América Latina* 2 (Marzo 1979): 103–24; Joseph Ramos, *Neoconservative Economics in the Southern Cone of Latin America, 1973–1983* (Baltimore: Johns Hopkins University Press, 1986), 127–28.

68 It may be noted, however, that state involvement in intervened banking and meat-packing firms also ceased. See Jorge Notaro, *La política económica en el Uruguay, 1968–1984* (Montevideo: CIEDUR, 1984), 47.

69 See Armando Arancibia and Wilson Peres, "La polémica en torno a las empresas públicas en América Latina," *Economia de América Latina* 2 (Marzo 1979): 13–44.

70 Jorge Schvarzer, "Empresas públicas y desarrollo industrial en Argentina," in ibid., 45–68; Arancibia and Peres, "La polémica," 36.

71 See Wisecarver, "Economic Regulation and Deregulation," in *The National Economic Policies of Chile*, ed. Walton, 145–202.

72 James Hanson and Jaime De Melo, "External Shocks, Financial Reforms, and Stabilization Attempts in Uruguay during 1974–83," *World Development*, vol. 13, no. 8 (1985): 939; Notaro, *La política económica*, 55.

73 Robert R. Kaufman, "Liberalization and Democratization in South America: Perspectives from the 1970s," in *Transitions from Authoritarian Rule: Comparative Perspectives*, ed. Guillermo O'Donnell, Philippe C. Schmitter, and Laurence Whitehead (Baltimore: Johns Hopkins University Press, 1986), 93.

74 See Joseph S. Tulchin, "Authoritarian Regimes and Foreign Policy: The Case of Argentina," *Latin American Nations in World*

Politics, ed. Heraldo Muñoz and Joseph S. Tulchin (Boulder, CO: Westview Press, 1984), 190; Edward Epstein, "Inflation and Public Policy in Argentina," paper presented at the annual meeting of the American Political Science Association, August 29–September 1, 1985, New Orleans, 19–20.

75 See Epstein, "Inflation and Public Policy"; Andrés Fontana, "Armed Forces and Neoconservative Ideology: State-Shrinking in Argentina, 1976–1981," paper presented at Research Conference on State-Shrinking: A Comparative Inquiry into Privatization, Institute of Latin American Studies, University of Texas, Austin, March 1–3, 1984.

76 Author's interview with José Martínez de Hoz, Buenos Aires, May 1986. See also Edward Epstein, "Inflation and Public Policy."

77 The minister of economics, José Martínez de Hoz, discusses this point in his account of the military regime's economic achievements. See *Bases para una argentina moderna, 1976–80* (Buenos Aires: n.p., 1981), 53. See also Andrés Fontana, "Armed Forces and Neoconservative Ideology."

78 On this point, see Nicolás Ardito Barletta, Mario I. Blejer, and Luis Landau, *Economic Liberalization and Stabilization Policies in Argentina, Chile, and Uruguay: Applications of the Monetary Approach to the Balance of Payments* (Washington, DC: World Bank, 1983).

79 See Notaro, *La política económica*.

CHAPTER 7

The Legacy of Military Rule

Military rule was the preponderant form of governance in Latin America during the 1970s. Within a decade, the political panorama of the region had changed completely. Beginning with Ecuador in 1979, a series of democratic transitions left less than 10 percent of the region's population under military domination. Even in Central America, elections and civilian presidents became the norm rather than the exception.

The key questions raised by this dramatic shift away from military rule have to do with its durability. Does the shift toward democracy in the 1980s represent more than a temporary phase in a long-term cycle of political instability? Are the new competitive or quasi-competitive regimes as likely to succumb to military intervention as did their predecessors? What, if anything, does the recent democratization wave signify with respect to the future of military rule in the region? Are military regimes a political species on the verge of extinction, or can we anticipate a resurgence of authoritarianism once the recent wave of democratization has run its course?

If Latin American democracy were merely a cyclical phenomenon, the answers to such questions would be simple. The problem is that the modern political history of the region cannot be read merely as a series of cyclical swings back and forth between competitive and military rule. Such countries as Costa Rica, Colombia, Cuba, Venezuela, and Mexico have failed to conform to such a pattern, and, as emphasized in chapter 1, the alternation of authoritarian and competitive rule in the region has occurred within the framework of a broader pattern of political evolution. Just as military rule assumed an increasingly exclusionary and repressive form during the 1970s

191

in response to high levels of industrialization and social differentiation, inclusionary forms of competitive rule have come to predominate over exclusionary ones in the 1980s. As a result, Latin American democracies today do not necessarily share either the strengths or weaknesses of their precursors. Few are threatened by the processes of urbanization, growing literacy, and the unionization of the countryside, which undermined the viability of oligarchical democracy during the 1960s. The vulnerabilities of inclusionary competitive rule are rather different.

From this perspective, the prospects for democratic stability in the late 1980s look much better than in the past. Very few oligarchical democracies remain in the region. On the other hand, social inequalities and foreign economic domination remain central structural characteristics of Latin America, and they post much more serious problems for the consolidation of inclusionary than exclusionary competitive rule. The same is true of U.S. domination of the region, which, although diluted by growing Western European influence, is still very much a part of the political scenery. In other words, the forces that undermined inclusionary democracy in the region in the past also threaten recently established competitive regimes.

The odds favoring the emergence of authoritarian over competitive rule, however, are not merely a function of larger structural forces or of the international political conjunctures created by U.S. foreign policy. Economic conditions and the political dynamic established by prior political events are also significant. The economic and political legacy of military rule consequently warrants consideration. In altering the conditions they inherit from their predecessors, military regimes bequeath a number of major political and economic problems to their successors. The scope of these problems has tended to vary considerably over time as well as with the structure of military rule, creating important contrasts between the past and the present with respect to the possibilities for democratic consolidation.

Civil-Military Tensions

Perhaps the least favorable legacy military regimes leave to their successors is the militarization of political life. Civilian politicians may breathe a sigh of relief when the armed forces abandon control of the government, but transitions from authoritarian rule rarely spell the end of military intervention in political affairs. After uniforms disappear from the presidential palace, the armed forces may continue to play a major role in determining who rules, how, and for whom. Indeed, in some cases, the capacity of the military as an institution to make its weight felt in the corridors of power may even be enhanced rather than diminished by a transition to a nominally democratic regime, creating considerable confusion about the boundaries between civilian and military rule. In the case of Argentina, for example, the armed forces as an institution exercised at least as much policy influence after the transition to an elected government in 1958 as under the dictatorship of Perón. The fragility of Argentine democracy, whose leaders were unable to act in the interest of their own survival, was a direct result. Examples of incomplete transitions from military rule also abound in the history of Central America and the Caribbean, where the inauguration of a civilian president has frequently corresponded to external pressures rather than endogenous developments. The rather formalistic regime transitions that occurred in Guatemala, El Salvador, Honduras, and Haiti during the 1980s represent cases in point.

Even when the breakdown of authoritarianism leads to the installation of a genuinely competitive regime, military rule leaves tensions between civil and military authorities in its wake. As illustrated by contemporary Latin American experience, these tensions characteristically revolve around issues of military authority and resources.[1] The Easter mutiny of 1987 in Argentina and its sequels (the military uprisings of mid-January and December 1988), the protracted political struggle over the amnesty law covering military violations of human rights in Uruguay, the coup rumors of April 1988 in Brazil, the March 1986 rebellion of air force General Frank Vargas Pazzos in Ecuador and subsequent military kidnapping of President León Febres Cordero, and the flagrant demonstra-

193

tion of military opposition to the creation of a unified defense ministry in Peru in April 1987 all provide examples of how the militarization of political life undermines successor regimes and complicates the process of consolidating any stable form of governance.[2] Partially because of such difficulties, military rule at one time enhances the odds of additional periods of authoritarianism.[3]

The legacy of military regimes, however, is hardly uniform. The capacity of the military to make claims on available political resources varies considerably from case to case. The problems are worst when military regimes have dramatically expanded the privileges of the armed forces. Mutual distrust and resentment between military and civil authorities, on the other hand, have been minimized when the claims of the military institution on available resources have remained relatively moderate under military rule. Which of these patterns emerges is mainly a function of how the military as an institution has been integrated into an authoritarian regime.

Table 7.1, which follows the classification of South American regimes described in chapter 2, presents data on shifting patterns of military expenditures as a means of assessing the capacity of the military to pursue its institutional interests. The correlation that emerges between institutional structures and patterns of spending underlines once again the importance of state structures for understanding the political outcomes of military rule. At one end of the spectrum are regimes with feudal institutional structures, which, by involving the armed forces deeply in governance, create incentives and opportunities for the military to make major claims on available political resources. Defense expenditures grew under all forms of military rule except the monarchical, but the rate of increase was most rapid and consistent under feudal military rule. Although the differences among the categories are less pronounced, under feudal military rule military expenditures also tended to grow as a proportion of GDP and remain high afterward, indicating that successor regimes confronted major obstacles in controlling military demands. In the cases of Bolivia and Peru, the ratio of military expenditures to GDP indicates that the costs of coaxing the military out of power were particularly high.

Table 7.1
Institutional Structures and Military Expenditures

	MILEX Aver. Annual % Change[a]	Preregime MILEX (% GDP)[b]	Regime MILEX (% GDP)[c]	Postregime MILEX (% GDP)[d]
Feudal				
Argentina, 1976–83	14.3	1.9	3.2	3.6
Bolivia, 1971–79	17.6	1.5	3.0	4.3
Bolivia, 1980–81	16.1	3.6	4.9	4.3
Ecuador, 1963–66	12.8	1.9	1.9	1.7
Ecuador, 1972–79	13.9	2.1	2.2	1.9
Peru, 1968–80	11.6	3.2	4.4	7.2
Monarchical				
Argentina, 1966–73	1.0	1.8	1.9	1.5
Bolivia, 1964–71	–1.1	2.4	1.8	1.9
Oligarchical				
Brazil, 1964–85	5.2	1.7	1.6	0.8[e]
Uruguay, 1973–85	2.8	2.6	2.8	2.3
Sultanistic				
Chile, 1973–88	9.4[f]	4.3	7.5[f]	n.a.
Paraguay, 1954–88[g]	5.9	n.a.	1.7	n.a.

Source: Stockholm International Peace Research Institute, *World Armaments and Disarmament: SIPRI Yearbook* (Stockholm: SIPRI, 1977–88); International Institute for Strategic Studies, *The Military Balance, 1987–1988* (London: IISS, 1987).

[a] Average for years in which military held power during the first six months of the year. Statistical differences among categories significant at the .001 level.
[b] Average for two years before military takeover.
[c] Average for years in which military held power during the first six months of the year.
[d] Average for two years subsequent to regime breakdown.
[e] Data for 1985 only.
[f] Data for 1974–86 only.
[g] Data for 1962–86 only.

Monarchical regimes represent the other end of the spectrum. In both the Argentine and Bolivian cases, there was little or no growth in military expenditures under military rule, and the ratio of military expenditures to GDP was lower after military rule than before. The sultanistic and oligarchical regimes fall somewhere in between. Expenditures grew more slowly than under feudal rule, and the capacity of the military to pursue its claims immediately subsequent to the breakdown of authoritarianism appears to have been more limited as well, depending on the degree of military involvement in the process of governance. The legacy of the two sultanistic regimes listed in table 7.1 remains to be seen, but the experience of the Philippines makes it difficult to be sanguine about the view that the removal of a personalistic ruler and his immediate entourage clears the slate for the construction or reconstitution of military professionalism around a set of democratic political loyalties. It also seems probable that the Chilean regime will leave more serious problems of civil-military relations to its successor than will the Paraguayan. As indicated by the ratio of defense expenditures to GDP, the claims of the military on available political resources have been much higher in Chile, and the involvement of the armed forces in the process of governance more significant.

These patterns suggest that no simple relationship exists between the ease of the transition from authoritarianism and the consolidation of successor civilian regimes. Feudal institutional arrangements, which promote regime breakdown by undermining the unity of the armed forces, leave particularly serious civil-military tensions in their wake. This pattern prevailed even in the case of the recent Argentine transition. Despite having been thoroughly discredited by their defeat at the hands of the British, the Argentine armed forces repeatedly challenged the democratic Alfonsín government and successfully pursued a number of key demands. By the same token, hierarchical institutional arrangements that make military regimes difficult to dislodge do not necessarily leave acute civil-military tensions in their wake.

Overall, the costs of coaxing the military out of power appear to be greatest where the armed forces as an institution have derived the most benefit from military rule. From the military perspective, however, the calculus concerning the costs and benefits of continuing military rule is not a simple one. The reason is that the role expansion that leads to the growth of institutional prerogatives and resources also undermines military unity and professionalism. Hence, while the tangible payoffs of continuing military rule are greatest for the military as an institution under a feudal regime, the institutional costs are highest in terms of military factionalism. Institutional autonomy and professional integrity are more easily maintained under oligarchical and monarchical rule, whereas sultanistic regimes at least preserve organizational unity and open up the possibility of shifting some of the long-term political costs of military rule from the military institution to its leadership.

In summary, the dynamic established by the militarization of political life has negative implications for the consolidation of successor regimes. The magnitude of the resulting problems, however, varies with the structure of military rule. Successor regimes confront particularly difficult problems where the military has governed through feudal types of institutional arrangements. This evidence indicates that *ceteris paribus* recent transitions opened much better prospects for the consolidation of competitive rule in Brazil and Uruguay than in Argentina, Bolivia, Ecuador, or Peru. It also underlines a significant contrast between Southern Europe and Latin America. Quite apart from questions of international position and social inequality, the relatively low level of institutional involvement of the military in Southern European authoritarianism made the process of democratic transition far easier there than in Latin America.[4]

The Economic Legacy of Military Rule

The odds favoring the consolidation of competitive institutions over future rounds of military rule are shaped by a second legacy of military rule—the economic conditions that military regimes bequeath to their successors. A dynamic economy creates opportunities for building a base of support for competitive institutions, papering over the cracks in multiclass political coalitions, and overcoming political opposition. When the economic pie is shrinking, however, political conflict mounts and compromise becomes more difficult.[5] The breakdown of competitive regimes in Latin America during the 1970s reflected this problem. Even the two oldest democracies in Latin America were undermined by a lack of economic dynamism, recurring balance of payments problems, and mounting inflation.

197

As indicated in chapter 3, comparative evidence provides no basis for asserting that military regimes manage the economy more effectively than others. In countries where military and democratic regimes have alternated in power, the success of the military in promoting growth and controlling inflation has been decidedly mixed. Even in the implementation of stabilization programs, where the coercive capacity of military regimes would appear to represent a critical advantage, authoritarian regimes have not outperformed their civilian predecessors or successors. At best, the odds that a military regime will manage an economic crisis more effectively than a civilian government are fifty-fifty.

The economic legacy of military rule is less mixed. As indicated by table 7.2, transitions from military rule typically have been associated with deteriorating economic conditions. The reasons are twofold. First, economic difficulties have often accelerated the demise of authoritarian rule. Second, the conflicts and uncertainties associated with regime transitions, whether those transitions involve the breakdown of authoritarianism or competitive rule, reduce investment confidence, provoke capital flight, and undermine policy coherence. The link between regime breakdown and deteriorating economic conditions, however, has been anything but constant over time. In the case of transitions from civilian to military rule, economic disruption was much more pronounced in the 1970s than in the 1960s, except in cases in which the transition involved the breakdown of oligarchical democracy. A similar tendency is evident with respect to transitions from regimes based on military power to competitive rule. The breakdown of authoritarianism in the 1980s left a legacy of acute economic disequilibrium without parallel in the past. Whether one looks simply at rates of growth and inflation, as in table 7.2, or considers a broader and more telling set of indicators of indebtedness, investment, and external imbalances, the economic burden that authoritarian regimes in Argentina, Bolivia, Brazil, Peru, and Uruguay bequeathed to their successors in the 1980s was truly staggering and anything but positive from the point of view of the consolidation of competitive rule. Yet new civilian authorities could draw two comforts from the economic situation. Much of the blame for it

Table 7.2

Regime Transitions and Economic Performance, 1960–88[a]

Transitions from Military Rule				Transitions to Military Rule			
Country	Year	GDP Growth	Inflation Rate	Country	Year	GDP Growth	Inflation Rate
Argentina	1962	–0.9	28.1	Argentina	1963	–3.7	24.0
	1973	3.2	61.2		1966	10.1	31.7
	1983	2.0	343.8		1976	–1.0	443.2
Bolivia	1979	1.8	19.7	Bolivia	1964	4.0	10.2
	1982	–8.7	133.3		1980	0.6	47.2
Brazil	1985	8.3	226.9	Brazil	1964	2.9	91.4
Dom. Rep.	1963	7.5	8.6	Dom. Rep.	1963	7.5	8.6
	1966	13.1	0.3				
Ecuador	1966	2.4	5.5	Ecuador	1963	3.9	5.9
	1979	5.3	10.3		1972	14.4	7.9
El Salv.	1984	2.3	11.5				
Guatemala	1986	0.0	36.9				
Honduras	1971	5.4	2.2	Honduras	1963	3.3	3.1
	1982	–2.0	9.0		1972	4.0	3.6
Nicaragua	1979	–26.4	48.2				
Peru	1963	4.9	5.9	Peru	1962	7.0	6.6
	1980	2.9	59.2		1968	0.0	19.0
Uruguay	1985	0.0	72.2	Uruguay	1973	–2.1	97.0

Source: Kenneth Ruddle and Philip Gillette, eds., *Latin American Political Statistics* (Los Angeles: University of California, 1972); *Keesing's Contemporary Archives*, 1970–88; International Monetary Fund, *Monthly Financial Statistics* (Washington, DC: IMF, 1963–88).

[a] Including partial and incomplete transitions to and from military rule.

could be shifted to their authoritarian predecessors, and the sheer magnitude of the crisis created few incentives for military establishments to reassume responsibility for economic management.

Although the outbreak of the regional debt crisis in the early 1980s immediately followed the breakdown of authoritarianism in several countries and fueled democratic transitions in others, the magnitude of the economic crises associated with recent regime transitions cannot be attributed solely to international forces. The tendency for more recent military regimes to leave monumental economic problems in their wake is evident even in the case of Peru, where a democratic transition occurred well before the onset of the debt crisis. The importance of the internal dimension is also evident from the data on

199

transitions involving the breakdown of competitive rule. Because of growing political participation and social complexity, regime transitions in Latin America are much more traumatic today than in the past. Except in a few of the less modernized countries, the political game is no longer restricted to a relatively small sector of society. Likewise, problems of economic management are complex, and the decisions that are reached affect the bulk of the population much more immediately than in the past. These arguments are buttressed by the pattern of cross-national variation evident in table 7.2. The economic crises associated with regime transitions have tended to be deepest in the most modernized and socially differentiated Latin American societies and least severe in the less industrialized and urbanized countries, such as Honduras and Ecuador. The key exception is Nicaragua, where the breakdown of authoritarian rule involved civil war and social revolution as opposed to a simple transition from military to competitive rule.

In objective terms then, the economic difficulties accompanying recent transitions from authoritarian rule created conditions unfavorable to regime consolidation, establishing a basis for the expectation that the most recent wave of democratization would prove no more durable than its predecessor some 20 years before. It is nevertheless possible that the impact of the intense crises associated with recent regime transitions may prove somewhat mixed. To the extent that economic difficulties force political leaders to reach accommodations with business elites, democracy may rest on more solid foundations than in the past. Likewise, to the extent that political actors continue to blame the military for intractable economic problems and/or recognize the increasing costs of transitions between military and competitive rule, the negative economic legacy of military rule may prove to have a stabilizing political effect, at least in the more socioeconomically advanced countries. The analysis now turns to this question of subjective impact. Precisely in this area, the greatest contrasts emerge between past and present prospects for the consolidation of democratic institutions.

Authoritarian Realities and Democratic Hopes

The third legacy of military rule is less a matter of institutional capacities, structural relationships, or economic facts than of attitudes and perceptions. Especially in the more modernized countries of Latin America, where military rule assumed a highly repressive form in the 1970s, recent authoritarian experiences have generated a new enthusiasm for democratic governance, a positive evaluation of competitive electoral processes, and a willingness to compromise and moderate demands in the interest of avoiding relapses into authoritarianism. Unlike the other legacies of the military regimes of the 1970s, this reorientation of attitudes establishes a positive basis for the consolidation of successor regimes. Never before in Latin America has military rule been so profoundly discredited, nor, as Guillermo O'Donnell has put it, "never has the ideological 'prestige' of political democracy been higher."[6]

The unprecedented support for competitive institutions, which emerged in the 1980s, was a direct outcome of military rule rather than a product of democratic transition and the related efforts of elected leaders to mobilize popular support. The evidence provided by public opinion surveys in Chile is revealing in this regard. With the prospect of a constitutionally scheduled plebiscite in sight, dozens of opinion polls were conducted by private companies, research institutes, and think tanks during the late 1980s. Continuing military rule biased the results of these polls in favor of authoritarianism by limiting access to information and providing respondents and researchers alike with a motive for caution. Nevertheless, the study of public opinion left little doubt about the lack of support for the Pinochet regime. As indicated in table 7.3, well before the defeat of Pinochet in the 1988 plebiscite, the Chilean public expressed an overwhelming preference for democratic government over authoritarianism.[7] Asked to choose specifically between the selection of the next president on the basis of a plebiscite or free elections, more than 70 percent opted for free elections and only 12 percent for the plebiscite formula backed by Pinochet.[8] These figures compare favorably with those reported in Spain prior to the transition to democracy. A year before Franco's death, 60 percent of the Spanish public declared

Table 7.3
Regime Preferences of Chileans under Military Rule (Percentages)

	Democracy	Authoritarianism	Indifferent	No Reponse
Santiago Residents, 1986	60.6	6.3	25.4	7.7
Santiago Residents, 1987	59.8	7.4	21.3	11.5
National Urban Sample, 1987	58.4	8.8	22.2	10.6

Source: Centro de Estudios de la Realidad Contemporánea, *Informe preliminar sobre primera encuesta nacional* (Santiago: CERC, 1988), 9.

themselves in favor of democratic representation and 18 percent in favor of one-man rule.[9]

In the case of highly exclusionary regimes, recent non-revolutionary transitions from authoritarianism have also revealed a major shift away from political extremes and a loss of support for the political forces most closely associated with military rule. Even in the Uruguayan case, which was characterized by an unusually high level of party system continuity between pre- and postauthoritarian elections, military rule produced a marked shift in the direction of moderation.[10] The same tendency became evident in Chile during the mid-1980s, despite fears that the prolongation of military rule would foster political extremism. After more than a decade of military rule, residents of greater Santiago identified much more strongly with the center than at any point stretching back to the 1950s.[11] This finding cannot be dismissed as a product of an authoritarian political context. To the extent that political fears provided leftists with incentives to disguise their political orientation, such fears also biased the results in favor of the right. Nevertheless, the tendency toward moderation was evident at both ends of the political spectrum.[12]

The Chilean data are particularly significant because they emphasize that shifts in the direction of moderation and pragmatism are less a cause of democratic transition than a consequence of authoritarianism. The reorientation of public opinion around the center, however, has important implications for the consolidation as distinct from the installation of competitive rule. The breakdown of democracy in the more modernized countries of Latin America in the past has corresponded to the progressive polarization of political forces.

Whether the realignment of political forces around competitive institutions and moderate political options will offset the negative legacies of military rule remains to be seen. It would certainly be premature to write the epitaph for Latin American militarism. In such countries as Ecuador and Peru, where military rule in the 1970s was not highly exclusionary, the political reaction in favor of competitive institutions appears to have been less profound than in the more advanced Latin American nations. In Central America, where the breakdown of military rule reflected international pressures, the survival of competitive rule hinges largely on the vagaries of U.S. policy.

Nevertheless, the democratic achievements of the 1980s contrast favorably with those resulting from the previous wave of military regime breakdowns. That wave reached its peak in 1958 with regime transitions in Venezuela, Colombia, and Argentina and had run its course by 1962, a year that was punctuated by military coups in Argentina and Peru. With the notable exception of Venezuela, its principal outcome was the establishment of unstable competitive regimes of an exclusionary character. In contrast, outside of Central America, the recent wave of regime transitions has produced inclusionary competitive regimes with much stronger claims to democratic legitimacy. The recent wave has also lasted longer, establishing new democratic precedents in several countries. Despite the deepest economic crisis in postwar history, during the 1980s, Argentina experienced its longest period of competitive rule since the ouster of President Hipólito Irigoyen in 1930. The 1980 Peruvian transition paved the way for the first transfer of executive power from one elected leader to another in the nation's history. The peaceful transmission of power from one political party to another in Bolivia after the 1982 transition was equally unprecedented. These achievements were offset by the continuation of military rule in other countries, but by the late 1980s, a transition from authoritarian rule had begun in Chile, and observers had even begun to talk seriously about prospects for democracy in Paraguay, a country with no history of competitive rule.[13]

The future of the new democracies in Latin America remains

clouded by the two most negative legacies of military rule: the militarization of political life and the historically unparalleled burden of debt. To the extent that these two pressures can be ameliorated by actions or influences from abroad, as is undoubtedly possible, a space has been created for political action that can support democracy in Latin America. Whatever the risks and uncertainties, democratic hopes seem much more firmly based in the region as the close of the twentieth century draws near than at any point in the past. This historic opportunity represents not an accidental conjuncture of favorable forces, but the result of a long trajectory of sociopolitical change. Military regimes remain an alternative to democracy, but the costs of military rule are more evident than ever. The advantage now lies with democracy.

Notes

1 For an extended discussion of these issues, see Alfred Stepan, *Rethinking Military Politics: Brazil and the Southern Cone* (Princeton: Princeton University Press, 1988).
2 All of these issues were covered in the *Latin American Weekly Report*. See No. 11 (March 14, 1986): 1; No. 4 (January 29, 1987): 10; No. 15 (April 16, 1987): 9; No. 17 (May 7, 1987): 6–8; No. 30 (August 6, 1987): 6; No. 7 (September 3, 1987): 7; No. 43 (November 5, 1987): 11; No. 42 (October 29, 1987): 2; No. 1 (January 7, 1988): 5; No. 4 (January 28, 1988): 1–3; No. 5 (February 4, 1988): 2; No. 11 (March 17, 1988): 4–5; No. 15 (April 21, 1988): 10; No. 17 (May 5, 1988): 3.
3 For evidence on this point, see Robert D. Putnam, "Toward Explaining Military Intervention in Latin American Politics," *World Politics* 20, no. 1 (1976): 83–110.
4 On this point, see Guillermo O'Donnell, Philippe C. Schmitter, and Laurence Whitehead, eds., *Transitions from Authoritarian Rule: Southern Europe* (Baltimore: Johns Hopkins University Press, 1986). See also Guillermo O'Donnell, "Introduction to the Latin American Cases," in *Transitions from Authoritarian Rule*, eds. O'Donnell, Schmitter, and Whitehead, 10–11.
5 For the application of these arguments to the situation in Latin America in the 1980s, see Richard E. Feinberg, "The Adjustment Imperative and U.S. Policy," in *Adjustment Crisis in the Third World*, eds. Richard Feinberg and Valeriana Kallab (New Brunswick: Transaction Books, 1984), 13.
6 Guillermo O'Donnell, "Introduction to the Latin American Cases," in *Transitions from Authoritarian Rule*, eds. O'Donnell, Schmitter, and Whitehead, 17.

7   Even the right-wing think tank, the Centro de Estudios Públicos, failed to uncover much support for authoritarianism. The published results of their survey of December 1986–January 1987 showed that 67.3 percent of their Santiago sample preferred democracy over the continuation of authoritarian rule. *Estudio social y de opinión pública en la población de Santiago* (Santiago: CEP, 1987), 140. A FLACSO poll of October–November 1986 showed an even higher proportion (77.0). *Opinión pública y cultura política* (Santiago: FLACSO, 1987), 241. See also FLACSO, "Encuesta comparativa para Latinoamérica: resultados generales," Material de Discusión, 106 (November 1987): 44, which shows 66.5 percent of an August 1987 sample of 788 Santiago residents agreeing that elected governments are better than any other form of government.

8   Centro de Estudios de la Realidad Contemporánea, *Informe preliminar sobre primera encuesta nacional* (Santiago: CERC, 1988), 13. The figure was virtually identical in the FLACSO poll of October–November 1987. See "Encuesta de opinión pública," Documento de Trabajo 371 (March 1988): 9.

9   Rafael López-Pintor, "Mass and Elite Perspectives in the Process of Transition to Democracy," in *Comparing New Democracies: Transition and Consolidation in Mediterranean Europe and the Southern Cone*, ed. Enrique A. Baloyra (Boulder, CO: Westview Press, 1987), 90.

10 Writing about the Uruguayan election of 1984, Juan Rial has commented: "The 1984 vote was a vote for moderation, pacification, and democracy. . . . Many of those who in 1973 had an extreme Left position supporting different types of radical actions now defended moderate positions. Many who had espoused an extreme Right view abandoned it for a centrist one. Very few dared to be marked by the stigma of defending the military regime." "Political Parties and Elections in the Process of Transition in Uruguay," in *Comparing New Democracies*, ed. Baloyra, 258. See also Juan Rial, "The Uruguayan Elections of 1984: A Triumph of the Center," in *Elections and Democratization in Latin America*, eds. Paul W. Drake and Eduardo Silva (San Diego: University of California, 1986), 245–71; Charles G. Gillespie, "Uruguay's Transition from Collegial Military-Technocratic Rule," in *Transitions from Authoritarian Rule*, eds. O'Donnell, Schmitter, and Whitehead, 173–95.

11 Carlos Huneeus, *Los chilenos y la política* (Santiago: n.p., 1987), 163.

12 Ibid. These results were the product of a question that asked respondents whether they identified most closely with the right, center, or left. The same tendency was evident when respondents were asked to place themselves on a ten-point scale, with one representing the extreme left of the political spectrum and ten the extreme right. Nearly 40 percent placed themselves at the exact

205

center. Huneeus, *Los chilenos y la política*, 168. These findings were not a product of the particular political moment of polling. When Santiago residents were asked in early 1988 whether they identified with the right, center, or left, 39.4 percent of the sample of 800 individuals selected the centrist position. The proportion was similar in Concepción (37.1) and even higher in Valparaíso (49.7). Centro de Estudios de la Realidad Contemporánea, *Informe preliminar sobre primera encuesta nacional* (Santiago: CERC, 1988), 9–10. Similarly, in a FLACSO poll taken in August 1987, 42.6 percent of the respondents classified themselves at the exact center of a ten-point scale. FLACSO, "Encuesta comparativa para Latinoamérica: resultados generales," Material de Discusión 106 (November 1987): 53.

13 See, in particular, Diego Abente, "Post-Stronismo and the Prospects for Democracy in Paraguay," paper presented at the XIV International Congress of the Latin American Studies Association, New Orleans, March 1988.

Index